Praise for *Data Quality Fundamentals*

Data engineers, ETL programmers, and entire data pipeline teams need a reference and testing guide like this! As I did, they will learn the building blocks, processes, and tooling that help ensure the quality of data-intensive applications.

This book adds fresh perspectives and practical test scenarios that expand the wisdom to test modern data pipelines.

—*Wayne Yaddow, Data and ETL Quality Analyst*

Your data investments, infrastructure, and insights don't matter at all if you can't trust your data. Barr, Lior, and Molly have done a tremendous job in breaking down the fundamentals of what trusting your data means and have created a very practical framework to implement data quality in enterprises. A must-read for anyone who cares about data quality.

—*Debashis Saha, Data Leader*
AppZen, Intuit, and eBay

As data architecture becomes increasingly distributed and the accountability for data increasingly decentralized, the focus on data quality will continue to grow. *Data Quality Fundamentals* provides an important resource for engineering teams that are serious about improving the accuracy, reliability, and trust of their data through some of today's most significant technologies and processes.

—*Mammad Zadeh, Data Leader and*
Former VP of Engineering at Intuit

Data Quality Fundamentals
A Practitioner's Guide to Building Trustworthy Data Pipelines

Barr Moses, Lior Gavish, and Molly Vorwerck

Beijing · Boston · Farnham · Sebastopol · Tokyo

Data Quality Fundamentals

by Barr Moses, Lior Gavish, and Molly Vorwerck

Published by O'Reilly Media, Inc., 1005 Gravenstein Highway North, Sebastopol, CA 95472.

O'Reilly books may be purchased for educational, business, or sales promotional use. Online editions are also available for most titles (*http://oreilly.com*). For more information, contact our corporate/institutional sales department: 800-998-9938 or *corporate@oreilly.com*.

Acquisitions Editor: Aaron Black
Development Editor: Jill Leonard
Production Editor: Gregory Hyman
Copyeditor: Charles Roumeliotis
Proofreader: Piper Editorial Consulting, LLC

Indexer: WordCo Indexing Services, Inc.
Interior Designer: David Futato
Cover Designer: Karen Montgomery
Illustrator: Kate Dullea

September 2022:   First Edition

Revision History for the First Edition

2022-09-01:   First Release

See *http://oreilly.com/catalog/errata.csp?isbn=9781098112042* for release details.

978-1-098-11204-2

[LSI]

To Rae and Robert, who keep things in perspective, no matter where we look.

To the Monte Carlo jellyfish and the data reliability pioneers—you know who you are. So grateful to be on this journey with you.

Table of Contents

Preface

If you've experienced any of the following scenarios, raise your hand (or, you can just nod in solidarity—there's no way we'll know otherwise):

- Five thousand rows in a critical (and relatively predictable) table suddenly turns into five hundred, with no rhyme or reason.
- A broken dashboard causes an executive dashboard to spit null values.
- A hidden schema change breaks a downstream pipeline.
- And the list goes on.

This book is for everyone who has suffered from unreliable data, silently or with muffled screams, and wants to do something about it. We expect that these individuals will come from data engineers, data analytics, or data science backgrounds, and be actively involved in building, scaling, and managing their company's data pipelines.

On the surface, it may seem like *Data Quality Fundamentals* is a manual about how to clean, wrangle, and generally make sense of data—and it is. But more so, this book tackles best practices, technologies, and processes around building more reliable data systems and, in the process, cultivating data trust with your team and stakeholders.

In Chapter 1, we'll discuss why data quality deserves attention now, and how architectural and technological trends are contributing to an overall decrease in governance and reliability. We'll introduce the concept of "data downtime," and explain how it harkens back to the early days of site reliability engineering (SRE) teams and how these same DevOps principles can apply to your data engineering workflows as well.

In Chapter 2, we'll highlight how to build more resilient data systems by walking through how you can solve for and measure data quality across several key data pipeline technologies, including data warehouses, data lakes, and data catalogs. These three foundational technologies store, process, and track data health preproduction, which naturally leads us into Chapter 3, where we'll walk through how to collect, clean, transform, and test your data with quality and reliability in mind.

Next, Chapter 4 will walk through one of the most important aspects of the data reliability workflow—proactive anomaly detection and monitoring—by sharing how to build a data quality monitor using a publicly available data set about exoplanets. This tutorial will give readers the opportunity to directly apply the lessons they've learned in *Data Quality Fundamentals* to their work in the field, albeit at a limited scale.

Chapter 5 will provide readers with a bird's-eye view into what it takes to put these critical technologies together and architect robust systems and processes that ensure data quality is measured and maintained no matter the use case. We'll also share how best-in-class data teams at Airbnb, Uber, Intuit, and other companies integrate data reliability into their day-to-day workflows, including setting SLAs, SLIs, and SLOs, and building data platforms that optimize for data quality across five key pillars: freshness, volume, distribution, schema, and lineage.

In Chapter 6, we'll dive into the steps necessary to actually react to and fix data quality issues in production environments, including data incident management, root cause analysis, postmortems, and establishing incident communication best practices. Then, in Chapter 7, readers will take their understanding of root cause analysis one step further by learning how to build field-level lineage using popular and widely adopted open source tools that should be in every data engineer's arsenal.

In Chapter 8, we'll discuss some of the cultural and organizational barriers data teams must cross when evangelizing and democratizing data quality at scale, including best-in-class principles like treating your data like a product, understanding your company's RACI matrix for data quality, and how to structure your data team for maximum business impact.

In Chapter 9, we'll share several real-world case studies and conversations with leading minds in the data engineering space, including Zhamak Dehghani, creator of the data mesh, António Fitas, whose team bravely shares their story of how they're migrating toward a decentralized (and data quality first!) data architecture, and Alex Tverdohleb, VP of Data Services at Fox and a pioneer of the "controlled freedom" data management technique. This patchwork of theory and on-the-ground examples will help you visualize how several of the technical and process-driven data quality concepts we highlight in Chapters 1 through 8 can come to life in stunning color.

And finally, in Chapter 10, we finish our book with a tangible calculation for measuring the financial impact of poor data on your business, in human hours, as a way to help readers (many of whom are tasked with fixing data downtime) make the case with leadership to invest in more tools and processes to solve these problems. We'll also highlight four of our predictions for the future of data quality as it relates to broader industry trends, such as distributed data management and the rise of the data lakehouse.

At the very least, we hope that you walk away from this book with a few tricks up your sleeve when it comes to making the case for prioritizing data quality and reliability across your organization. As any seasoned data leader will tell you, data trust is never built in a day, but with the right approach, incremental progress can be made—pipeline by pipeline.

Conventions Used in This Book

The following typographical conventions are used in this book:

Italic
> Indicates new terms, URLs, email addresses, filenames, and file extensions.

`Constant width`
> Used for program listings, as well as within paragraphs to refer to program elements such as variable or function names, databases, data types, environment variables, statements, and keywords.

> This element signifies a tip or suggestion.

> This element signifies a general note.

Using Code Examples

Supplemental material (code examples, exercises, etc.) is available for download at *https://oreil.ly/data-quality-fundamentals-code*.

If you have a technical question or a problem using the code examples, please send an email to *bookquestions@oreilly.com*.

This book is here to help you get your job done. In general, if example code is offered with this book, you may use it in your programs and documentation. You do not need to contact us for permission unless you're reproducing a significant portion of the code. For example, writing a program that uses several chunks of code from this book does not require permission. Selling or distributing examples from O'Reilly books does require permission. Answering a question by citing this book and quoting example code does not require permission. Incorporating a significant amount of example code from this book into your product's documentation does require permission.

We appreciate, but generally do not require, attribution. An attribution usually includes the title, author, publisher, and ISBN. For example: "*Data Quality Fundamentals* by Barr Moses, Lior Gavish, and Molly Vorwerck (O'Reilly). Copyright 2022 Monte Carlo Data, Inc., 978-1-098-11204-2."

If you feel your use of code examples falls outside fair use or the permission described herein, feel free to contact us at *permissions@oreilly.com*.

O'Reilly Online Learning

 For more than 40 years, *O'Reilly Media* has provided technology and business training, knowledge, and insight to help companies succeed.

Our unique network of experts and innovators share their knowledge and expertise through books, articles, and our online learning platform. O'Reilly's online learning platform gives you on-demand access to live training courses, in-depth learning paths, interactive coding environments, and a vast collection of text and video from O'Reilly and 200+ other publishers. For more information, visit *https://oreilly.com*.

How to Contact Us

Please address comments and questions concerning this book to the publisher:

O'Reilly Media, Inc.
1005 Gravenstein Highway North
Sebastopol, CA 95472
800-998-9938 (in the United States or Canada)
707-829-0515 (international or local)
707-829-0104 (fax)

We have a web page for this book, where we list errata, examples, and any additional information. You can access this page at *https://oreil.ly/data-quality-fundamentals*.

Email *bookquestions@oreilly.com* to comment or ask technical questions about this book.

For news and information about our books and courses, visit *https://oreilly.com*.

Find us on LinkedIn: *https://linkedin.com/company/oreilly-media*.

Follow us on Twitter: *https://twitter.com/oreillymedia*.

Watch us on YouTube: *https://www.youtube.com/oreillymedia*.

Acknowledgments

This book was a labor of love, and for that reason, we have many people to thank.

First, we'd like to thank Jess Haberman, our fearless acquisitions editor, who believed in us every step of the way. When Jess came to us with the idea for a book on data quality, we were taken aback—in the best way possible. We had no idea that a topic—data reliability—that's so near and dear to our hearts would find life outside of our personal blog articles. With her dedication and encouragement, we were able to draft a proposal that set itself apart from what was already published in the space and ultimately write a book that would bring value to other data practitioners struggling with data downtime.

We must also thank Jill Leonard, our development editor, who has served as our Yoda of the entire writing process. From providing invaluable guidance on flow and copy, to being available for pep talks and brainstorming sessions ("Should this chapter go here? What about there? What even *is* a preface?"), Jill was the Jedi who saw us through to the finish line. Our mutual love of cats only helped seal the bond.

We are forever indebted to our technical reviewers, Tristan Baker, Debashis Saha, Wayne Yaddow, Scott Haines, Sam Bail, Joy Payton, and Robert Ansel, for their sharp edits and valuable feedback on multiple drafts of the book. Their passion for bringing DevOps best practices and good data hygiene to the field is an inspiration, and we've been grateful to work with them.

We'd like to acknowledge—and thank a million times over—Ryan Kearns, a contributor to this book whose name could have been on the byline. From spearheading several chapters to offering critical insights on the technologies and processes discussed, this book would not have come together without his assistance. We learn from him every day and are so lucky to call him a dear colleague. In the coming years, Ryan will undoubtedly become one of the most important voices in data engineering and data science.

There were several industry experts and trailblazers we interviewed for this book and various other projects we've pursued over the past year. In no particular order, we'd like to thank Brandon Beidel, Alex Tverdohleb, António Fitas, Gopi Krishnamurthy, Manu Raj, Zhamak Dehghani, Mammad Zadeh, Greg Waldman, Wendy Turner Williams, Zosia Kossowski, Erik Bernhardsson, Jessica Cherny, Josh Wills, Kyle Shannon, Atul Gupte, Chad Sanderson, Patricia Ho, Michael Celentano, Prateek Chawla, Cindi Howson, Debashis Saha, Melody Chien, Ankush Jain, Maxime Beauchemin, DJ Patil, Bob Muglia, Mauricio de Diana, Shane Murray, Francisco Alberini, Mei Tao, Xuanzi Han, and Helena Munoz.

We'd also like to thank Brandon Gubitosa, Sara Gates, and Michael Segner for their assistance with outlines and drafts and for always encouraging us to "kill our darlings."

We're indebted to our parents, Elisha and Kadia Moses, Motti and Vira Gavish, and Gregg and Barbara Vorwerck, for encouraging us to pursue our passions for data engineering and data quality, from launching a company and category dedicated to the concept, to writing this book. We'd also like to thank Rae Barr Gavish (RBG) for being our number one fan, and Robert Ansel for being our resident SRE, WordPress consultant, and DevOps guru.

And we're forever indebted to our customers, who are helping us pioneer the data observability category and through the process laying the foundations for the future of reliable data at scale.

CHAPTER 1

Why Data Quality Deserves Attention—Now

Raise your hand (or spit out your coffee, sigh deeply, and shake your head) if this scenario rings a bell.

Data is a priority for your CEO, as it often is for digital-first companies, and she is fluent in the latest and greatest business intelligence tools. Your CTO is excited about migrating to the cloud, and constantly sends your team articles highlighting performance measurements against some of the latest technologies. Your downstream data consumers including product analysts, marketing leaders, and sales teams rely on data-driven tools like customer relationship management/customer experience platforms (CRMs/CXPs), content management systems (CMSs), and any other acronym under the sun to do their jobs quickly and effectively.

As the data analyst or engineer responsible for managing this data and making it usable, accessible, and trustworthy, rarely a day goes by without having to field some request from your stakeholders. But what happens when the data is wrong?

Have you ever been about to sign off after a long day running queries or building data pipelines only to get pinged by your head of marketing that "the data is missing" from a critical report? What about a frantic email from your CTO about "duplicate data" in a business intelligence dashboard? Or a memo from your CEO, the same one who is so bullish on data, about a confusing or inaccurate number in his latest board deck?

If any of these situations hit home for you, you're not alone.

This problem, often referred to as "data downtime," happens to even the most innovative and data-first companies, and, in our opinion, it's one of the biggest challenges facing businesses in the 21st century. Data downtime refers to periods of time where data is missing, inaccurate, or otherwise erroneous, and it manifests in stale dashboards, inaccurate reports, and even poor decision making.

The root of data downtime? Unreliable data, and lots of it.

Data downtime can cost companies upwards of millions of dollars per year (*https://oreil.ly/FF8kC*), not to mention customer trust. In fact, ZoomInfo found in 2019 that one in five companies lost a customer due to a data quality issue.

As you're likely aware, your company's bottom line isn't the only thing that's suffering from data downtime. Handling data quality issues consumes upwards of 40% of your data team's time (*https://oreil.ly/HEpED*) that could otherwise be spent working on more interesting projects or actually innovating for the business.

This statistic probably comes as no surprise to you. It certainly didn't to us.

In a former life, Barr Moses served as VP of Operations at a customer success software company. Her team was responsible for managing reporting for the broader business, from generating dashboards for her CEO to use during All Hands meetings to setting strategy to reduce customer churn based on user metrics. She was responsible for managing her company's data operations and making sure stakeholders were set up for success when working with data.

Barr will never forget the day she came back to her desk from a grueling, hours-long planning session to find a sticky note with the words "The data is wrong" on her computer monitor. Not only was this revelation embarrassing; unfortunately, it also wasn't uncommon. Time and again she and her team would encounter these silent and small, but potentially detrimental, issues with their data.

There had to be a better way.

Poor data quality and unreliable data have been problems for organizations for decades, whether it's caused by poor reporting, false information, or technical errors. And as organizations increasingly leverage data and build more and more complex data ecosystems and infrastructure, this problem is only slated to increase.

The concept of "bad data" and poor data quality has been around nearly as long as humans have existed, albeit in different forms. With Captain Robert Falcon Scott and other early Antarctic explorers, poor data quality (or rather, data-uninformed decision making) led them to inaccurately forecast where and how long it would take to get to the South Pole, their target destination.

Several in more recent memory stick out, too. Take the infamous Mars Climate Orbiter crash in 1999. A NASA space probe, the Mars Climate Orbiter crashed as a result of a data entry error that produced outputs in non-SI (International System) units versus SI units, bringing it too close to the planet. This crash cost NASA a whopping $125 million. Like spacecraft, analytic pipelines can be extremely vulnerable to the most innocent changes at any stage of the process. And this just scratches the surface.

Barr's unfortunate sticky note incident got her thinking: "I can't be alone!" Alongside Lior Gavish, Barr set out to get to the root cause of the "data downtime" issue. Together, they interviewed hundreds of data teams about their biggest problems, and time and again, data quality sprang to the top of the list. From ecommerce to healthcare, companies across industries were facing similar problems: schema changes were causing data pipelines to break, row or column duplicates were surfacing on business critical reports, and data would go missing in dashboards, causing them significant time, money, and resources to fix. We also realized that there needed to be a better way to communicate and address data quality issues as part of an iterative cycle of improving data reliability—and building a culture around driving data trust.

These conversations inspired us to write this book to convey some of the best practices we've learned and developed related to managing data quality at each stage of the data pipeline, from ingestion to analytics, and share how data teams in similar situations may be able to prevent their own data downtime.

For the purpose of this book, "data in production" refers to data from source systems (like CRMs, CMSs, and databases from any of the other analogies previously mentioned) that has been ingested by your warehouse, data lake, or other data storage and processing solutions and flows through your data pipeline (extract-transform-load, or ETL) so that it can be surfaced by the analytics layer to business users. Data pipelines can handle both batch and streaming data, and at a high level, the methods for measuring data quality for either type of asset are much the same.

Data downtime draws corollaries to software engineering and developer operations, a world in which application uptime or downtime (meaning, how frequently your software or service was "available" or "up" or "unavailable" or "down") is measured scrutinously to ensure that software is accessible and performant. Many site reliability engineers use "uptime" as a measurement because it correlates directly to the customer impact of poor software performance on the business. In a world where "five nines" (in other words, 99.999% uptime) of reliability is becoming the industry standard, how can we apply this to data?

In this book, we will address how modern data teams can build more resilient technologies, teams, and processes to ensure high data quality and reliability across their organizations.

In this chapter, we'll start by defining what data quality means in the context of this book. Next, we'll frame the current moment to better understand why data quality is more important for data leaders than ever before. And finally, we'll take a closer look at how best-in-class teams can achieve high data quality at each stage of the data pipeline and what it takes to maintain data trust at scale. This book focuses primarily on data quality as a function of powering data analytical data pipelines for building decision-making dashboards, data products, machine learning (ML) models, and other data science outputs.

What Is Data Quality?

Data quality as a concept is not novel—"data quality" has been around as long as humans have been collecting data!

Over the past few decades, however, the definition of data quality has started to crystallize as a function of measuring the reliability, completeness, and accuracy of data as it relates to the state of what is being reported on. As they say, you can't manage what you don't measure, and high data quality is the first stage of any robust analytics program. Data quality is also an extremely powerful way to understand whether your data fits the needs of your business.

For the purpose of this book, we define data quality as the health of data at any stage in its life cycle. Data quality can be impacted at any stage of the data pipeline, before ingestion, in production, or even during analysis.

In our opinion, data quality frequently gets a bad rep. Data teams know they need to prioritize it, but it doesn't roll off the tongue the same way "machine learning," "data science," or even "analytics" does, and many teams don't have the bandwidth or resources to bring on someone full time to manage it. Instead, resource-strapped companies rely on the data analysts and engineers themselves to manage it, diverting them from projects that are perceived to be more interesting or innovative.

But if you can't trust the data and the data products it powers, then how can data users trust your team to deliver value? The phrase, "no data is better than bad data" is one that gets thrown around a lot by professionals in the space, and while it certainly holds merit, this often isn't a reality.

Data quality issues (or, data downtime) are practically unavoidable given the rate of growth and data consumption of most companies. But by understanding how we define data quality, it becomes much easier to measure and prevent it from causing issues downstream.

Framing the Current Moment

Technical teams have been tracking—and seeking to improve—data quality for as long as they've been tracking analytical data, but only in the 2020s has data quality become a top-line priority for many businesses. As data becomes not just an output but a financial commodity for many organizations, it's important that this information can be trusted.

As a result, companies are increasingly treating their data like code, applying frameworks and paradigms long-standard among software engineering teams to their data organizations and architectures. Development operations (DevOps), a technical field dedicated to shortening the systems development life cycle, spawned industry-leading best practices such as site reliability engineering (SRE), CI/CD (continuous integration / continuous deployment), and microservices-based architectures. In short, the goal of DevOps is to release more reliable and performant software through automation.

Over the past few years, more and more companies have been applying these concepts to data in the form of "DataOps." DataOps refers to the process of improving the reliability and performance of your data through automation, reducing data silos and fostering quicker, more fault-tolerant analytics.

Since 2019, companies such as Intuit (*https://oreil.ly/NhMtB*), Airbnb (*https://oreil.ly/fbHlY*), Uber (*https://oreil.ly/0GhQC*), and Netflix (*https://oreil.ly/Ai2zC*) have written prolifically about their commitment to ensuring reliable, highly available data for stakeholders across the business by applying DataOps best practices. In addition to powering analytics-based decision making (i.e., product strategy, financial models, growth marketing, etc.), data produced by these companies powers their applications and digital services. Inaccurate, missing, or erroneous data can cost them time, money, and the trust of their customers.

As these tech behemoths increasingly shed light on the importance and challenges of achieving high data quality, other companies of all sizes and industries are starting to take note and replicate these efforts, from implementing more robust testing to investing in DataOps best practices like monitoring and data observability.

But what has led to this need for higher data quality? What about the data landscape has changed to facilitate the rise of DataOps, and as such the rise of data quality? We'll dig into these questions next.

Understanding the "Rise of Data Downtime"

With a greater focus on monetizing data coupled with the ever-present desire to increase data accuracy, we need to better understand some of the factors that can lead to data downtime. We'll take a closer look at variables that can impact your data next.

Migration to the cloud

Twenty years ago, your data warehouse (a place to transform and store structured data) probably would have lived in an office basement, not on AWS or Azure. Now, with the rise of data-driven analytics, cross-functional data teams, and most importantly, the cloud, cloud data warehousing solutions such as Amazon Redshift, Snowflake, and Google BigQuery have become increasingly popular options for companies bullish on data. In many ways, the cloud makes data easier to manage, more accessible to a wider variety of users, and far faster to process.

Not long after data warehouses moved to the cloud, so too did data lakes (a place to transform and store unstructured data), giving data teams even greater flexibility when it comes to managing their data assets. As companies and their data moved to the cloud, analytics-based decision making (and the need for high-quality data) became a greater priority for businesses.

More data sources

Nowadays, companies use anywhere from dozens to hundreds of internal and external data sources to produce analytics and ML models. Any one of these sources can change in unexpected ways and without notice, compromising the data the company uses to make decisions.

For example, an engineering team might make a change to the company's website, thereby modifying the output of a data set that is key to marketing analytics. As a result, key marketing metrics may be wrong, leading the company to make poor decisions about ad campaigns, sales targets, and other important, revenue-driving projects.

Increasingly complex data pipelines

Data pipelines have become increasingly complex with multiple stages of processing and nontrivial dependencies between various data assets as a result of more advanced (and disparate) tooling, more data sources, and increasing diligence afforded to data by executive leadership. Without visibility into these dependencies, however, any change made to one data set can have unintended consequences impacting the correctness of dependent data assets.

In short, a lot goes on in a data pipeline. Source data is extracted, ingested, transformed, loaded, stored, processed, and delivered, among other possible steps, with many APIs and integrations between different stages of the pipeline. At each juncture, there's an opportunity for data downtime, just like there's an opportunity for application downtime whenever code is merged. Additionally, things can go wrong even when data isn't at a critical juncture, for instance, when data is migrated between warehouses or manually entered in a source system.

More specialized data teams

As companies increasingly rely on data to drive smart decision making, they are hiring more and more data analysts, data scientists, and data engineers to build and maintain the data pipelines, analytics, and ML models that power their services and products, as well as their business operations.

While data analysts are primarily responsible for gathering, cleaning, and querying data sets to help functional stakeholders produce rich, actionable insights about the business, data engineers are responsible for ensuring that the underlying technologies and systems powering these analytics are performant, fast, and reliable. In industry, data scientists typically collect, wrangle, augment, and make sense of unstructured data to improve the business. The distinction between data analysts and data scientists can be a little vague, and titles and responsibilities often vary depending on the needs of the company. For instance, in the late 2010s, Uber changed all data analysts' titles to data scientists after an organizational restructure.

As data becomes more and more foundational to business, data teams will only grow. In fact, larger companies may support additional roles including data stewards, data governance leaders, operations analysts, and even analytics engineers (a hybrid data engineer-analyst role popular with startups and mid-sized companies who may not have the resources to support a large data team).

With all of these different users touching the data, miscommunication or insufficient coordination is inevitable and will cause these complex systems to break as changes are made. For example, a new field added to a data table by one team may cause another team's pipeline to fail, resulting in missing or partial data. Downstream, this bad data can lead to millions of dollars in lost revenue, erosion of customer trust, and even compliance risk.

Decentralized data teams

As data becomes central to business operations, more and more functional teams across the company have gotten involved in data management and analytics to streamline and speed up the insights gathering process. Consequently, more and more data teams are adopting a distributed, decentralized model that mimics the industry-wide migration from monolithic to microservice architectures that took the software engineering world by storm in the mid-2010s.

What is a decentralized data architecture? Not to be confused with the data mesh (*https://oreil.ly/Vga7I*), which is an organizational paradigm that leverages a distributed, domain-oriented design, a decentralized data architecture is managed by a central data platform team, with analytical and data science teams distributed across the business. Increasingly, we're finding that more and more teams leaning into the embedded data analyst model are relying on this type of architecture.

For instance, your 200-person company may support a team of 3 data engineers and 10 data analysts, with analysts distributed across functional teams to better support the needs of the business. These analysts will report to operational teams or centralized data teams but own specific data sets and reporting functions. Multiple domains will generate and leverage data, leading to the inevitability that data sets used by multiple teams become duplicated, go missing, or go stale over time. If you're reading this book, you're probably no stranger to the experience of using a data set that's no longer relevant, unbeknownst to you!

Other Industry Trends Contributing to the Current Moment

In addition to the aforementioned factors that frequently lead to data downtime, several industry shifts are also occurring as a result of technological innovation that are driving transformation of the data landscape. These shifts are all contributors to this heightened attention to data quality.

Data mesh

Much in the same way that software engineering teams transitioned from monolithic applications to microservice architectures, the data mesh is, in many ways, the data platform version of microservices. It's important to note that the concept of data mesh is nascent, and there is much discussion in the data community regarding how (or whether it makes sense) to execute on one at both a cultural and technical level.

As first defined by Zhamak Dehghani, a Thoughtworks consultant and the original architect of the term, a data mesh, illustrated in Figure 1-1, is a sociotechnical paradigm that recognizes the interactions between people and the technical architecture and solutions in complex organizations. The data mesh embraces the ubiquity of data in the enterprise by leveraging a domain-oriented, self-serve design. It utilizes Eric Evans's theory of domain-driven design, a flexible, scalable software development paradigm that matches the structure and language of your code with its corresponding business domain.

Unlike traditional monolithic data infrastructures that handle the consumption, storage, transformation, and output of data in one central data lake, a data mesh supports distributed, domain-specific data consumers and views "data-as-a-product," with each domain handling their own data pipelines. The tissue connecting these domains and their associated data assets is a universal interoperability layer that applies the same syntax and data standards.

Data meshes federate data ownership among domain data owners who are held accountable for providing their data as products, while also facilitating communication between distributed data across different locations.

While the data infrastructure is responsible for providing each domain with the solutions with which to process it, domains are tasked with managing ingestion, cleaning, and aggregation of the data to generate assets that can be used by business intelligence applications. Each domain is responsible for owning their pipelines, but there is a set of capabilities applied to all domains that stores, catalogs, and maintains access controls for the raw data. Once data has been served to and transformed by a given domain, the domain owners can then leverage the data for their analytics or operational needs.

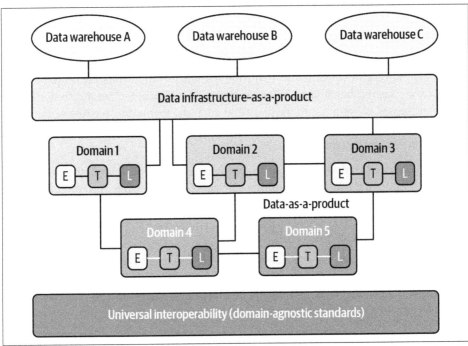

Figure 1-1. The data mesh, pioneered by Zhamak Dehghani, pushes for a decentralized, domain-oriented data architecture that relies on high-quality reliable data and universal governance

The data mesh paradigm is successful only if the data is reliable and trustworthy, and if this "universal interoperability layer" is applied across domains. The only way data can be reliable and trustworthy? Close attention to data quality through testing, monitoring, and observability.

Many companies are adopting the data mesh paradigm, particularly larger organizations with the need for multiple data domains. For instance, in a January 2021 blog article (*https://oreil.ly/oxTyk*) written by Intuit's former VP of Data Engineering, Mammad Zadeh, and Raji Arasu, Intuit's SVP of Core Services & Experiences, Intuit positions itself as a "AI-driven expert platform company," whose platform "collects, processes, and transforms a steady stream of data into a connected mesh of high-quality data." Another example is JPMorgan Chase (*https://oreil.ly/Tga4W*), which built a data mesh architecture to help them delineate data ownership between discrete analytics functions and improve visibility into data sharing across the enterprise.

Regardless of your perspective on the data mesh, it's certainly taken the data community by storm and surfaced great conversation—and blog articles (*https://oreil.ly/rcFTp*)—on the future of our distributed data architectures and team structures.

Streaming data

Streaming data refers to the process of transmitting a continuous flow of data into your pipeline to quickly generate real-time insights. Traditionally, data quality was enforced via testing batch data before it entered production pipelines, but increasingly, businesses are seeking more real-time analysis. While this has the potential to make insights faster, it also opens up greater questions and challenges related to data quality since streaming data is data "in motion."

Increasingly, organizations are adopting both batch processing and stream processing, which forces data teams to rethink their approach to testing and observing their data.

Rise of the data lakehouse

Data warehouse or data lake? That is the question—at least if you ask a data engineer. Data warehouses, a structured data repository, and data lakes, a pool of raw, unstructured data, both rely on high-quality data for processing and transformation. Increasingly, data teams are opting to use both data warehouses and data lakes to accommodate the growing data needs of their business. Meet: the data lakehouse.

Data lakehouses first came onto the scene when cloud warehouse providers began adding features that offer lake-style benefits, such as Redshift Spectrum or Databricks Lakehouse. Similarly, data lakes have been adding technologies that offer warehouse-style features, such as SQL functionality and schema. Today, the historical differences between warehouses and lakes are narrowing so you can access the best of both worlds in one package.

This migration to the lakehouse model suggests that pipelines are growing more and more complex, and while some might choose one dedicated vendor to tackle both, others are migrating data to multiple storage and processing layers, leading to more opportunities for pipeline data to break even with ample testing.

Summary

The rise of the cloud, distributed data architectures and teams, and the move toward data productization have put the onus on data leaders to help their companies drive toward more trustworthy data (leading to more trustworthy analytics). Achieving reliable data is a marathon, not a sprint, and involves many stages of your data pipeline. Further, committing to improving data quality is much more than a technical challenge; it's very much organizational and cultural, too. In the next chapter, we'll discuss some technologies your team can use to prevent broken pipelines and build repeatable, iterative processes and frameworks with which to better communicate, address, and even prevent data downtime.

CHAPTER 2

Assembling the Building Blocks of a Reliable Data System

With Ryan Kearns

While solving data quality issues in production is a critical skill set for any data practitioner, data downtime can often be prevented almost entirely with the right systems and processes in place.

Like software, data can rely on any number of operational, programmatic, or even data-related influences at various stages in the pipeline, and all it takes is one schema change or code push to send a downstream report into disarray.

As we'll discuss in Chapter 8, solving for data quality and building more reliable pipelines is broken into three key components: process, technologies, and people. In this chapter, we'll tackle the technology component of this equation, mapping together the disparate pieces of the data pipeline and what it takes to measure, fix, and prevent data downtime at each step.

Data systems are ridiculously complex, with various stages in the data pipeline contributing to this chaos. And as companies increasingly invest in data and analytics, the pressure to build at scale puts serious pressure on data engineers to account for quality before data even enters the pipeline.

In this chapter, we'll highlight the various metadata-powered building blocks—from data catalogs to data warehouses and lakes—to ensure your data infrastructure is set up for success when it comes to ensuring high-quality data at each stage of the pipeline.

Understanding the Difference Between Operational and Analytical Data

If you ask a data engineer for the broadest possible distinction between data within their organization, you might hear the terms "operational data" and "analytical data." The operational versus analytical distinction is just one of many ways to cleave the data in your ecosystem. But it's an important one, and one you'll need to understand if you're interested in adopting a culture of data quality.

While we'll dive into operational data a bit here, it's important to note that for the purposes of this book, we have been and will continue to focus on data quality as it relates to analytical data. Managing the quality and reliability of operational data often lies in the realm of DevOps, site reliability engineering, and other software disciplines more concerned with building software products that are informed by analytical data.

Operational data

> Data produced operationally—that is, by the day-to-day ongoing operations at your organization (*https://oreil.ly/kZmui*). Inventory snapshots at moments in time, customer impressions, and transaction records are all examples of operational data.

Analytical data

> Data used analytically. This is to say, it's the type of data behind data-driven business decisions. Marketing churn, clickthrough rates, and impressions by global region are all examples of analytical data categories.

In a nutshell, operational data records data from actual business processes for quick updates to systems and processes, while analytical data is used for more robust and efficient analysis. One easy way of thinking about this is that operational data *runs* your business while analytical data *manages* your business. Given that analytical data drives business intelligence in a way operational data does not, one might be tempted to suspect this data is more important or more "central" to an organization's success. Yet more often than not, analytical data rests on a backbone of operational data transformations and aggregations.

 This operational versus analytical distinction is the same one made by the comparison between transaction-processing and analytic data systems (OLTP versus OLAP), e.g., in *Designing Data-Intensive Applications* (O'Reilly).

What Makes Them Different?

As you likely guessed, analytical and operational data are different in a few critical ways that inform how we manage their reliability, as depicted in Figure 2-1.

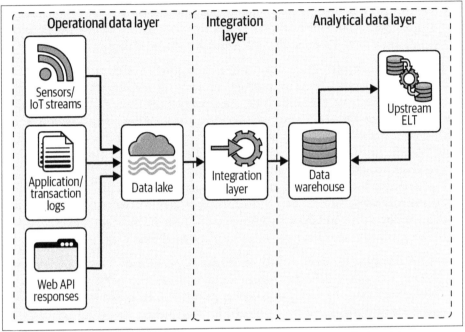

Figure 2-1. An example data platform, illustrating just one way to distinguish operational and analytical data

Almost always, operational data appears *upstream* from analytical data in your data pipelines. This is because analytical data can and often does contain aggregations or augmentations of operational datastores. The clickthrough rate of a given user from her browser at 5 a.m. is one operational datum, and the clickthrough rate for your December marketing campaign is a corresponding analytical datum.

One crucial reason for why the operational versus analytical data distinction is important is what's called the *throughput versus latency trade-off*. The throughput–latency constraint affects any system with fixed computational power. Traditionally *throughput* refers to the quantity of data processed within some unit of time, and *latency* refers to the delay before data is processed.

Think of a popular internet cafe with a line outside. How long before someone at the end of the line receives their coffee? This process involves standing in line, ordering, paying, and then waiting for the barista to make the drink. The sum total of this time describes the cafe's *latency*. Conversely, the number of customers able to enjoy their coffees indoors in, say, an hour's time describes the *throughput* of the cafe.

Unfortunately, these two measures of data processing performance are doomed to compete. We cannot have both high throughput and low latency for our internet cafe. But why, you ask? It's not like throughput and latency describe *opposite* ideals. The answer has to do with how data processing systems are architected in reality (*https://oreil.ly/nf0nq*)—specifically, with a *limited* number of request handlers.

Imagine, again, our internet cafe. We have a fixed number of employees at our cafe, and those robot serve-o-trons we ordered are on backlog due to the chip shortage. As managers, we have to decide how many employees should staff the espresso machines and registers, and how many should go around bussing tables. Notice the trade-off yet? Suppose we try at all costs to optimize our cafe latency. This would involve staffing nearly *all* of our employees at the registers and espresso machines, so that drinks could be ordered and picked up as fast as possible. Yet if we do this, we're guaranteed to drastically reduce our throughput, since no one is around to bus tables and make space for the new customers. If, by contrast, we relegate most of our workers to hover around tables, snatching empty cups the moment they're forfeited, our latency will increase—because no one is operating the cash register!

In certain cases, the balance to strike is obvious. Operational—that is, transactional (*https://oreil.ly/IZfuX*)—databases require certain information like order details to be fetched on page load as quickly as possible. As a result, their architectures, through various design decisions, will be optimized for low latency. Analytical databases, by contrast, cater to users conducting large aggregations across massive data sets, and so they must optimize for high throughput. This heuristic won't pass for flawless advice about which services to employ for what, but it at least explains why you won't generally query Snowflake or Redshift from a customer UI or run trillion-row aggregations in your MySQL or Postgres instance.

Data Warehouses Versus Data Lakes

Data warehouses and data lakes—perhaps no two words receive as much headspace in the day-to-day vernacular of a data engineering team. While warehouses and lakes are not interchangeable, these technologies are rapidly converging, with each offering the best of both worlds.

Many organizations genuinely require both kinds of systems within their data pipelines, but they're used for quite different things. Generally, data *warehouses* store data in a structured (row-column) format. Such data is highly transformed (the result of defined preprocessing procedures) and present only because it has a determinate *reason* for being there—at least, in theory.

Data *lakes* by contrast store *anything*—structured data, semi-structured data, unstructured data. Unlike warehouses, data lakes need not have highly specified procedures through which data enters—you can dump any format you like into a lake and directly access it. The result is a system that is typically higher volume and often more complex in terms of its governance and data.

Data Warehouses: Table Types at the Schema Level

Data warehouses require "schema on write" access, meaning we set the structure of the data at the instant it enters the warehouse. Further transformations of this data must make its new structure explicit at every step.

Data warehouses are fully integrated and managed solutions, making them simple to build and operate out of the box. Unlike data lakes, data warehouses typically require more structure and schema, which often forces better data hygiene and results in less complexity when reading and consuming data.

The modern data warehouse owes its conception in part to the Kimball Group, who developed the Data Warehouse / Business Intelligence Lifecycle Methodology (*https://oreil.ly/uxbcY*) in the 1980s. This innovation in systems design championed *business value* across all levels of the enterprise, including the stages of data ingestion and preprocessing most often occupied by engineers. Kimball was influential in identifying data storage techniques as *business assets* instead of mere technological preferences.

Modern data warehouses follow this methodology with their schema-on-write architectures and ready integrations to business intelligence tools like Looker and Tableau. Simply put, data in a data warehouse has *reasons for being there*, and those reasons should correspond to a business objective of some kind.

Today, common data warehouse technologies include:

Amazon Redshift
> The first widely popular (and readily available) cloud data warehouse, Amazon Redshift sits on top of Amazon Web Services (AWS) and leverages source connectors to pipe data from raw data sources into relational storage. Redshift's columnar storage structure and parallel processing make it ideal for analytic workloads.

Google BigQuery
> Like Redshift, Google BigQuery leverages its mothership's proprietary cloud platform (Google Cloud Platform, or GCP), uses a columnar storage format, and takes advantage of parallel processing for quick querying. Unlike Redshift, BigQuery is a serverless solution that scales according to usage patterns.

Snowflake

Unlike Redshift or GCP, which rely on their proprietary clouds to operate, Snowflake's cloud data warehousing capabilities are powered by AWS, Google, Azure, and other public cloud infrastructures. Unlike Redshift, Snowflake allows users to pay separate fees for compute and storage, making the data warehouse a great option for teams looking for a more flexible pay structure.

Owing to its prepackaged functionalities and strong support for SQL, data warehouses facilitate fast, actionable querying, making them great for data analytics teams.

While data warehouses can be extremely valuable for business analytics use cases, there are a few drawbacks you should keep in mind, particularly as related to managing data quality:

Limited flexibility

Data warehouses are not the most flexible data storage solution on the market. This is not to say they don't scale well—many of the best modern solutions famously do—but instead that the format of data in warehouses is limited. Entries into a data warehouse must be coerced into tabular form with a definite schema. Semi-structured data like JSON, and the querying thereof, is typically not naturally supported, and bad data often falls through the cracks.

SQL-only support

Querying a data warehouse will require the use of a query language like SQL. There's generally no support for data manipulation with imperative languages like Python, useful for machine learning due to a strong library ecosystem. Thus, many machine learning implementations require data to be moved *out* of a warehouse, via SQL, for further processing. Again, this movement of data is where it often breaks and volume, freshness, and schema anomalies occur.

Frictional workflows

A small team of data scientists, working closely together on a quickly iterating product, might find the cleanliness afforded by the schema-on-write system more cumbersome than beneficial. When you want to work fast, it's to your benefit to have lax standards as to the structure of your data. That structure will be constantly changing, and constant schema change is not something a data warehouse happily supports.

For these reasons, it's not uncommon for data teams to adopt both data warehouses and lakes for analytical workloads, each serving a different purpose.

Data Lakes: Manipulations at the File Level

Data lakes, another increasingly popular storage and compute option for modern data systems, also rely on high-quality analytical data to deliver optimal results.

Unlike data warehouses, data lake architectures permit "schema on read" access. This means we infer the structure of the data when we're ready to use it.

Data lakes are the do-it-yourself version of a data warehouse, allowing teams to pick and choose the various metadata, storage, and compute technologies they want to use depending on the needs of their systems. Data lakes are ideal for data teams looking to build a more customized platform, often supported by a handful (or more) of data engineers. With data lakes, data scientists, ML engineers, and data engineers can draw from a much larger pool of data that includes both semi-structured and unstructured formats.

The concept of a data lake was first brought to life by James Dixon, the founder and former CTO of software company Pentaho, which he described (*https://oreil.ly/ M2rLh*) as "a large body of water in a more natural state. The contents of the data lake stream in from a source to fill the lake, and various users of the lake can come to examine, dive in, or take samples."

Very early data lakes were built primarily on Apache Hadoop MapReduce and HDFS, leveraging Apache Hive to query their data with a SQL engine. In the early 2010s, Apache Spark made data lakes much more tenable, providing a generalized framework for distributed computations across large data sets in the data lake.

Some common features of data lakes include:

Decoupled storage and compute
Not only can this functionality allow for substantial cost savings, but it also facilitates parsing and enriching of the data for real-time streaming and querying.

Support for distributed compute
Distributed computing helps support the performance of large-scale data processing because it allows for better segmented query performance, more fault-tolerant design, and superior parallel data processing.

Customization and interoperability
Owing to their "plug and chug" nature, data lakes support data platform scalability by making it easy for different elements of your stack to play well together as the data needs of your company evolve and mature.

Largely built on open source technologies
This facilitates reduced vendor lock-in and affords great customization, which works well for companies with large data engineering teams.

Ability to handle unstructured or weakly structured data
Data lakes can support raw data, meaning that you have greater flexibility when it comes to working with your data, ideal for data scientists and data engineers. Working with raw data gives you more control over your aggregates and calculations.

Support for sophisticated non-SQL programming models
> Unlike most data warehouses, data lakes support Apache Hadoop, Apache Spark, PySpark, and other frameworks for advanced data science and machine learning.

While data warehouses provide structure that makes it easy for data teams to efficiently operationalize data (i.e., gleaning analytic insights and supporting machine learning capabilities), that structure can make them inflexible and expensive for certain applications. On the other hand, data lakes are infinitely flexible and customizable to support a wide range of use cases, but with that greater agility comes a host of other issues related to data organization and governance.

Here are a few salient challenges data teams face when trying to achieve more reliable data across their lake environments:

Data integrity
> Resources in a data lake, being manipulated at the file level, have no guarantees as to their data's schema. If you're transforming data in a lake with some assumption as to its schema, you're doing something called "blind ETL," which is incredibly dangerous. Transformations may fail at any point due to unforeseen upstream changes.

Swampification
> Swampification refers to the tendency for data lakes to incur technical debt and tacit knowledge over time. Often, you'll have to rely on a skilled data engineer or data scientist for knowledge about where certain data resides, who its stakeholders are, and how it might be expected to change. Lean too heavily on this and your data lake "swampifies," meaning no one can get any work done because data literacy comes at a high learning curve.

More endpoints
> Data reliability is often a bigger challenge in data lakes because there are more ways that data can be collected, manipulated, and transformed. More steps in the pipeline introduces more opportunity for error.

Data lakes are often used as collection points for large quantities of unstructured data, such as application data or auto-generated data for the purposes of some machine learning task. This data can either remain in its raw format in the lake or be intended to feed some upstream resource, possibly in a data warehouse or business intelligence tool, via an integration layer like AWS Glue.

Alternatively, smaller teams might operate with a data lake as their sole data store for the purposes of moving quickly and not settling on a robust infrastructure—though practitioners of this should always be wary of the "data swamp" problem.

What About the Data Lakehouse?

Data lakehouses first came onto the scene when cloud warehouse providers began adding features that offer lake-style benefits, such as Redshift Spectrum or Delta Lake. Similarly, data lakes have been adding technologies that offer warehouse-style features, such as SQL functionality and schema. Today, the historical differences between warehouses and lakes are narrowing so you can access the best of both words in one package.

The following functionalities are helping data lakehouses further blur the lines between the two technologies:

High-performance SQL
> Technologies like Presto and Spark provide a SQL interface at close to interactive speeds over data lakes. This opened the possibility of data lakes serving analysis and exploratory needs directly, without requiring summarization and ETL into traditional data warehouses.

Schema
> File formats like Parquet introduced more rigid schema to data lake tables, as well as a columnar format for greater query efficiency.

Atomicity, consistency, isolation, and durability (ACID)
> Lake technologies like Delta Lake and Apache Hudi introduced greater reliability in write/read transactions, and took lakes a step closer to the highly desirable ACID properties that are standard in traditional database technologies.

Managed services
> For teams that want to reduce the operational lift associated with building and running a data lake, cloud providers offer a variety of managed lake services. For example, Databricks offers managed versions of Apache Hive, Delta Lake, and Apache Spark while Amazon Athena offers a fully managed lake SQL query engine and Amazon's Glue offers a fully managed metadata service.

With the rise of real-time data aggregation and streaming to inform lightspeed analytics (think Silicon Valley tech giant speeds: Uber, DoorDash, and Airbnb), data lakehouses are likely to rise in popularity and relevance for data teams across industries in the coming years.

Syncing Data Between Warehouses and Lakes

Different data warehouses and lakes are bridged by a *data integration layer*. Data integration tools, such as AWS Glue, Fivetran, and Matillion, collect data from disparate sources, unify this data, and transform it into an upstream source. A classic use case of data integration would be to collect lake data and load it in a structured format into one's data warehouse.

Extract-transform-load, or ETL, is one well-known process within data integration. ETL generally describes integration steps where data is first *extracted* from one or more data stores, *transformed* into a new structure or format, and finally *loaded* into a destination data store.

Now that we've discussed these core elements of the modern data pipeline, let's dive into how they all work together and what we can do to ensure high data quality at each step.

Collecting Data Quality Metrics

So far, we've covered various distinctions like operational versus analytical data, transactional versus analytical databases, and data lakes versus data warehouses. Understanding all of these distinctions helps us know exactly where our data may reside. We also get a sense of the various advantages and risks of different storage formats and steps in one's data pipeline. But when it comes to data quality, which metrics specifically should we be taking into account?

In this next section we'll talk about *data quality metrics*—what they are, where they might be found, and how you know you're leveraging them correctly.

What Are Data Quality Metrics?

You can't fix what you can't measure. Likewise, you can't have data quality without data quality metrics, in other words, key performance indicators (KPIs) or other indicators that your data is healthy and reliable enough to be used by stakeholders.

We advocate measuring data quality in terms of data downtime—periods of time when your data is partial, erroneous, missing, or otherwise inaccurate. As mentioned previously, we call it "downtime" to harken back to the early days of the internet. Back then, online applications were a nice-to-have, and if they were down for a while, it was not a big deal. You could afford downtime, since businesses were not overly reliant on them. We're now two decades into the Internet Age (or beyond it, depending on whom you ask!), and online applications are mission-critical to almost every business. As a result, companies measure downtime meticulously and invest a lot of resources in avoiding service interruptions.

Similarly, companies are increasingly reliant on data to run their daily operations and make mission-critical decisions. But we aren't yet treating data downtime with the diligence it demands. While a handful of companies are putting service-level agreements (SLAs) in place to hold data teams accountable to accurate and reliable data, it is not the norm yet. In the coming years, we expect there will be increased scrutiny around data downtime and increased focus on minimizing it.

In assessing whether your data is down, you might build a list of questions:

- Is the data up-to-date?
- Is the data complete?
- Are fields within expected ranges?
- Is the null rate higher or lower than it should be?
- Has the schema changed?

This list might not be exhaustive for your own data quality needs, but it's a good place to start. It moves us from answering one broad and difficult question ("Is my data down?") to a sequence of more specific ones. We're well on our way to data quality *metrics*, which should answer questions like the preceding with quantitative and measurable results.

How to Pull Data Quality Metrics

The answers to the preceding questions come from analysis of specific data *assets*, which mostly take the form of the resources we discussed earlier in this chapter—data warehouses, lakes, the transformation layers between them, and so on.

How do we go about formulating data quality metrics from a warehouse environment? Recall from "Data Warehouses: Table Types at the Schema Level" on page 17 that data warehouses are differentiated by their structured content and "schema-on-write" architecture.

Scalability

Tracking a large number of tables and big data sets can become tricky. You'll need to think about batching your calls, optimizing your queries for scale, deduplicating, normalizing the various schemas, and storing all this information in a scalable store so you can make sense of it. This requires building a dedicated data pipeline that you operate, update, and maintain over time.

 Don't forget to keep track of your Snowflake credit consumption (you don't want to be getting a call from your CFO).

Monitoring across other parts of your stack

Building truly reliable data pipelines and achieving data observability requires more than collecting metrics. In fact, as the modern data stack evolves, it has become critical to keep tabs on the reliability of real-time streaming data, data lakes, dashboards, ML models, and other assets.

Monitoring data quality metrics as your data stack grows to incorporate additional technologies and data sources is a fundamental challenge. Since data can break literally anywhere in your pipeline, you will need a way to pull metrics and metadata from not just your warehouse but other assets too.

Investing in solutions that allow these integrations to play nice with each other and your end users, whether that's your data engineers, analytics engineers, ML teams, or data scientists, should be a top priority. True data observability (*https://oreil.ly/Zbtj3*) extends beyond the warehouse to provide insights into the health of data in your lakes, ETL, business intelligence dashboards, and beyond before broken data snowballs into bigger problems down the road.

In the following section, we highlight how you'd go about pulling data quality metrics from Snowflake to measure data health in the warehouse. While we leverage Snowflake for this specific example, pulling data quality information from Redshift, BigQuery, and other popular OLAP-based warehouses follows a similar process.

Example: Pulling data quality metrics from Snowflake

Snowflake is one of the most popular cloud data warehousing tools, and its design has prioritized data quality and integrity from the very beginning. One of the most important features of the warehouse when it comes to building more reliable data pipelines is the ability to pull data quality metrics directly from the warehouse and visualize them for easy analysis (see Figure 2-2).

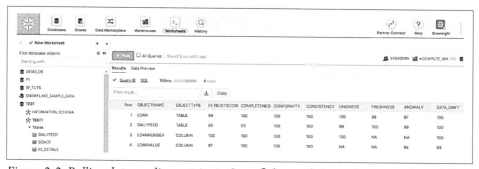

Figure 2-2. Pulling data quality metrics in Snowflake can help render a snapshot of data health in the warehouse at a given point in time

Here are the four steps you need to take to successfully glean data quality metrics from Snowflake. (Keep in mind that this tutorial is applicable to other brands of data warehouse as well, with a few adjustments.)

Step 1: Map your inventory. For the purposes of this tutorial, let's assume you have a single database on Snowflake called ANALYTICS (although, as with most data stacks, this is rarely the case). To run the following queries in your environment, simply replace ANALYTICS with the name of the database you are looking to track. To list the databases in your account, you can run SHOW DATABASES.

Your first step will be to map all the tables you have in your warehouse so you know what needs to be tracked in the first place. While you do so, mapping schema can be a powerful tool in understanding what's in each table, and how that changes over time.

Here's how to do that with Snowflake, as depicted in Example 2-1.

Example 2-1. Query to pull a list of tables with their relevant metadata

```
SELECT
 TABLE_CATALOG,
 TABLE_SCHEMA,
 TABLE_NAME,
 TABLE_OWNER,
 TABLE_TYPE,
 IS_TRANSIENT,
 RETENTION_TIME,
 AUTO_CLUSTERING_ON,
 COMMENT
FROM "ANALYTICS".information_schema.tables
WHERE
 table_schema NOT IN ('INFORMATION_SCHEMA')
 AND TABLE_TYPE NOT IN ('VIEW', 'EXTERNAL TABLE')
ORDER BY TABLE_CATALOG, TABLE_SCHEMA, TABLE_NAME;
```

This query will fetch a list of all tables along with helpful metadata about their settings. The *comment* property is particularly useful if you've been diligent about documenting your data with COMMENT (*https://oreil.ly/CZvoU*).

To get the schema for your tables—understanding how it evolves can really help prevent and troubleshoot data breakages—you might use the query in Example 2-2.

Example 2-2. Retrieving the schema for tables in Snowflake

```
SELECT
 '"' || TABLE_CATALOG || '"."' || TABLE_SCHEMA || '"."' || TABLE_NAME
   || '"' AS FULL_NAME,
 COLUMN_NAME,
 DATA_TYPE,
 COLUMN_DEFAULT,
 IS_NULLABLE,
 COMMENT,
 CHARACTER_MAXIMUM_LENGTH,
 NUMERIC_PRECISION,
 NUMERIC_SCALE,
 DATETIME_PRECISION
FROM "ANALYTICS".information_schema.columns;
```

Please note that the preceding snippets will help with tables, but we intentionally left out views and external tables. To pull metadata for those, we recommend using the following queries:

```
SHOW VIEWS IN DATABASE "ANALYTICS";
SHOW EXTERNAL TABLES IN DATABASE "ANALYTICS";
```

While it might add complexity to your implementation, these queries will fetch valuable information that is not available when querying `information_schema.tables`. For example, you will have the text property for views—which will provide insight about the underlying SQL query for your views.

Step 2: Monitor for data freshness and volume. Tracking volume and freshness for your tables is incredibly important (*https://oreil.ly/ICi96*) in understanding Snowflake data observability and the overall health of your data pipelines. Thankfully, Snowflake tracks that information as writes are made to tables in the warehouse. You can pull how many bytes and rows tables have, as well as the time they were most recently updated using this query (Example 2-3).

Example 2-3. Query generating results correlating to the freshness of the table

```
SELECT
 TABLE_CATALOG,
 TABLE_SCHEMA,
 TABLE_NAME,
 ROW_COUNT,
 BYTES,
 CONVERT_TIMEZONE('UTC', CREATED) as CREATED,
 CONVERT_TIMEZONE('UTC', LAST_ALTERED) as LAST_ALTERED
FROM "ANALYTICS".information_schema.tables
WHERE
 table_schema NOT IN ('INFORMATION_SCHEMA')
 AND TABLE_TYPE NOT IN ('VIEW', 'EXTERNAL TABLE')
ORDER BY TABLE_CATALOG, TABLE_SCHEMA, TABLE_NAME;
```

By storing these metrics and observing how they change over time, you can map how frequently tables get updated, how much data is to be expected in each update, and, most importantly, identify missing or anomalous updates.

Measuring the freshness and volume of views is not straightforward, as it is a function of the tables included in the underlying queries. As far as external tables go, we recommend using freshness information from `SHOW EXTERNAL TABLES....`

Step 3: Build your query history. Having a solid history of all the queries running in your Snowflake environment is an invaluable tool when troubleshooting issues—it lets you see exactly how and when a table was most recently written to. More broadly, an analysis of your query logs can help map lineage (dependencies between tables), understand which users use which assets, and even optimize the performance and cost of your Snowflake instance.

Example 2-4 is the query we use to extract query logs—notice we'll be filtering out system and faulty queries to reduce noise. This can provide vital information about who was using a given table and for what purpose.

Example 2-4. Extracting query logs

```
SELECT
    "QUERY_TEXT",
    "DATABASE_NAME",
    "SCHEMA_NAME",
    "QUERY_TYPE",
    "USER_NAME",
    "ROLE_NAME",
    "EXECUTION_STATUS",
    "START_TIME",
    "END_TIME",
    "TOTAL_ELAPSED_TIME",
    "BYTES_SCANNED",
    "ROWS_PRODUCED",
    "SESSION_ID",
    "QUERY_ID",
    "QUERY_TAG",
    "WAREHOUSE_NAME",
    "ROWS_INSERTED",
    "ROWS_UPDATED",
    "ROWS_DELETED",
    "ROWS_UNLOADED"
FROM snowflake.account_usage.query_history
WHERE
    start_time BETWEEN to_timestamp_ltz('2021-01-01 00:00:00.000000+00:00')
      AND to_timestamp_ltz('2021-01-01 01:00:00.000000+00:00')
    AND QUERY_TYPE NOT IN ('DESCRIBE', 'SHOW')
    AND (DATABASE_NAME IS NULL OR DATABASE_NAME NOT IN ('UTIL_DB', 'SNOWFLAKE'))
    AND ERROR_CODE is NULL
ORDER BY start_time DESC;
```

You might also find it valuable to take a look at the history of copy and load operations to understand how data is loaded and moved around (Example 2-5). This can provide insights into table freshness.

Example 2-5. Query to gather information about how the data is loaded

```
SELECT
    "FILE_NAME",
    "STAGE_LOCATION",
    "LAST_LOAD_TIME",
    "ROW_COUNT",
```

```
        "FILE_SIZE",
        "ERROR_COUNT",
        "STATUS",
        "TABLE_CATALOG_NAME",
        "TABLE_SCHEMA_NAME",
        "TABLE_NAME",
        "PIPE_CATALOG_NAME",
        "PIPE_SCHEMA_NAME",
        "PIPE_NAME",
        "PIPE_RECEIVED_TIME"
FROM snowflake.account_usage.copy_history
WHERE
    LAST_LOAD_TIME between to_timestamp_ltz('2021-01-01 00:00:00.000000+00:00')
        AND to_timestamp_ltz('2021-01-01 01:00:00.000000+00:00')
    AND STATUS != 'load failed'
ORDER BY LAST_LOAD_TIME DESC;
```

In the next step, we take our analysis of data quality in Snowflake a step further by running queries to monitor for null and zero values—signals that something might be wrong.

Step 4: Health check. Finally, for some of your critical tables, you might want to run data quality checks to make sure all fields are populated properly and have healthy values. By tracking health metrics over time and comparing them to past batches, you can find a range of data quality issues as soon as they appear in your data. Example 2-6 queries a historical record of your Snowflake data, which will help you understand where there might be anomalies in a given table.

Example 2-6. Querying a historical record of Snowflake data

```
SELECT
    DATE_TRUNC('HOUR', created_on) as bucket_start,
    DATEADD(hr, 1, DATE_TRUNC('HOUR', created_on)) as bucket_end,

    COUNT(*) as row_count,

    -- string field
    COUNT(account_id) / CAST(COUNT(*) AS NUMERIC) as account_id___completeness,
    COUNT(DISTINCT account_id) as account_id___approx_distinct_count,
    COUNT(DISTINCT account_id) / CAST(COUNT(*) AS NUMERIC)
        as account_id___approx_distinctness,
    AVG(LENGTH(account_id)) as account_id___mean_length,
    MAX(LENGTH(account_id)) as account_id___max_length,
    MIN(LENGTH(account_id)) as account_id___min_length,
    STDDEV(CAST(LENGTH(account_id) as double)) as account_id___std_length,
    SUM(IFF(REGEXP_COUNT(TO_VARCHAR(account_id),
      '^([-+]?[0-9]+)$', 1, 'i') != 0, 1, 0)) / CAST(COUNT(*) AS NUMERIC)
        as account_id___text_int_rate,
    SUM(IFF(REGEXP_COUNT(TO_VARCHAR(account_id),
```

```
    '^([-+]?[0-9]*[.]?[0-9]+([eE][-+]?[0-9]+)?)$', 1, 'i') != 0, 1, 0))
  / CAST(COUNT(*) AS NUMERIC) as account_id___text_number_rate,
SUM(IFF(REGEXP_COUNT(TO_VARCHAR(account_id),
  '^([0-9a-fA-F]{8}-[0-9a-fA-F]{4}-[0-9a-fA-F]{4}-[0-9a-fA-F]{4}
  -[0-9a-fA-F]{12})$', 1, 'i') != 0, 1, 0)) / CAST(COUNT(*) AS NUMERIC)
  as account_id___text_uuid_rate,
SUM(IFF(REGEXP_COUNT(TO_VARCHAR(account_id),
  '^(\\s+)$', 1, 'i') != 0, 1, 0)) / CAST(COUNT(*) AS NUMERIC)
  as account_id___text_all_spaces_rate,
SUM(IFF(UPPER(account_id) IN ('NULL', 'NONE', 'NIL', 'NOTHING'), 1, 0))
  / CAST(COUNT(*) AS NUMERIC) as account_id___text_null_keyword_rate,
```

Next, you can track the accuracy of a specific numeric field (or distribution) of your data, as highlighted in Example 2-7. In this example, we're specifically gathering information on the distribution of our data across two fields: account_id and num_of_users.

Example 2-7. Gathering data distribution information for account_id and num_of_users

```
-- numeric field
COUNT(num_of_users) / CAST(COUNT(*) AS NUMERIC)
  as num_of_users___completeness,
SUM(IFF(num_of_users = 0, 1, 0)) / CAST(COUNT(*) AS NUMERIC)
  as num_of_users___zero_rate,
SUM(IFF(num_of_users < 0, 1, 0)) / CAST(COUNT(*) AS NUMERIC)
  as num_of_users___negative_rate,
COUNT(DISTINCT num_of_users) / CAST(COUNT(*) AS NUMERIC)
  as num_of_users___approx_distinctness,
AVG(num_of_users) as num_of_users___numeric_mean,
MIN(num_of_users) as num_of_users___numeric_min,
MAX(num_of_users) as num_of_users___numeric_max,
STDDEV(CAST(num_of_users as double)) as num_of_users___numeric_std,
ARRAY_CONSTRUCT(APPROX_PERCENTILE(num_of_users, 0.00),
  APPROX_PERCENTILE(num_of_users, 0.20),
  APPROX_PERCENTILE(num_of_users, 0.40),
  APPROX_PERCENTILE(num_of_users, 0.60),
  APPROX_PERCENTILE(num_of_users, 0.80),
  APPROX_PERCENTILE(num_of_users, 1.00))
  as num_of_users___approx_quantiles
FROM analytics.prod.client_hub
WHERE
  DATE_TRUNC('HOUR', measurement_timestamp)
    >= DATEADD(day, -1, CURRENT_TIMESTAMP())
GROUP BY bucket_start, bucket_end
ORDER BY bucket_start ASC;
```

In this example, we are collecting health metrics for two fields in our client_hub table.

For the field `account_id`, a string, we track metrics like completeness (% of non-null values), distinctness (% of unique values) and universally unique identifier (UUID) rate (% of records that match a UUID format). Tracking those over time would help identify common issues like accounts that have no IDs, duplicate records, and IDs that have the wrong format.

For the numeric field `num_of_users` we track other kinds of metrics like zero rate (% of records with the value 0), mean, and quantiles. These metrics—when observed over time—can help us identify common issues like missing data causing our counts to zero out, or bugs that would cause our user counts to be way off.

For scalability, note that we track only recent data (one day in this example) and assume that past data was previously queried and stored. This practice—along with sampling if necessary—will let you track some sizable data sets efficiently and cost effectively.

The information you pull to track data quality metrics needs to be readily available to other members of the team, particularly when things break or you're in the throes of conducting root cause analysis on your data pipelines (*https://oreil.ly/Z3Nm5*). Baking in automatic notifications when issues are detected and a centralized (and easy-to-navigate) UI to better handle these workflows can spell the difference between fast resolution and a days-long data disaster.

Using Query Logs to Understand Data Quality in the Warehouse

A powerful source of metadata accessible in warehouse environments is *query logs*— records of the transformations made on the warehouse. Query logs let you answer questions such as:

- Who is accessing this data?
- Where does it come from upstream? Where is it going downstream?
- How often, on average, is this particular transformation executed?
- How many rows are affected?

This information comes packaged in system tables in most major data warehouse vendors. The Snowflake `QUERY_HISTORY` (*https://oreil.ly/NcspE*) family of tables, Big-Query's AuditLogs resources, and the Redshift `STL_QUERY` (*https://oreil.ly/00KBm*) table family are places to start. A Google search for "[vendor-name] query logs" is probably sufficient for finding the analogue from your warehouse provider.

Query log tables typically (1) store only some single number of days of query history, and (2) contain way more information than you'll need for your data quality initiative. This means that a robust solution handling query logs for data quality metrics will need to be proactive and store the desired metrics and aggregations in a more permanent location. If we look at Snowflake and Redshift, the metrics appearing ready-made for you will include:

- The user ID who executed the query
- The SQL text of the query, as well as a hash that identifies it
- The query's total elapsed time, from start to end
- An error code if one was produced
- The size of the input/output of the query, in rows or in bytes

This may not sound like a lot by itself, but think of the questions that now have answers if we apply our metadata collection in an intelligent way:

- When was this table last queried?
- Was that update part of a regular cadence, or does it break a pattern?
- What's the load on this warehouse as a function of the time of day?
- Is this query taking progressively longer than it was two months ago?
- Who (or what bot) has access to this resource who shouldn't?

Your query logs can answer these questions and more. Next we'll take a look at how.

Using Query Logs to Understand Data Quality in the Lake

Data lakes, as we discussed in "Data Lakes: Manipulations at the File Level" on page 18 differ from warehouses mainly in terms of the flexibility of storage format they permit. Lakes permit "schema-on-read" access protocols (*https://oreil.ly/SZpui*), which allow data to be stored in raw file formats and manipulated as such. This has obvious advantages, as we discussed earlier, but comes with the increased risk of the lake "swampifying." Because schemas aren't coerced by the system when data is inserted, many data quality metrics present in warehouse architectures are harder or impossible to get in these cases. But there's no need to lose hope, because there's plenty a modern data lake can do to assure data quality.

Some metadata in your lake you'll get for free. Lakes collect and store object metadata when new data is added. Some of this metadata you'll benefit from "accidentally"—for example, Amazon S3 happens to require storing object insertion times and payload size for their own object management. Yet you can harness this metadata to answer questions like "When was this object last updated?" or "What is the average file size of files of this type, and has it recently been increasing?"

System metadata present in most modern data lakes will include:

- Object insertion times
- Object size in bytes
- Object file format, if recognized
- Whether encryption is enabled

In addition to metadata the system stores on your behalf, you can specify additional object headers at the time of creation. Here, the solution for data quality is more open-ended. Think about what's missing from system-defined metadata that you'll need to assess data downtime.

Some examples include:

- Which job pipeline or user was responsible for this object's creation?
- What schema is the object using or relying on? For example, you can hash the schema of an upstream transformation to tell whether the resource is configured for a certain ETL workflow, or whether one side of the transformation has been deprecated.

Keep in mind, however, that another common (and perhaps more holistic) way to answer the question of "Who was responsible for this object's creation?" is to enforce more tightly controlled access permissions and grant write permissions only to a single pipeline. While ambitious, this approach ensures that data quality is handled more proactively.

Another key element of your data stack that plays a role in understanding data quality is the data catalog.

Designing a Data Catalog

Analogous to a physical library catalog, data catalogs serve as an inventory of metadata and give investors the information necessary to evaluate data accessibility, health, and location. Companies like Alation, Collibra, and Informatica tout solutions that not only keep tabs on your data but also integrate with machine learning and automation to make data more discoverable, collaborative, and now, in compliance with organizational, industry-wide, or even government regulations.

Since data catalogs provide a single source of truth about a company's data sources, it's very easy to leverage data catalogs to manage the data in your pipelines. Data catalogs can be used to store metadata that gives stakeholders a better understanding of a specific source's lineage, thereby instilling greater trust in the data itself. Additionally, data catalogs make it easy to keep track of where personally identifiable information can both be housed and sprawl downstream, as well as who in the organization has the permission to access it across the pipeline.

Data catalogs are designed to answer questions such as:

- Where should I look for my data?
- Does this data matter?
- What does this data represent?
- Is this data relevant and important?
- How can I use this data?

If you were the first to ever design a data catalog at your company, certainly the most low-tech approach to answering the preceding questions would be to amass all of your data information into one enormous spreadsheet. And traditionally, this was how data cataloging was solved—with Excel.

The issues with manual data cataloging are easy to identify, though. With large warehouses sporting tens of thousands of tables, the need for automation is unavoidable. Traditional data catalogs and governance methodologies typically rely on data teams to do the heavy lifting of manual data entry, holding them responsible for updating the catalog as data assets evolve. This approach is not only time-intensive but also requires significant manual toil that could otherwise be automated, freeing time for data engineers and analysts to focus on projects that actually move the needle.

Moreover, a greater majority of data stored today is unstructured and highly fluid—the type of data perfect for ingestion into machine learning pipelines, and the type of data you'd store in a data lake. It's simply impossible to maintain a manual catalog of these forms of data, unless you'd like to relegate a handful of engineers to the task full time. On top of this, rather than simply describing the data that consumers access and use, there's a growing need also to understand the data based on its intention and purpose. How a producer of data might describe an asset would be very different from how a consumer of this data understands its function, and even between one consumer of data to another there might be a vast difference in terms of understanding the meaning ascribed to the data. All told, manual data catalogs just no longer cut it.

Fortunately, data cataloging can be a matter of *discovering* and *organizing* the proper metadata that explains your data pipeline. We've already established that this is something we can automate.

Building a Data Catalog

Let's say you did want to build a data catalog from scratch (may the force be with you!)—how would you go about getting started?

Before building or investing in a catalog, you need to partner with downstream stakeholders on the operations and analytics teams to understand which data is most important to the business and, as such, needs to be documented and cataloged. Many teams tackle this first step (alignment) with a spreadsheet that highlights the data source, what it connects to, and when it was last updated.

After alignment, teams should assign owners who are accountable for keeping their column (and data!) up to date. Some teams assign ownership based on source, schema, or even data domain.

At its most basic, a data catalog is a collection of data about your data (metadata) that provides context and insight into the location, ownership, and potential use cases of the data. To actually populate the data catalog, as depicted in its most basic state in Table 2-1, data teams can manually comb through every table in the data warehouse or use automated SQL parsers to do the work for them. Sqlparse (*https://oreil.ly/5zhUG*), ANTLR (*https://oreil.ly/XTGr5*), Apache Calcite (*https://oreil.ly/wl7ok*), and MySQL's SQL Parser (*https://oreil.ly/55PCH*) are all popular open source SQL parsing solutions.

Table 2-1. A basic, rough-and-dirty data catalog

Table name	Dashboard/report	Last updated	Owner	Notes
LIOR_GOOD_TABLE_3.csv	Exec Forecasting V3 (Looker)	March 3, 2022	Lior Gavish (*lior@internet.org*)	Lior's table; used for executive financial forecasts, i.e., ARR
MEETINGS_DOWNTIME_2022.csv	Report 1234 (Tableau)	February 2, 2022	Barr Moses (*barr@internet.org*)	Outages occurred during in-person meetings
DONT_USE_4_MV.csv	Dashboard Yikes (Chartio)	October 30, 2021	Molly Vorwerck (*molly@internet.org*)	Who knows?
RYANS_DATA.csv	Marketing Model (Looker)	March 3, 2022	Ryan Kearns (*ryan@internet.org*)	For demand generation models to inform ad spend across social channels

SQL parsers separate pieces of a SQL statement (i.e., keywords, identifiers, clauses, etc.) into a data structure that other routines can process.

Once you've parsed the SQL, you need somewhere to store and process it. Open source databases like the open ELK stack (*https://oreil.ly/JarRL*), PostgreSQL (*https://oreil.ly/QdVve*), MySQL (*https://oreil.ly/TwfWw*), and MariaDB (*https://oreil.ly/M027O*) are great options when building a data catalog from the ground up.

While each parser and database application will function differently, Example 2-8 is an illustration of code you can write to pull a query (in this case, pulling a query from a CSV file using ANTLR, and porting the "output" of the query into MySQL) that ports information about data in a given database.

Example 2-8. Database query to gather metadata for storage in a catalog or discovery tool

```
String sql = "SELECT CUST_NAME FROM CUSTOMERS WHERE CUST_NAME LIKE 'Kash%'";

MySqlLexer lexer = new MySqlLexer(CharStreams.fromString(sql));
MySqlParser parser = new MySqlParser(new CommonTokenStream(lexer));
ParseTree root = parser.dmlStatement();

System.out.println(root.toStringTree(parser));
```

The output of this query renders metadata about data in a given database, to be stored in a data catalog or discovery tool, as shown in Example 2-9.

Example 2-9. Output from query in Example 2-8

```
(dmlStatement
  (selectStatement
    (querySpecification SELECT
    (selectElements
        (selectElement
        (fullColumnName
        (uid
          (simpleId CUST_NAME)))))
    (fromClause FROM
    (tableSources
        (tableSource
        (tableSourceItem
        (tableName
          (fullId
          (uid
          (simpleId CUSTOMERS))))))) WHERE (expression (predicate

    (predicate
        (expressionAtom
        (fullColumnName
        (uid (simpleId CUST_NAME))))) LIKE
    (predicate
        (expressionAtom
        (constant
        (stringLiteral 'Kash%')))))))))))
```

Open source query language tools like GraphQL (*https://oreil.ly/WbFAK*), REST (*https://oreil.ly/MT2pR*), and Cube.js (*https://oreil.ly/LlBTt*) will allow you to query

SQL in the database and render it in a cataloging visualization service such as Amundsen (*https://oreil.ly/Svhlg*), Apache Atlas (*https://oreil.ly/Q1X7F*), DataHub (*https://oreil.ly/CCH6M*), or CKAN (*https://oreil.ly/K2HVG*).

Data catalogs work well when you have rigid models, but as data pipelines grow increasingly complex and unstructured data becomes the gold standard, our understanding of the data (what it does, who uses it, how it's used) doesn't reflect reality.

Next-generation catalogs will have the capabilities to learn, understand, and infer the data, enabling users to leverage its insights in a self-service manner. Most importantly, data catalogs will support automated data discovery and active metadata. Imagine being able to use Slack, Teams, or any other communication channel to query data in your warehouse—exciting, right? Well, we're not too far off.

In addition to cataloging data, data management strategies must also incorporate data discovery, a new approach to understanding the health of your distributed data assets in real time. Borrowing from the distributed domain-oriented architecture proposed by Zhamak Dehghani and Thoughtworks' data mesh model, data discovery posits that different data owners are held accountable for their data as products, as well as for facilitating communication between distributed data across different locations. Once data has been served to and transformed by a given domain, the domain data owners can leverage the data for their operational or analytic needs.

Data discovery replaces the need for a data catalog by providing a domain-specific, dynamic understanding of your data based on how it's being ingested, stored, aggregated, and used by a set of specific consumers. As with a data catalog, governance standards and tooling are federated across these domains (allowing for greater accessibility and interoperability), but unlike a data catalog, data discovery surfaces a real-time understanding of the data's current state as opposed to its ideal or "cataloged" state.

Data discovery can answer these questions not just for the data's ideal state but for the current state of the data across each domain:

- What data set is most recent? Which data sets can be deprecated?
- When was the last time this table was updated?
- What is the meaning of a given field in my domain?
- Who has access to this data? When was it last used? By whom?
- What are the upstream and downstream dependencies of this data?
- Is this production-quality data?
- What data matters for my domain's business requirements?
- What are my assumptions about this data, and are they being met?

A data quality–first catalog has the following features:

Self-service discovery and automation
  Data teams should be able to easily leverage their data catalog without a dedicated support team. Self-service, automation, and workflow orchestration for your data tooling removes silos between stages of the data pipeline and, in the process, makes it easier to understand and access data. Greater accessibility naturally leads to increased data adoption, reducing the load for your data engineering team.

Scalability as data evolves
  As companies ingest more and more data and unstructured data becomes the norm, the ability to scale to meet these demands will be critical for the success of your data initiatives. Data discovery leverages machine learning to gain a bird's-eye view of your data assets as they scale, ensuring that your understanding adapts as your data evolves. This way, data consumers are set up to make more intelligent and informed decisions instead of relying on outdated documentation (aka data about data that becomes stale, how meta!) or worse—gut-based decision making.

Data lineage for distributed discovery
  Data discovery relies heavily on automated table and field-level lineage to map upstream and downstream dependencies between data assets. Lineage helps surface the right information at the right time (a core functionality of data discovery) and draw connections between data assets so you can better troubleshoot when data pipelines do break. This is becoming an increasingly common problem as the modern data stack evolves to accommodate more complex use cases. In Chapter 7, we'll dive into how you can actually build lineage for your own data pipelines.

The truth is—in one way or another—your team is probably already investing in data discovery, whether it's through manual work your team is doing to verify data, custom validation rules your engineers are writing, or simply the cost of decisions made based on broken data or silent errors that went unnoticed. Modern data teams have started leveraging automated approaches to ensure highly trustworthy data at every stage of the pipeline, from data quality monitoring to more robust, end-to-end data observability platforms that monitor and alert for issues in your data pipelines. Such solutions notify you when data breaks so you can identify the root cause quickly for fast resolution and prevent future downtime.

Data discovery empowers data teams to trust that their assumptions about data match reality, enabling dynamic discovery and a high degree of reliability across your data infrastructure, regardless of domain.

Summary

To achieve truly discoverable data, it's important that your data is not just "cataloged" but also accurate, clean, and fully observable for ingestion to consumption—in other words, reliable. Only by understanding your data, the state of your data, and how it's being used—at all stages of its life cycle, across domains—can we even begin to trust it. In our next chapter, we'll discuss how to manage data quality across the pipeline and share the fundamentals of how to collect, clean, transform, and test your data at scale.

CHAPTER 3

Collecting, Cleaning, Transforming, and Testing Data

With Ryan Kearns

Now that we have a better understanding of the various tools necessary to prioritize data reliability, let's discuss how to ready your data for production use cases with data quality in mind.

In Chapter 2, we discussed some of the domain terminology and walked through a taxonomy of where data quality nuggets (mostly metadata) are to be found. Still, to get a thorough sense of data quality in your data pipeline, you need to look *end to end*, at the *entire* life cycle of data as it persists at your organization.

In this chapter, we'll walk through how to manage data before and while it's in the pipeline through four key steps that impact overall data quality: data collection, cleaning, transformation, and testing. While data collection and cleaning concern the first step of the production pipeline, transformation and testing tackle data quality while it's midway through its journey to becoming actionable analytics.

Collecting Data

When it comes to collecting data, perhaps no aspect of the pipeline is as important as the *entrypoint*, the most upstream location in any data pipeline. We define an entrypoint as an *initial point of contact where data from the outside world enters your pipeline*. If you're familiar with Docker containerization, you might be familiar with the ENTRYPOINT keyword. This is the initial command run whenever we start a container. Likewise, "entrypoint" in software engineering parlance often refers to the initial point of execution in a program, like the main method. The spirit is similar in data engineering.

Data at your entrypoint is the most raw it will be, as it contains all of the noise and irregularity typical of the outside world it's modeling. Such data might be collected from application or service logs, clickstream sources, or live sensors. Your data will probably be highly heterogeneous—meaning, it'll be both structured and unstructured, opening up the opportunity for issues down the (pipe)line.

The sources where we collect our data are rarely up to us as data engineers. Most often they depend on some business objective or upstream tool, like an analytics service or an API. The sources of data fall into three mostly exhaustive categories, and we will go through each of them here. Understanding the unique advantages and disadvantages of each type can be helpful when designing a processing solution.

Application Log Data

Application logs refer to data produced by actions within some software application. The application can be client facing or internal, and the actions can be user initiated or programmatic. Alongside descriptions of the events, which are often timestamped, you might find error or warning messages produced by the application software. Importantly, unlike in system logs—which might record the sequence of events as an operating system boots—what is included or excluded from application logs is up to the developers of the application. As a result, logs may not represent an exhaustive history of the application's use. Still, they remain a critical data source for many business uses.

Here are a few examples to demonstrate this data collection use case:

- A user reading a blog spends 10 minutes on a webpage, clicks three outgoing links in the blog's text, and scrolls all the way to the bottom of the document.

- An engineer creates a virtual machine instance on your cloud computing service. They select the instance type with six vCPUs, but that type is not available in their region, so they have to navigate back and change the config.

- A machine learning model is fitting to a data set. Logs record the different training epochs, the current accuracy, and a link to the external dashboard where the loss is plotted.

Your business will likely collect application logs from a variety of sources and in plenty of different formats. Some elements to consider when dealing with log data:

Structure
> You're likely to consume application logs in ASCII or binary formats, since they're simply serializable text. This places *very* little constraint on how application logs are structured, though, or even on how long they are (and how large your log files will be as a result). Since application programmers decide what goes into logs, their structure can be highly variable.

Timestamps

Most application log text will be discrete events, with descriptions, separated by \n characters. If the programmers are doing their job right, these events will be timestamped. Timestamps, unlike event descriptions, should be highly standardized, most often in the ISO standard format (yyyy-mm-ddThh:mm:ss[.mmm]) or something similar.

Log levels

Good application logs use *levels* to codify, roughly, the type of log each event is. Frequently used log levels are INFO: this log contains purely descriptive information; WARN: this log is an application warning but not a failing error; and ERROR: this log is a programmatic failure in the application.

Purpose

Application logs aren't collected willy-nilly. Pushing around all that data costs money, so the logs should surely be *useful* for something. In fact, you're probably collecting application logs for one of two reasons:

Diagnostics

How often does this request time out? Are page loads slowing down? Are we using a deprecated library function? All of these questions address diagnostic criteria and are answered by intelligently collecting and parsing logs. If you are collecting log data for a diagnostic purpose, then answers to your questions could be in very specific WARN- or ERROR-level logs. Also, the vast majority of your collection will probably be unrelated to that *one* specific question you have *right now*.

Auditing

Who issued that request? How many times? How did the system respond? And does this behavior also occur on weekends, or is the pattern different? Unlike diagnostic logging, *audit logging* is all about recording a history of events within the application. Many INFO-level logs will be useful for this task, and the power of auditing often comes from large aggregations of application sessions.

API Responses

Your own application can't do everything. That's why you relegate certain functionalities to different applications. The standard method for doing this is with an *application programming interface*, or API. APIs are intermediaries between two programs. They require specifically formatted *requests* and they deliver *responses*, which for our purposes are just semi-structured data.

In addition to application logs, you may store data pulled from API endpoints. There are some important differences in the format of these data types to be aware of. With API data, pay attention to:

Structure

API response objects are *objects*—they may be serializable, like logs, but they unpack into a structured or semi-structured format. One common object format you will see, particularly with web APIs, is the JavaScript Object Notation (JSON). JSON objects are highly flexible, but they're constrained by structure in important ways. Everything within a JSON object (or file) is either a *key-value pair* or a *list of values*. This is significantly different from log data, which can be just a stream of text! Other API response types have similar formats, for example the HTTP response specifications, like HTTP/1.1, which may contain JSON or XML in the HTTP request or response body as well.

Response codes

Since API requests can succeed or fail, most API specifications have codes for different types of responses. The most famous you'll hear about are HTTP status codes (200 OK, 404 Not Found, 500 Internal Server Error), but there are other code standards (for example, SOAP APIs, which can use HTTP or other transport protocols). These codes are meaningful—for example, the rate of HTTP 500 responses is a key indicator for whether a server is having an outage. If you store API response data you should think about such code specifications if they exist.

Purpose

The world of possible API use cases is enormous, so we cannot predict all the use cases one might run into. But APIs are used in myriad ways, and the details of one's particular use will affect what the data stored about it means. For example, HTTP responses often include response codes, some key-value pair information, and sometimes a long "body," which is the content requested. If we're interested in, say, the rate of server errors, we will care fundamentally about the response code. If instead we're pulling data from an external server via an API, the response code may be irrelevant. Instead, we'll just want the body. In short, the use case can affect which information in the API response object is meaningful. Some information transferred may be useless in your specific context.

Sensor Data

A third form of data you may collect come from *sensors*, such as Internet of Things devices or research equipment. Sensors aren't necessarily applications since their internal logic may be brutally simple. For example, a temperature sensor just records the temperature with some hardware and sends it off for collection—without the added benefit of INFO-level logs. If you work with sensor data there are some important considerations to be aware of:

Noise

Data collected from real-world sensors will likely be *incredibly* noisy. This isn't necessarily something to focus on at the collection phase. However, it underlines the importance of throughput when dealing with sensors. A little bit of sensor data is, simply put, probably garbage. Downstream processing (which we'll talk about in the next section) will do lots of outlier removal, smoothing, and other transformations on sensor data, so a steady and consistent stream is almost always imperative.

Failure modes

Sensors aren't smart like applications, which means they may not know to tell you when they fail. For example, a temperature sensor that has broken won't send "ERROR: Device offline," but may instead start sending crazy temperature values—or just nothing at all. This makes dealing with sensors more challenging than applications. You cannot rely on the goodwill of an application designer in the same way and may have to be more clever checking things like the volume of data received or the time delta between batches.

Purpose

Sensor data, like application logs and API responses, is used for lots of downstream tasks. Much sensor data today is processed with machine learning systems. For this purpose, the volume of data collected can be an important factor. The best ML systems often consume and fit to the largest data sets. As a result, the throughput of sensor data used for ML is extremely important. But also, pay attention to when your sensor data is used for inference-based tasks: for example, alerting a user when there's movement at their doorstep. In these cases, *latency* should be of utmost importance instead.

After you properly collect your data, the next step is to clean it.

Cleaning Data

Ask any data professional: one of the biggest hurdles to high data quality is data cleaning—in other words, removing inaccurate or unrepresentative data from an otherwise usable data set. There are many flavors of data cleaning, too, depending on the type of data and state of data processing and data product development.

As we just saw with sensors, data at an entrypoint isn't likely to be *clean*. After all, your data only *just* arrived from the chaos of the outside world! There will be omissions, error messages, extreme values, and incompatible formats, but with the right approach to data cleaning, these issues can easily be prevented. Data cleaning is a field of recent interest, especially in machine learning. There has been a lot of effort spent deciding how to do it right. The following explores some of the common ways data needs to be cleaned, and what you can do about each case:

Outlier removal

The world is noisy, so your data will be noisy, too. But *too* noisy data often causes ML pipelines to fail or business dashboards to look wildly inaccurate. In some contexts, you'll want to identify and remove outliers from your data as early as possible. Obviously this doesn't make sense if, say, your downstream task is *outlier detection*. But consider something like sensor data again—a temperature reading of 99999° probably *shouldn't* be passed along in good faith. Consider statistical techniques like standard scoring (*https://oreil.ly/N60ol*), or more snazzy algorithmic techniques like isolation forests (*https://oreil.ly/J9kTW*), to remove your outliers. If your data set is large, pay special attention to the time complexity of your detection procedure. We'll discuss anomaly detection in depth in Chapter 5.

Assessing data set features

Look at the structure of the data you've collected. Is everything (even remotely) relevant? As we talked about with HTTP status codes, sometimes whole sections of your data are irrelevant for a downstream task. Throw them out! Granted, the cost of cloud storage is decreasing, but storing meaningless data is more than just a storage problem. Other engineers might get confused why a certain field is present. In general, more features means more documentation or more domain knowledge necessary to understand your system, both of which can complicate your analysis and impact data quality. Think hard about what data set features are required to solve your problem.

Normalization

Some data points can be examined in isolation, and that's OK. Other data is most meaningful when compared to *other* data of the same type. In those cases, it often helps you (and your ML system) to *normalize* the data during a cleaning or transformation step. Popular choices for normalization include L1 ("Manhattan") Norm (*https://oreil.ly/0zwO2*), L2 ("Unit") Norm (*https://oreil.ly/BOhNm*), demeaning (*https://oreil.ly/mMk3D*), and unit variance (*https://oreil.ly/aY8Cy*), and the best choice will depend on the use case for the data.

Data reconstruction

Sometimes, certain fields from your collected data are missing. This is bound to happen with things like error-prone API calls or sensors that can go offline. In many cases these omissions can be fine, but sometimes you might require all fields to have *some* value associated with them. In these cases it is often possible to recover missing values, with a bit of noise, using techniques like interpolation (*https://oreil.ly/AJFGz*), extrapolation (*https://oreil.ly/FsNTx*), or categorizing/labeling similar data (*https://oreil.ly/sAwB3*).

Time zone conversion

You might consider time zone conversion as a kind of normalization. But this step is so important for many data cleaning tasks that it deserves its own entry. Your application users or sensors may be worldwide, meaning they will be recording local timestamps that differ from each other. Comparing timestamps *to* one another is possible only with some standard of truth. Often, this is Coordinated Universal Time (UTC). UTC is not a time *zone*, but a time *standard* (countries using Greenwich Mean Time [GMT] happen to always agree with UTC, but they don't *use* UTC). If you don't do this, and snap off time zone information at collection like some kind of maniac, then you can never know when two international events happened relative to one another. Also, many software bugs can be traced back to time zone confusions (Y2K being maybe the most famous example), so check your time zones carefully to ensure that they convert/capture time as UTC.

Type coercions

Most structured data is *typed*, meaning it has to obey a certain format. Frequently in computing, we need to blur the line between these formats for applications to function. Floating-point numbers might be truncated to integers, characters might become strings, and so on. If a downstream application requires data in a certain type, consider *coercing* it, in other words, the automatic or implicit conversion of values from one data type to another, to that type as part of the cleaning process. Type coercion is also essential if you're combining data from different formats. Many libraries and applications have their own data types for different things, and often they need to be explicitly cast to a new, more agreeable format.

And the list of ways you can (and often should) clean data goes on. The next step? Data processing.

Batch Versus Stream Processing

It's a debate as old as time (well, at least in data engineering): whether to process data in batches or to stream data in real time.

There are two primary ways of collecting analytical data: batch processing versus stream processing. Fundamentally, batch processing collects data over a period of time, "batching" large quantities of data in discrete packets, while stream processing is a lengthier process and processes data almost immediately.

Up until the mid-2010s, batch processing was the most common approach to processing analytical data. Significantly cheaper than stream processing, batch was sufficient for even the most timely processing needs. As companies across industries become increasingly reliant on real-time data, technologies like Apache Kafka and Amazon Kinesis make streaming data more accessible and affordable at scale.

Batch processing is the time-tested standard and is still a popular and common way for companies to ingest large amounts of data. But when organizations want to gain real-time insights, batch processing falls short.

That's where stream processing fills the gap. It's a game-changer to have access to data in real time and can lead to an increased return on investment for products and services that rely on data to be constantly updated.

A simple example of batch versus stream processing is credit card processing. On the vendor side, it may take several hours or even days to process payments over a certain period of time, an activity often handled in batch. For instance, you may have purchased a new scarf at your local boutique on Monday, but the charge doesn't settle until Wednesday evening. On the credit card provider side, once transactions are authorized, potentially fraudulent transactions can be immediately identified and alerts triggered to the credit card holder. However, if the data about these transactions isn't accurate and up-to-date (i.e., in the case of using batch streaming), fraud detection can be delayed or missed altogether.

Apache Hadoop is one of the most popular open source batch processing frameworks for distributed storage and processing of large data sets. Hadoop operates by splitting files into smaller packets of data and then distributing these more manageable chunks across nodes in a cluster. Managed alternatives to Hadoop include Google BigQuery, Snowflake (as described in Chapter 2), Microsoft Azure, and Amazon Redshift.

Stream processing refers to real-time ride-sharing app requests, for example, when someone requests an Uber or Lyft through the app and is connected with an available driver in real time (or rather, as quickly as a driver becomes available!). Using real-time streaming data, these ridesharing applications can piece together real-time location, pricing, and driver data to instantly connect a user with a ride.

For stream processing, some of the most common open source technologies include solutions from Apache such as Spark, Kafka, Flink, Storm, Samza, and Flume. While there are many solutions available, one of the most widely used options is Apache Spark and Kafka. Apache Spark employs a micro-batch processing approach, which splits incoming streams into smaller packets; Apache Kafka analyzes events as they unfold in closer to near real time. Managed alternatives include Databricks, Cloudera, and Azure. For more information, we recommend you read *Streaming Systems: The What, Where, When, and How of Large-Scale Data Processing* (O'Reilly), which goes into much more detail about these approaches, technologies, and use cases.

Data Quality for Stream Processing

When you boil it down, the major difference between batch and stream processing is the amount of data being processed per batch and the speed at which it's being processed. While batch processing is concerned with gathering as much data as possible—even if it means there are lags—stream processing is concerned with collecting data as quickly as possible, leading to some lossiness. As a result, data quality (meaning, the health of data at a given stage in the pipeline) tends to be higher for batch streaming systems, but when data is streamed in real time, the margin for error (and low data quality) increases.

For example, marketing teams position ads based on users' behavior, using data that flows in real time between a brand's products, CRMs, and advertising platforms. One small schema change to an API can lead to erroneous data, causing companies to overspend, miss out on potential revenue, or serve irrelevant ads that create a poor user experience.

This scenario and the credit card fraud monitoring example from earlier just scratch the surface of what's possible when bad data powers your perfectly good pipelines. So, how do you solve for data quality with stream processing?

Traditionally, data quality was enforced through testing: you were ingesting data in batches and would expect the data to arrive in the interval that you deemed necessary (i.e., every 12 hours or every 24 hours). Your team would write tests based on their assumptions about the data, but it's not possible to write tests to account for all possible outcomes.

A new error in data quality would arise, and engineers would rush to conduct root cause analysis before the issue affected downstream tables and users. Data engineers would eventually fix the problem and write a test to prevent it from happening again.

In short, testing was hard to scale and, as we found after talking to hundreds of data teams, only covered about 20% of possible data quality issues—your known unknowns. With increasing complexity in today's modern data ecosystem—where companies ingest anywhere from dozens to hundreds of internal and external data sources—traditional methods of processing and testing have begun to look outdated.

Even so, in the mid-2010s, when organizations began ingesting data in real time with Amazon Kinesis, Apache Kafka, Spark Streaming, and other tools, they followed this same approach. While this move to real-time insights was great for business, it opened up a whole new can of worms for dealing with data quality.

If ensuring reliability for batch data is difficult, imagine running and scaling tests for data that evolves by the minute—or second! Missing, inaccurate, or late fields can have a detrimental impact on downstream systems, and without a way to catch data issues in real time, the effects can magnify across the business.

While traditional data quality frameworks such as unit testing, functional testing, and integration testing might cover the fundamentals, they cannot scale alongside data sets that are hard to predict and evolve in real time. In order to ensure that the data feeding these real-time use cases is reliable, data teams need to rethink their approach to data quality when dealing with stream processing.

Now that we know the challenges, in the following sections, we share how to manage data quality for stream processing systems, specifically through utilizing AWS Kinesis and Apache Kafka.

AWS Kinesis

Amazon's Kinesis service, as depicted in Figure 3-1, is a popular serverless streaming tool for applications reliant on real-time data. Capacity for Kinesis scales "on-demand," reducing the need to provision and scale resources before data volume increases.

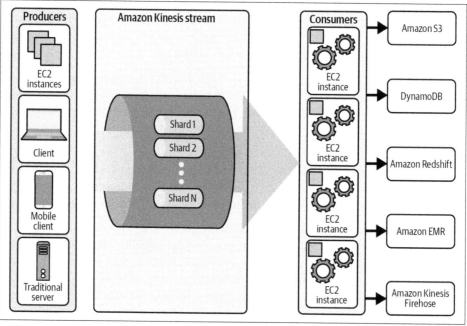

Figure 3-1. AWS Kinesis streams data to various structured consumers, including data warehouses, databases, and bespoke big data platforms

Kinesis (and other streaming services) can be configured to capture data from other AWS services, microservices, application logs, mobile data, and sensor data, among others. The service can scale to stream gigabytes of data per second.

Working with Amazon Kinesis has several advantages:

On-demand availability
AWS sets an industry standard for on-demand provisioning, meaning resource groups can scale up when loads increase. This makes the service more reliable and robust against unexpected spikes in data volume, and eliminates the need for an experienced data engineer to handle cluster and partition management.

Cost efficiency
Kinesis's payment plan scales in proportion to resource usage. This is a general benefit to serverless architectures of other kinds as well but is of special interest for a streaming service, where the volume of data throughput might change drastically as a function of time.

Thorough SDK
Kinesis supports development in Java, Android, .NET, and Go, significantly more languages than some competitors (for comparison, Kafka supports only Java).

Integration to AWS infrastructure
One of the key reasons to prefer Kinesis to alternatives is if you already have existing integration into the AWS stack. Amazon's hegemony has its advantages; for example, Kinesis is dramatically easier to integrate with S3, Redshift, and other Amazon data services than third-party or open source alternatives.

Apache Kafka

Apache Kafka is an open source event streaming platform. Kafka Streams, specifically, is the client library supporting streaming data to and from Kafka clusters. The service provides a data streaming and integration layer as well as streaming analytics. Kafka streaming services are optimized for low latency—the service touts latencies as low as 2 milliseconds, subject to network-limited throughput.

Kafka Streams offers several advantages:

Open source community
Kafka is open source software, meaning the tool is free to use. Moreover, a vibrant online community exists to share best practices and learnings via forums, meetups, and online reference materials.

Increased customizability
While Kafka has a higher learning curve than more integrated streaming solutions like Kinesis, users have greater configurability including manually specifying the data retention period (Kinesis keeps this fixed at 7 days).

High throughput
In testing, Kafka has been shown to support throughput of up to 30,000 records per second, where Kinesis supports only single thousands of records per second.

Streaming solutions like AWS Kinesis and Apache Kafka can port data directly to analytical systems in real time or to the warehouse for storage, processing, and transformation. Sometimes, data teams will choose to "stream" these inputs directly to downstream systems, i.e., in the case of a ridesharing app or real-time fraud detection tool. Given the high latency of streaming systems, however, this type of analytical data is often prone to more errors, and it can be much more difficult to make sense of it in real or near real time. This is why batch processing is often the method of choice for analytical use cases.

When it comes to choosing between AWS Kinesis and Apache Kafka, it really boils down to your data team's needs. Given the ease of setup for a managed solution like AWS Kinesis, smaller data teams looking for quick time-to-value will benefit from a software as a service (SaaS) product, while larger teams with more specific requirements may find that leveraging open source Apache Kafka will fit the bill.

Whether you choose to collect your data in batch or streaming, it's time to actually make sense of it through transformations. When it comes to managing data quality, often the first step in this journey is data normalization.

Normalizing Data

We call the first operational data transformation layer the *data normalization* stage, though this nomenclature may vary at your organization. In general, a data transformation is a program for moving data from one or more source formats to a destination format. Normalization is often the first of many such transformations your data will go through on its way down the pipeline. Since normalization occurs on entrypoint data, where noise, ambiguity, and heterogeneity are at their maximum, there are special challenges to consider at this step.

Handling Heterogeneous Data Sources

More often than not, data practitioners are gathering data from disparate sources in an attempt to paint a holistic picture of their user, product, or application—some of it useful, but much of it useless.

Here are several key features that most likely describe your data at the normalization point in the pipeline:

Optimized for latency
   Data from streaming endpoints is optimized to be available immediately upon creation. As we discussed earlier, this comes at the expense of *throughput* given fixed network performance, which in practice determines the *completeness* of your data. This means to expect data batches that are incomplete, as they'll be pushed through the pipeline immediately regardless of their terminal status.

Nonhierarchical format

Data heading into data normalization will probably reside in a nonhierarchical, "flat" storage format for efficiency and ease of use. Rather than a clean warehouse + schema + table storage regimen, you're more likely to have data "dumped" in some central repository like an S3 bucket for transformation.

Raw file format

In addition to being stored "flat," entrypoint data likely reflects the original file format from wherever it was streamed. We don't bother converting application log data and sensor data into tabular form; this would be much too expensive, and most of this data doesn't need such conversion to be useful.

Optional data fields

Unlike warehouse data, where schemas require a value for every field, raw file data like JSON can have optional fields. You may need to infer what the absence of that field means—NULL? 0? The current timestamp, or a time delta of 0? Depending on the field in question anything might be the default, and its absence may or may not be a problem for upstream processing.

Heterogeneity

All of the preceding features point to a certain kind of heterogeneity. Data will come from *various* sources, in those various original file formats, and may be different amounts complete compared to previous data of the same form.

Learning to make sense of your data against a predictable kind of heterogeneity is key at this stage in the pipeline and ensures that once data is stored and processed, it can easily be transformed for maximal impact.

Warehouse data versus lake data: heterogeneity edition

You may notice that a lot of the preceding features describe data in lake format. Recall from Chapter 2 our discussion on the difference between data warehouses and data lakes. Lakes are often the preferred storage solution for entrypoint data because they have much less rigid constraints on the type of data they can accept. This is why you will often see a separation where streaming services (AWS Kinesis, Apache Kafka, etc.) collect unstructured and semi-structured data from different source locations, dump said data into a lake format, and then rely on an initial level of operational transformations to lift pieces of this data into structured form on a warehouse. AWS Lambda functions for AWS Kinesis, or Apache Kafka consumers for Kafka Streams, are the typical ways to apply this kind of normalization. Also, a transformation layer like AWS Glue (*https://oreil.ly/1TTHB*) becomes helpful at this stage if you're moving data across to your warehouse at regular intervals.

Schema Checking and Type Coercion

Schema checking and type coercion are two more techniques you'll want to apply in data normalization. *Schema checking* refers to the process where we validate that the structure of data is as we expect. Are the requisite fields present, and do they contain data in the format we require? *Type coercion* is something that happens—sometimes explicitly, sometimes implicitly—when data is not in the format required and must be "coerced" into a new format. In some programming languages this behavior is referred to as "casting."

Why should you check your schemas? More often than not, data arrives in some packaged format—JSON, comma separated values, and so on. Schemas let us know what to expect when we "unpackage" our data for the first time. Changing schemas are a major source of data breakage. Maybe a field you learned to rely on is no longer present in that one API call due to a versioning update. Maybe your engineering team renamed a field for consistency—the data presented is "the same," but your custom scripts are no longer working. We need to check for these sorts of errors proactively, which often means keeping records of expected schemas and recording when they change in some way that's visible.

Type coercion can be a more sinister form of data failure. In some applications, types can be coerced or cast implicitly without throwing errors. Casting a string "4" to an integer 4 is no big deal—but what about casting floating point number 4.00 to integer 4? Now we're throwing out significant digits, which seems bad. Even worse would be integer casting float 4.99 to integer 4 (this is called *integer rounding* and it doesn't round like you learned in math class—it just truncates everything after the decimal place). In some data applications one may need to look out for type coercion and conversion problems—they sound basic but are definitely capable of producing some malicious bugs.

Syntactic Versus Semantic Ambiguity in Data

This discussion leads us to a distinction that's not so technical in nature but deserves mention to anyone data-literate. Data can be ambiguous—everyone knows that—but this ambiguity comes in importantly different flavors. *Syntactic ambiguity* refers to confusion in the way data is presented. Maybe the same metric appears in multiple places under different field names in a data warehouse. Your colleague's "clickthrough_annual" might be your "clickthrough_rate_yr," just renamed in some operational transformation. Likewise, the same metric might appear as an integer in your data lake but a float in your warehouse—say, always ending with ".00" so the *value* of the data isn't changed, just its type. These are syntactic ambiguities in data and can present friction to data teams.

More pernicious are *semantic ambiguities*, which refer to confusions in the *purpose* of data in a system. A data engineer might think field X is present in a table because it tracks a pipeline performance metric. A business analyst might look at the same field, decide by its vague-sounding name that it tracks the business objective they're interested in, and add it to a dashboard. This field is semantically ambiguous because employees cannot agree on the field's purpose. Worse than presenting friction, something like this case might lead to data *mis*representing key metrics for the organization. Documentation is a key tool for avoiding situations like these and should also be proactive in nature. Ambiguity can creep up quickly in a way that's hard to root out, especially as teams scale quickly.

Managing Operational Data Transformations Across AWS Kinesis and Apache Kafka

While operational data transforms handle data in a raw state, this doesn't mean you need to run totally blind. Many data streaming and processing applications provide built-in alerting and the ability to configure more complex alerting as needed. In the following sections we'll go through some concrete technical examples of popular built-in data quality checks.

AWS Kinesis

AWS Kinesis streams are managed via AWS Lambda functions. You can configure Lambdas for various preprocessing tasks, and their ubiquity allows for some data quality assurance to be built into that preprocessing (*https://oreil.ly/wZMTx*). AWS Lambda functions can be written in .NET (PowerShell, C#), Go, Java, Node.js, Python, and Ruby, and need only to be uploaded to your AWS console to be invoked.

To connect AWS Lambda to a running instance of AWS Kinesis, you'll select "Connect to a Source" in the Kinesis application page and then select "Record pre-processing with AWS Lambda." There you'll have the opportunity to create a new Lambda function that runs before any application SQL code is executed or Amazon creates schema snapshots of the incoming data.

Apache Kafka

Apache Kafka is an application with a high learning curve, meaning it exposes lots of granular settings for the Kafka Streams, Producers, and Consumers in a given application. Confluent, Instacluster, and AWS offer fully managed versions of Apache Kafka that make it easier for teams to get up and running with the powerful streaming framework and that often handle some necessary data downtime prevention out of the box.

It would take too long for us to go through these exhaustively, but suffice it to say that Apache Kafka presents plenty of configurability for data quality purposes (in fact, as a managed solution with Confluent, Apache Kafka offers a schema registry (*https://oreil.ly/yZjfS*), which enables schema checking and evolution to prevent data quality issues). For more information on how to optimize Apache Kafka for improved data quality, check out the project's docs (*https://oreil.ly/mJ4FG*).

By default, Apache Kafka streams report streaming metrics through JMX, the Java Management Extensions specification. You can visualize JMX data with graphical tools like JConsole. Or, you can opt to go directly to the `KafkaStreams` Java class instance and access metrics with the `KafkaStreams#metrics()` method.

In general, the checks you'll be doing at the operational transformation step align with the priority for latency over throughput at this step. In other words, you might avoid the kinds of throughput-intensive aggregation checks, like data drift, at this stage. Instead, set your monitoring sights on lower latency verifications, like comparing historical schemas to incoming ones or tracking the volume of bytes scanned as they vary over time. A lot of the operational "monitoring" done here won't even ensure data quality at all, since it will be focused on ensuring that incoming data doesn't overwhelm the existing capacity, storage, and memory constraints.

Running Analytical Data Transformations

We use the phrase *analytical data transformations* to designate data transformations done on analytical data. This can also apply to the data integration layer between operational and analytical sources, such as AWS Glue configured between an S3 data lake and a Redshift data warehouse. Since analytical data differs from operational data in several key ways, there will be corresponding differences to look out for when transforming this data.

Ensuring Data Quality During ETL

In many contexts you may hear the phrase "ETL" used as synonymous with analytical data transformations. ETL stands for "extract-transform-load" and describes a three-step process that's becoming more ubiquitous for organizations with complex data:

1. In the *extract* step, raw data is exported from some number of upstream sources and moved into a staging area. Examples of such sources might include MySQL and NoSQL servers, CRM systems, or raw files in a data lake.

2. Next, in the *transform* step, the meatiest component of ETL, data in the staging area is combined and processed per the specification of a data engineer. In some cases, the transform step may be menial and virtually consist of copying the source data. In other cases, transformations might be quite intensive. We'll talk about what these transformations can consist of in the next section.

3. Finally, in the *load* step, we move the transformed data out of the staging area and into the destination, often a specific table in a data warehouse.

Ensuring Data Quality During Transformation

As we said earlier, the "transform" step in either ETL or ELT can be the most intensive and varies between different applications. ETL refers to the process of loading data first into the staging server and then the target system, while ELT (extract-load-transform) requires that data is loaded directly into the target system. While ETL offers data engineers the opportunity to validate data before it's pushed to production, ELT makes for quicker processing—and if you're not appropriating testing and monitoring, lower data quality.

There can be several reasons for transforming source data:

- You may simply be renaming fields to fit the target location's schema requirements.
- You may want to *filter*, *aggregate* and *summarize*, *deduplicate*, or otherwise clean and consolidate source data.
- You may need to perform both *type* and *unit* conversions, for example, standardizing different currency fields to all be US dollars and float types.
- You may perform *encryption* at this step for sensitive data fields or to meet industry or government regulations.
- Most important for our purposes, you may conduct *data governance audits* or *data quality checks* at this step.

Alerting and Testing

Like all software and data applications, ETL systems like dbt, WhereScape, or Informatica are prone to failure. You need a robust testing and alerting system to run such applications in high-volume production environments. In this section, we'll talk about the type of alerting that's typical for ETL/ELT systems and some best practices for data quality. Many data transforming systems have built-in mechanisms for data quality. These may take the form of unit tests, visibility metrics into pipeline health, alerting, or others. In the next sections we'll go through some of the built-in tools to popular transforming tools, as well as some add-on tools that provide data quality.

Testing your data plays a crucial role in discovering data quality issues before it even enters a production data pipeline. With testing, engineers anticipate something might break and write logic to detect the issue preemptively.

Data testing is the process of validating your organization's assumptions about the data, either before or during production. Writing basic tests that check for things such as uniqueness and not null are ways organizations can test out the basic assumptions they make about their source data. It is also common for organizations to ensure that data is in the correct format for their team to work with and that the data meets their business needs.

Some of the most common data quality tests include:

Null values
Are any values unknown (NULL)?

Volume
Did I get any data at all? Did I get too much or too little?

Distribution
Is my data within an accepted range? Are my values in range within a given column?

Uniqueness
Are any values duplicated?

Known invariants
Are these two objects fundamentally different from each other—e.g., is profit always the difference between revenue and cost?

From our own experience, two of the best tools out there to test your data are dbt tests and Great Expectations (as a more general-purpose tool). Both tools are open source and allow you to discover data quality issues before they end up in the hands of stakeholders. While dbt is not a testing solution per se, their out-of-the-box tests work well if you're already using the framework to model and transform your data.

To run data quality tests, you need to do two simple things:

- Load the transformed data into a temporary staging table/data set.
- Run tests to ensure that the data in the staging table falls within the thresholds demanded of production (i.e., you need to answer "yes" to the question: is this what reliable data looks like?).

If a data quality test fails, an alert is sent to the data engineer or analyst responsible for that asset, and the pipeline is not run. This allows data engineers to catch unexpected data quality issues before impacting end users/systems. Data testing can be done before transformation and after each step in the transformation process.

dbt Unit Testing

dbt is one of the most popular choices for modern ELT, and its tool extends the ability to add unit tests to transformed tables. The dbt run command executes model transformations using SQL, and dbt test runs unit tests on transformed models. dbt unit tests can be defined in custom SQL queries and assigned to individual models within *.yml* schema files.

A dbt unit test in SQL is designed to fetch "failing" rows, e.g., records that do not match the tester's assertion. This is a common testing paradigm with SQL where you produce a query identifying the condition you want to avoid and basically "assert" it is empty. This is a flexible and effective testing technique, though it does have its limitations, which we'll discuss at the end of this section.

In our opinion, the notion of a "unit test" versus an "integration test" is a little blurry in dbt. On one hand, dbt models are standalone SQL statements—they take input data, apply transformations, and load some result of the transformations into a destination table. Since this transformation logic can fail in a standalone fashion, it makes sense to define "unit tests" assessing the quality of each dbt model individually. At the same time, dbt (and really any ELT) models sit within long sequences of transformations, so it also makes sense to test their integration into the whole pipeline. This is why you may find yourself writing both unit and integration tests for dbt models, often side by side in the same `tests` repository. That's OK! Documentation is key.

There are two kinds of dbt tests:

Singular tests

These are standalone SQL tests referencing particular models. If you write a singular test in SQL and save it to a testing directory (indicated by your `test-paths` config variable), it will be run whenever you call `dbt test`. Example 3-1 checks a single dbt model (`'fct_payments'`) to verify that no payment records have negative values.

Example 3-1. Singular test to verify payment records. Source: dbt documentation (https://oreil.ly/huapD)

```
tests/assert_total_payment_amount_is_positive.sql
-------------------------------------------------
-- Refunds have a negative amount, so the total amount should
-- always be >= 0.
-- Therefore, return records where this isn't true to make the test fail.
select
    order_id,
    sum(amount) as total_amount
from {{ ref('fct_payments' )}}
group by 1
having not(total_amount >= 0)
```

Generic tests

These are "templatized" tests that can be reused on different models. They take the form of parameterized SQL queries, which can take arguments. In your *.yml* schema files, you can apply generic tests to particular models and also feed in parameters like column names or thresholds/SLAs. Example 3-2 takes a model and column name, and fails whenever values from that column are NULL after the model runs.

Example 3-2. Generic test checking for NULLs. Source: dbt documentation (https:// oreil.ly/huapD)

```
tests/test_not_null.sql
------------------------
{% test not_null(model, column_name) %}

    select *
    from {{ model }}
    where {{ column_name }} is null

{% endtest %}
```

dbt ships with four default generic tests: `unique`, `not_null`, `accepted_values`, and `relationships`. `unique` tests that no two rows have the same value for a particular column. `not_null` tests that no values for a particular column are NULL. `accepted_values` ensures that all values for a column are one of a finite set, and `relationships` checks "referential integrity" between tables, basically ensuring one-to-one correspondence for critical fields like `ids`.

While generally great as testing standards for ELT go, dbt tests are not a magic bullet (like all testing software). Some limitations you may note with dbt testing are:

Technical debt and upkeep

dbt tests are maintained manually as code, by developers at your organization. ELT models have a tendency to "drift" as business and data needs evolve, and updates to the models themselves mean updates to the tests on them. Complex tests may ensure high-quality data, but they'll become a time sink on engineering resources, costing close to the time required developing the models themselves.

Test fatigue and tacit knowledge

A test failure has to be *meaningful* to be effective. A developer might add a test to a model that is not well-founded, thinking that tested code is "better" than untested code. Another dev may come along (months later) and push changes that break the test. If they can't understand why the test was there, they might go ahead and remove it just so their CI build completes and they can get on with the ticket. In this engineering culture, tests are a roadblock to get over to get development done, rather than serving as insights into the performance of models. If you catch yourself viewing tests in this way, be careful—such ill-conceived tests add nothing to data quality and simply slow developers down. It would honestly be better to do no testing at all, if there's no intention of taking them seriously.

Limited visibility

A dbt test might fail due to upstream problems. For example, a schema mismatch in the operational data store, like a misconfigured AWS Glue Lambda function, could break data well before it reaches your data warehouse. In this case, your failing test is a good *indicator* something is wrong, but it doesn't quite afford a quick fix. You'll still need to drill into your stack to get rid of the bug, because your ELT testing scheme is not properly end to end.

Great Expectations Unit Testing

Great Expectations (*https://oreil.ly/zFwJz*) is an open source tool, providing another way to "assert what you expect" from your data in the form of unit tests. It is more extensible than dbt testing as tests are written in Python, and it can be applied to various ETL/ELT solutions.

Great Expectations provides a library of common "unit tests" you can apply to data and makes it easy to apply these tests in flexible ways. For example, here's how you might ensure the `zip_code` column represents a valid zip code:

```
expect_column_values_to_be_between(
    column="zip_code",
    min_value=1,
    max_value=99999
)
```

Great Expectations allows unit tests to be run on a range of different data volumes, from single small batches of data to complete transformations. After applying tests, the tool can render a human-readable results page called a "Data Doc," which presents helpful analytics on the rates of failure of different tests and allows random sampling of failing rows. An example is shown in Figure 3-2.

Great Expectations has a number of advantages compared to competitors in data unit testing:

General ease of use

Great Expectations ships as a Python package, extends a useful command-line interface, and uses tools like Jupyter for data validation. The software is quite easy to use and natural for data scientists most familiar with the Python ecosystem. Also, while the number of data sources Great Expectations integrates with is immense, you can indicate all sources in a single *.yaml* configuration file and abstract away information about data ingestion.

Slack integration

> Great Expectations explains in their docs how to set up highly configurable Slack alerts when validation steps are completed. The same configuration can send emails as well, and in general the Great Expectations notification scheme seems to be well-conceived and not fatiguing.

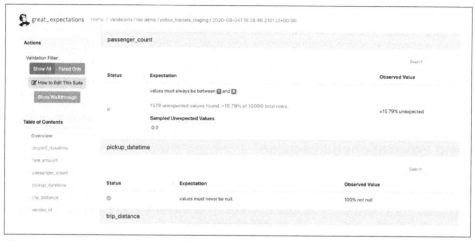

Figure 3-2. An example Data Doc from Great Expectations, showcasing a failing test and analytics describing the failure

Yet, as with any tool, there are some limitations of the Great Expectations tool to be aware of:

Limited to Python

> Great Expectations is a Python tool, meaning if your data environment uses predominantly SQL, R, or some other language, you may be out of luck.

Separate from transformation / job orchestration tool

> Unlike dbt unit tests, which are intimately linked to both the transformation (dbt models) and orchestration (dbt Cloud) pieces of the data engineering stack, Great Expectations is a wholly separate tool with a different learning curve. This slight distance might be a reason to prefer something integrated like dbt tests, should your organization have limited use for the analytics in Data Docs or extensive customization in testing.

Deequ Unit Testing

Deequ is an open source library built by AWS that runs unit tests for data. The software is built atop Apache Spark, so it has a lot of format flexibility. Anything that can fit into a Spark DataFrame—CSV data, JSON, warehouse table data, application log data—can be unit tested in Deequ. The developers also ship a PyDeequ package for use in Python, which can be found on GitHub and PyPI.

Like dbt testing and Great Expectations, Deequ works by asserting test conditions and returning failing rows, or batches, of data. Since Deequ can be integrated within a transformation and streaming environment in AWS, the application is designed to "quarantine" bad data before feeding it to upstream sources. This can make Deequ a better integrated tool for deployment in addition to testing.

Technically, the entrypoint for a Deequ testing suite is the `VerificationSuite` class, as depicted in Example 3-3. With a `VerificationSuite` object, you can assign data to be tested with `.onData(data)` and add individual unit test `Checks` with `addCheck()`. For example, you can test that the data tested has a particular size, has unique and non-NULL columns, and has quantiles within respected ranges. When called, Deequ turns the `VerificationSuite` into a series of Spark jobs to run and report errors when assumptions are violated.

Example 3-3. Some example Deequ code (in Scala) defining simple unit tests on a dummy data set

```scala
import com.amazon.deequ.VerificationSuite
import com.amazon.deequ.checks.{Check, CheckLevel, CheckStatus}

val verificationResult = VerificationSuite()
  .onData(data)
  .addCheck(
    Check(CheckLevel.Error, "unit testing my data")
      .hasSize(_ == 5) // we expect 5 rows
      .isComplete("id") // should never be NULL
      .isUnique("id") // should not contain duplicates
      .isComplete("productName") // should never be NULL
      // should only contain the values "high" and "low"
      .isContainedIn("priority", Array("high", "low"))
      .isNonNegative("numViews") // should not contain negative values
      // at least half of the descriptions should contain a url
      .containsURL("description", _ >= 0.5)
      // half of the items should have less than 10 views
      .hasApproxQuantile("numViews", 0.5, _ <= 10))
  .run()
```

Choosing to run Deequ over other unit testing software like dbt tests and Great Expectations has the following advantages:

Integration with AWS
    If you're an AWS shop and keep the majority of your data engineering within the AWS stack, then Deequ could be for you. Deequ integration with AWS Glue is easy and extensively well documented online in technical blogs.

High scalability

Running on top of Scala allows Deequ to take advantage of Scala job orchestration and parallelism, making it highly efficient. Data is stored in Scala Data Frames, which are already purpose-built for the big data ecosystem and its challenges.

Stateful calculation

Deequ can calculate metric metadata, store said metadata in place, and then recalculate key metrics as more data is ingested. This incremental approach to metric calculation makes the library capable of working with data sets it could not afford to recalculate in their entirety, which is a useful feature with massive streaming data sets that tend to be common in data engineering workflows.

Built-in anomaly detection

One place Deequ particularly stands out is its built-in capacity for advanced anomaly detection. Great Expectations can be configured to "detect" anomalies based on rates of change or simple thresholding. However, Deequ's anomaly detection runs a bit deeper, allowing detection on running metric averages and deviations. It's not as high powered as something a data scientist could build in-house, but it provides an additional layer of sophistication to an already well-integrated tool.

Of course, Deequ has some disadvantages worth mentioning:

Scala's learning curve

Scala is not a friendly language for those immediately outside the data engineering community. For your org, this may be no problem whatsoever. Yet it is relevant to consider that data scientists and other Python-happy folks would find more ease of use from Great Expectations or PyDeequ.

Limited applicability to integration testing

Unlike dbt testing, which runs per model and naturally integrates testing assertions across an ELT pipeline, Deequ runs flexibly on any batch of data you give it. Deequ indeed doesn't claim to be integration testing software at all. If you wanted to leverage Deequ for testing that looks more like integration testing, you may have to dedicate considerably more development time compared with dbt testing.

Lack of intuitive UI

The authors of Deequ don't pride their software on a snazzy looking interface. The software is very no frills and functional for data engineering purposes. If your organization derives a lot of benefit from a digestible report like the Data Doc from Great Expectations or Slack notification routing, then Deequ may be a bit barebones for this purpose.

Testing is an important part of the data quality workflow, but it's not the only proactive measure teams should be taking when solving for data quality. Next, we'll discuss how to leverage Apache Airflow to build circuit breakers and other checks at the orchestration layer.

Managing Data Quality with Apache Airflow

Tools like Apache Airflow, Luigi, Matillion, and Stitch give teams the ability to better manage data quality at the orchestration layer, which programmatically authors, schedules, and monitors workflows across your data pipelines. Given the multiple "checkpoints" in a workflow (often referred to as a DAG, or directed acyclic graph), opportunities for failures or errant changes to the structure of the data are not uncommon.

For the purposes of this chapter, we'll focus on how to improve data quality with Apache Airflow, one of the most popular data engineering orchestration tools available today.

The most common types of data downtime for Apache Airflow (and other orchestration) DAGs are deteriorating queries and errant Python code. Buggy code is probably caused by human error (pesky indenting!), while deteriorating queries happen when Apache Airflow jobs run but take longer than expected; these are usually an indication that the pipeline isn't scaling.

Apache Airflow users can schedule service-level agreements (SLAs) for the maximum amount of time a task should take; if the task runs longer, it is visible as an "SLA missed" in the Apache Airflow UI or can be communicated via Slack, Microsoft Teams, email, or your preferred channels with a little bit of custom Python.

Scheduler SLAs

To set an SLA for an Apache Airflow task, users must pass a `datetime.timedelta` object to the Task/Operator's SLA parameter. If you want to run your own logic for the SLA, you can include an `sla_miss_callback` to be triggered when an SLA is missed.

The function signature of an `sla_miss_callback` requires five parameters:

`dag`
    Parent DAG object for the DAG run in which tasks missed their SLA

`task_list`
    List of all tasks that missed their SLA since the last time the `sla_miss_callback` ran

blocking_task_list

> Any task in the DAG run that is not in a SUCCESS state at the time that the sla_miss_callback runs, i.e., runs that failed

slas

> List of SlaMiss objects associated with the tasks in the task list

blocking_tis

> List of the TaskInstance objects associated with the tasks in the blocking _task_list thresholds

Example 3-4 presents an sla_callback query, as pulled from the Apache Airflow docs (*https://oreil.ly/LpVMY*). An Airflow callback query can pause data pipelines if they don't meet certain SLAs.

Example 3-4. sla_callback query

```python
def sla_callback(dag, task_list, blocking_task_list, slas, blocking_tis):
    print(
        "The callback arguments are: ",
        {
            "dag": dag,
            "task_list": task_list,
            "blocking_task_list": blocking_task_list,
            "slas": slas,
            "blocking_tis": blocking_tis,
        },
    )

@dag(
    schedule_interval="*/2 * * * *",
    start_date=pendulum.datetime(2021, 1, 1, tz="UTC"),
    catchup=False,
    sla_miss_callback=sla_callback,
    default_args={'email': "email@example.com"},
)
def example_sla_dag():
    @task(sla=datetime.timedelta(seconds=10))
    def sleep_20():
        """Sleep for 20 seconds"""
        time.sleep(20)

    @task
    def sleep_30():
        """Sleep for 30 seconds"""
        time.sleep(30)

    sleep_20() >> sleep_30()

dag = example_sla_dag()
```

Another increasingly popular approach to preventing data incidents at the orchestration layer is to apply a "circuit breaker" methodology to running data pipelines. In short, circuit breaking entails that pipelines stop running when data does not meet a set of quality thresholds.

Circuit breakers are common practice in CI/CD workflows as a means of preventing systems from breaking due to new software deployments, and many of the same concepts can be applied to data pipelines, too. In data ecosystems, teams can integrate circuit breakers on top of testing and other steps in the CI/CD process, like versioning.

For instance, a useful circuit breaker could be implemented after a metrics update completes to run integrity tests before allowing any downstream jobs to execute, as depicted in Figure 3-3. This could prevent false positive notifications from being sent to data analysts or data scientists if recent metrics are experiencing any data downtime. Another common use case for circuit breakers is to pause data workflows in the middle of a pipeline if upstream data feeding the pipeline is found to be inaccurate.

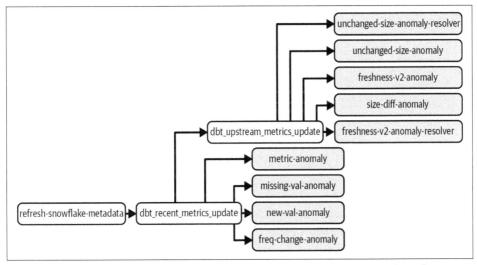

Figure 3-3. Circuit breakers prevent unreliable data in batch or real time from flowing into production data pipelines if certain data quality thresholds are not met

Circuit breakers prevent data products from mixing high- and low-quality data, ensuring an implicit guarantee that the available data will be reliable. There are two states in the data circuit breaker pattern (Figure 3-3):

- Circuit closed: data is flowing through the pipeline.
- Circuit open: data is not flowing through the pipeline.

According to Sandeep Uttamchandi (*https://oreil.ly/Wd4a1*), a former Chief Data Architect at Intuit, using circuit breakers requires three core solutions:

- Data lineage
- Data profiling across the pipeline
- Ability to automatically trigger the circuit via issues unearthed through profiling

In the wild, we've seen circuit breakers used to prevent freshness, volume, and distribution issues across siloed data pipelines, but similar principles can be applied with automation at scale.

Installing Circuit Breakers with Apache Airflow

Installing circuit breakers for your Apache Airflow DAGs is a more proactive way to prevent data quality issues by actually stopping the data pipelines at the orchestration layer if data doesn't meet requirements for freshness, volume, and schema thresholds. Not only does circuit breaking prevent bad data from corrupting your otherwise perfectly good pipelines, but it also ensures you don't run into backfilling costs when DAGs with (silent) data quality issues are run. An example is shown in Figure 3-4.

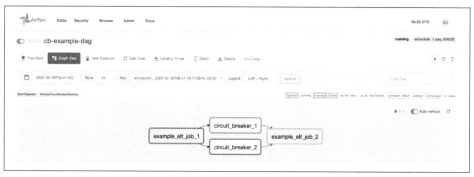

Figure 3-4. Installing a custom Python circuit breaker is one way to pause a broken data pipeline and prevent data quality issues from migrating downstream

There are a few ways to "circuit break" your Apache Airflow DAGs:

- Set the catchup parameter of a DAG to False.
- Include the `LatestOnlyOperator` operator inside the DAG, stopping the DAG from running.
- Insert custom Python code into the orchestration layer to trigger "breaks" and surface relevant metadata related to root cause analysis directly in a data observability platform or data catalog.

Circuit breaking is a valuable—and potentially cost-saving—tool for fast-moving data teams, but it is often used only for the most critical of data downtime incidents. Next, we'll discuss SQL check operators, a more commonly used and proactive way to manage data quality using Apache Airflow.

SQL Check Operators

SQL check operators are another way to manually check data quality across an Apache Airflow DAG or even the entire data pipeline. Functioning the same way as Great Expectations, dbt, or other data quality tests, SQL check operators validate that the content of a given DAG matches expectations across several key elements, including values, intervals, and thresholds. Additionally, Apache Airflow will let you run custom SQL check operators that return a single row from a given SQL query to check and see if any of the returned values in that row are False.

The following is an example of a SQL check operator that you can apply to your own Apache Airflow DAGs:

```
SQLCheckOperator(
    task_id="orange_carddata_row_quality_check",
    sql="row_quality_blue_bankdata_check.sql",
    params={"dropoff_datetime": "2021-01-01"},
)
```

As with a circuit breaker, you can configure custom Python code to stop the pipeline if the check doesn't pass.

Still, "pipeline stopping" should only be used for data incidents that can have serious ramifications for your company. If not implemented strategically and prudentially, circuit breaking and SQL check operators can stop entire pipelines from running unrelated—and perfectly high-quality—jobs, preventing the flow of analytical data to downstream systems.

Summary

Tackling data downtime isn't just about responding to stakeholders when null values surface in downstream dashboards or revisiting your Snowflake queries when you receive a frantic email from your CEO about "missing data." Data downtime can—and should!—be prevented proactively by integrating data quality checks at each stage in the data pipeline, from ingestion in the warehouse or lake down to the business intelligence layer.

While data quality can't be solved by technology alone, collecting, cleaning, ingesting, processing, and orchestrating data with reliability in mind can certainly help. Fortunately, many of the technologies listed in this chapter can proactively identify when assumptions about your data don't meet reality and, with the right integrations and customizations, send alerts about these incidents to the proper communication channels.

Still, even with the most ironclad SQL checks in place, unknown unknowns can fall through the cracks. As with many things in life, data will never be perfectly reliable, and the sooner we accept this fact, the better. Here is where anomaly detection comes into the picture. In Chapter 4, we'll dive into these critical technologies and end-to-end processes, and share how to build your own data quality monitors that extend beyond the traditional capabilities of anomaly detection. Then, in Chapter 5, we'll highlight how to architect for greater data reliability by engineering more reliable data workflows, including CI/CD, alerting and triaging, and incident management.

Monitoring and Anomaly Detection for Your Data Pipelines

With Ryan Kearns

Imagine that you've just purchased a new car. Based on the routine prepurchase check, all systems are working according to the manual, the oil and brake fluid tanks are filled nearly to the brim, and the parts are good as new—because, well, they are.

After grabbing the keys from your dealer, you hit the road. "There's nothing like that new car smell!" you think as you pull onto the highway. Everything is fine and dandy until you hear a loud pop. *Yikes.* And your car starts to wobble. You pull onto the shoulder, turn on your hazard lights, and jump out of the car. After a brief investigation, you've identified the alleged culprit of the loud sound—a flat tire. No matter how many tests or checks your dealership could have done to validate the health of your car, there's no accounting for unknown unknowns (i.e, nails or debris on the highway) that might affect your vehicle.

Similarly, in data, all of the testing and data quality checks under the sun can't fully protect you from data downtime, which can manifest at all stages of the pipeline and surface for a variety of reasons that are often unaffiliated with the data itself.

When it comes to understanding when data breaks, your best course of action is to lean on monitoring, specifically anomaly detection techniques that identify when your expected thresholds for volume, freshness, distribution, and other values don't meet expectations.

Anomaly detection (*https://oreil.ly/m8q3B*) refers to the identification of events or observations that deviate from the norm—for instance, fraudulent credit card behavior or a technical glitch, like a website crash. Assuming your website is normally up and running, of course.

A number of techniques, algorithms, and frameworks exist and are used (and developed) by industry giants like Meta, Google, Uber, and others. For a technical deep dive, we recommend Preetam Jinka and Baron Schwartz's report *Anomaly Detection for Monitoring* (O'Reilly).

Up until recently, anomaly detection was considered a nice-to-have—not a need-to-have—for many data teams. Now, as data systems become increasingly complex and companies empower employees across functions to use data, it's imperative that teams take both proactive and reactive approaches to solving for data quality.

While automobiles are vastly different from data pipelines, cars and other mechanical systems have their own monitoring and anomaly detection capabilities, too. Most contemporary vehicles alert you when oil, brake fluid, gas, tire pressure, and other vital entities are lower than they should be and encourage you to take action. Data monitoring and anomaly detection function in much the same way.

In this chapter, we'll walk through how to build your own data quality monitors for a data warehouse environment to monitor and alert to the pillars of data observability: freshness, volume, distribution, and schema. In the process, we'll introduce important concepts and terms necessary to bulk up your understanding of important anomaly detection techniques.

Knowing Your Known Unknowns and Unknown Unknowns

There are two types of data quality issues in this world: those you can predict (known unknowns) and those you can't (unknown unknowns). Known unknowns are issues that you can easily predict, i.e., null values, specific freshness issues, or schema changes triggered by a system that updates regularly. These issues may not happen, but with a healthy dose of testing, you can often account for them before they cause issues downstream. In Figure 4-1, we highlight popular examples of both.

Unknown unknowns refer to data downtime that even the most comprehensive testing can't account for, issues that arise across your entire data pipeline, not just the sections covered by specific tests. Unknown unknowns might include:

- A distribution anomaly in a critical field that causes your Tableau dashboard to malfunction
- A JSON schema change made by another team that turns 6 columns into 600
- An unintended change to ETL (or reverse ETL, if you fancy) leading to tests not running and bad data being missed
- Incomplete or stale data that goes unnoticed until several weeks later, affecting key marketing metrics

- A code change that causes an API to stop collecting data feeding an important new product
- Data drift over time, which can be challenging to catch, particularly if your tests look only at the data being written at the time of your ETL jobs, which don't normally take into account data that is already in a given table

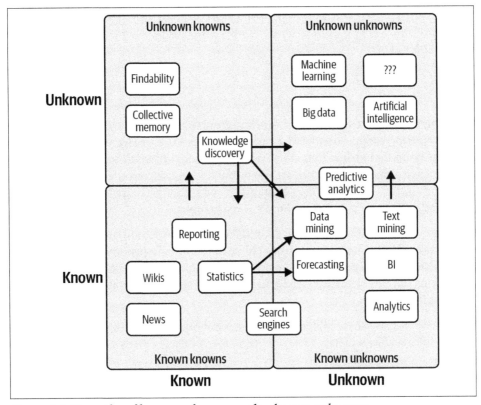

Figure 4-1. Examples of known unknowns and unknown unknowns

While testing and circuit breakers can handle many of your known unknowns, monitoring and anomaly detection can cover your bases when it comes to unknown unknowns.

Frequently, data teams leverage monitoring and anomaly detection to identify and alert to data behavior that deviates from what's historically expected of a given data pipeline. By understanding what "good" data looks like, it's easier to proactively identify "bad" data.

Now that we've outlined the differences between these two types of data issues, let's dive into what anomaly detection for unknown unknowns looks like in practice.

Building an Anomaly Detection Algorithm

To crystalize how anomaly detection works, let's walk through a real-world tutorial in building an anomaly detector for a very anomalous data set.

Keep in mind that there are any number of technologies and approaches you can use to build data quality monitors, and the choices you make will depend on your tech stack. In this example, we leverage the following languages and tools:

- SQLite and SQL
- Jupyter Notebooks
- Python

Our sample data ecosystem uses mock astronomical data (*https://oreil.ly/gLO5n*) about habitable exoplanets. For the purpose of this exercise, we generated the data set with Python, modeling anomalies from real incidents we've come across in production environments. This data set is entirely free to use, and the *utils* folder in the repository (*https://oreil.ly/VZEgg*) contains the code that generated the data, if you're interested in learning more about how it was assembled.

We'll use SQLite 3.32.3 (*https://oreil.ly/zz0wR*), which should make the database (*https://oreil.ly/zNocO*) accessible from either the command prompt or SQL files with minimal setup. The concepts extend to really any query language, and these implementations can be extended to MySQL, Snowflake, and other database environments with minimal changes.

In the following, we share table information about our EXOPLANETS data set, including five specific database entries:

```
$ sqlite3 EXOPLANETS.db
sqlite> PRAGMA TABLE_INFO(EXOPLANETS);
_id              | TEXT | 0 | | 0   ❶
distance         | REAL | 0 | | 0   ❷
g                | REAL | 0 | | 0   ❸
orbital_period   | REAL | 0 | | 0   ❹
avg_temp         | REAL | 0 | | 0   ❺
date_added       | TEXT | 0 | | 0   ❻
```

A database entry in EXOPLANETS contains the following info:

❶ _id: a UUID corresponding to the planet

❷ distance: distance from Earth, in light-years

❸ g: surface gravity as a multiple of *g*, the gravitational force constant

❹ `orbital_period`: length of a single orbital cycle in days

❺ `avg_temp`: average surface temperature in degrees Kelvin

❻ `date_added`: the date our system discovered the planet and added it automatically to our databases

Note that one or more of `distance`, `g`, `orbital_period`, and `avg_temp` may be NULL for a given planet as a result of missing or erroneous data.

If we query `sqlite> SELECT * FROM EXOPLANETS LIMIT 5;` we can pull five rows from our database. In Example 4-1, we share five database entries (*https://oreil.ly/ ZTS1q*) in our `EXOPLANETS` data set, to highlight the format and distribution of the data.

Example 4-1. Five rows from the EXOPLANETS data set

```
_id,distance,g,orbital_period,avg_temp,date_added
c168b188-ef0c-4d6a-8cb2-f473d4154bdb,34.6273036348341,,476.480044083599, ...
e7b56e84-41f4-4e62-b078-01b076cea369,110.196919810563,2.52507362359066, ...
a27030a0-e4b4-4bd7-8d24-5435ed86b395,26.6957950454452,10.2764970016067, ...
54f9cf85-eae9-4f29-b665-855357a14375,54.8883521129783,,173.788967912197, ...
4d06ec88-f5c8-4d03-91ef-7493a12cd89e,153.264217159834,0.922874568459221, ...
```

Note that this exercise (*https://oreil.ly/M7Y7a*) is retroactive—we're looking at historical data. In a production data environment, anomaly detection is real time and applied at each stage of the data life cycle, and thus will involve a slightly different implementation than what is done here.

For the purpose of this exercise, we'll be building data observability algorithms for freshness and distribution, but in future articles, we'll address the rest of our five pillars—and more.

Monitoring for Freshness

The first pillar of data observability we monitor for is freshness, which can give us a strong indicator of when critical data assets were last updated. If a report that is regularly updated on the hour suddenly looks very stale, this type of anomaly should give us a strong indication that something is inaccurate or otherwise wrong.

First, note the `DATE_ADDED` column. SQL doesn't store metadata on when individual records are added. So, to visualize freshness in this retroactive setting, we need to track that information ourselves. Grouping by the `DATE_ADDED` column can give us insight into how `EXOPLANETS` updates daily. As depicted in Example 4-2, we can query for the number of new IDs added per day.

Example 4-2. A query about the number of new exoplanets added to our data set per day

```
SELECT
  DATE_ADDED,
  COUNT(*) AS ROWS_ADDED
FROM
  EXOPLANETS
GROUP BY
  DATE_ADDED;
```

You can run this yourself with `$ sqlite3 EXOPLANETS.db < queries/freshness/ rows-added.sql` in the repository. We get the data in Example 4-3 back.

Example 4-3. Data pulled from Example 4-2

```
date_added     ROWS_ADDED
2020-01-01     84
2020-01-02     92
2020-01-03     101
2020-01-04     102
2020-01-05     100
... ...
2020-07-14     104
2020-07-15     110
2020-07-16     103
2020-07-17     89
2020-07-18     104
```

Based on this graphical representation of our data set, it looks like EXOPLANETS consistently updates with around 100 new entries each day, though there are gaps where no data comes in for multiple days.

Recall that with freshness, we want to ask the question "Is my data up to date?"—thus, knowing about those gaps in table updates is essential to understanding the reliability of our data. The following query, Example 4-4, operationalizes freshness (as depicted in Figure 4-2) by introducing a metric for DAYS_SINCE_LAST_UPDATE. (Note: since this tutorial uses SQLite3, the SQL syntax for calculating time differences will be different in MySQL, Snowflake, and other environments.)

Example 4-4. Query that pulls the number of days since the data set was updated

```
WITH UPDATES AS(
  SELECT
    DATE_ADDED,
    COUNT(*) AS ROWS_ADDED
  FROM
    EXOPLANETS
```

```
  GROUP BY
    DATE_ADDED
)

SELECT
  DATE_ADDED,
  JULIANDAY(DATE_ADDED) - JULIANDAY(LAG(DATE_ADDED) OVER(
    ORDER BY DATE_ADDED
  )) AS DAYS_SINCE_LAST_UPDATE
FROM
  UPDATES;
```

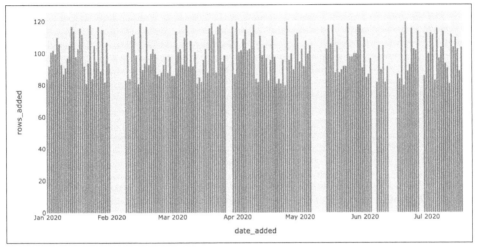

Figure 4-2. Rendering freshness patterns within our data set using a Jupyter Notebook

The resulting table, Example 4-5, says, "On date X, the most recent data in EXOPLANETS was Y days old." This is information not explicitly available from the DATE_ADDED column in the table—but applying data observability gives us the tools to uncover it. This is visualized in Figure 4-3, where freshness anomalies are depicted by the high Y values. This denotes table update lags, which we can query for with a simple detector.

Example 4-5. Exoplanet data freshness table from query in Example 4-4

```
DATE_ADDED     DAYS_SINCE_LAST_UPDATE
2020-01-01
2020-01-02     1
2020-01-03     1
2020-01-04     1
2020-01-05     1
...            ...
2020-07-14     1
2020-07-15     1
```

```
2020-07-16     1
2020-07-17     1
2020-07-18     1
```

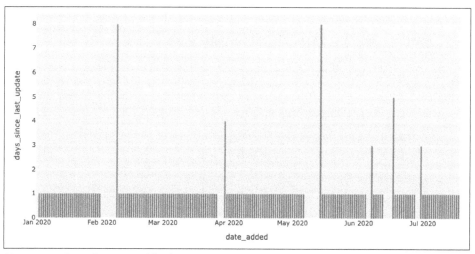

Figure 4-3. Visualization of freshness anomalies depicted by high Y values

Now, we have the data we need to detect freshness anomalies. All that's left to do is to set a threshold parameter for Y—how many days old is too many? A parameter turns a query, Example 4-6, into a detector, since it decides what counts as anomalous (read: worth alerting) and what doesn't.

Example 4-6. Modified query to alert to data that sits beyond expected freshness for exoplanet data

```
WITH UPDATES AS(
  SELECT
    DATE_ADDED,
    COUNT(*) AS ROWS_ADDED
  FROM
    EXOPLANETS
  GROUP BY
    DATE_ADDED
),

NUM_DAYS_UPDATES AS (
  SELECT
    DATE_ADDED,
    JULIANDAY(DATE_ADDED) - JULIANDAY(LAG(DATE_ADDED)
      OVER(
        ORDER BY DATE_ADDED
      )
    ) AS DAYS_SINCE_LAST_UPDATE
```

```
   FROM
      UPDATES
)

SELECT
   *
FROM
   NUM_DAYS_UPDATES
WHERE
   DAYS_SINCE_LAST_UPDATE > 1;
```

The data returned to us, Example 4-7, represents dates where freshness incidents occurred.

Example 4-7. Data returned from Example 4-6 query

```
DATE_ADDED    DAYS_SINCE_LAST_UPDATE
2020-02-08    8
2020-03-30    4
2020-05-14    8
2020-06-07    3
2020-06-17    5
2020-06-30    3
```

On 2020–05–14, the most recent data in the table was 8 days old! Such an outage may represent a breakage in our data pipeline and would be good to know about if we're using this data for anything high impact (and if we're using this in a production environment, chances are, we are). As illustrated in Figure 4-4, we can render freshness anomalies by setting thresholds for what is an acceptable amount of time since the last update.

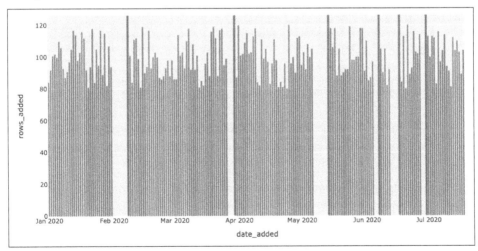

Figure 4-4. Visualization of freshness anomalies using thresholds

Note in particular the last line of the query: DAYS_SINCE_LAST_UPDATE > 1;.

Here, 1 is a model parameter—there's nothing "correct" about this number, though changing it will impact what dates we consider to be incidents. The smaller the number, the more genuine anomalies we'll catch (high recall), but chances are, several of these "anomalies" will not reflect real outages. The larger the number, the greater the likelihood all anomalies we catch will reflect true anomalies (high precision), but it's possible we may miss some.

For the purpose of this example, we could change 1 to 7 and thus catch only the two worst outages (on 2020–02–08 and 2020–05–14). Any choice here will reflect the particular use case and objectives; it is an important balance to strike that comes up again and again when applying data observability at scale to production environments.

In Figure 4-5, we leverage the same freshness detector but with the SQLite query DAYS_SINCE_LAST_UPDATE > 3; serving as the threshold. Two of the smaller outages now go undetected.

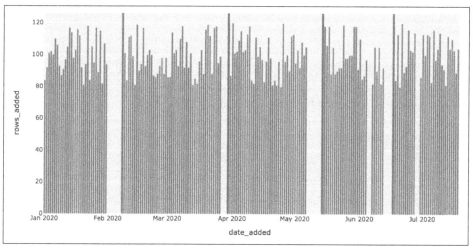

Figure 4-5. Narrowing the search for anomalies (DAYS_SINCE_LAST_UPDATE > 3)

Now, we visualize the same freshness detector, but with DAYS_SINCE_LAST_UPDATE > 7; now serving as the threshold. All but the two largest outages now go undetected (Figure 4-6).

Just like planets, optimal model parameters sit in a "Goldilocks Zone" or "sweet spot" between values considered too low and too high.

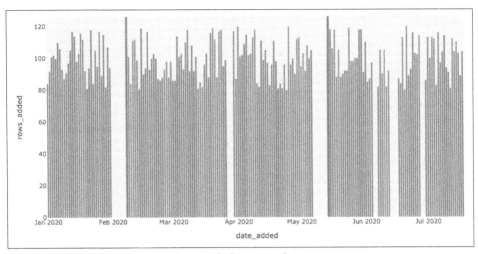

Figure 4-6. Further narrowing the search for anomalies
(DAYS_SINCE_LAST_UPDATE > 7)

Understanding Distribution

Next, we want to assess the field-level, distributional health of our data. Distribution tells us all of the expected values of our data, as well as how frequently each value occurs. One of the simplest questions is, "How often is my data NULL?" In many cases, some level of incomplete data is acceptable—but if a 10% null rate turns into 90%, we'll want to know.

In statistics, we like to assume that sets of observations are drawn from baseline distributions that obey mathematical rules. Call the former "sample distributions" and the latter "true distributions." Statistics has an observation about natural processes, called the central limit theorem (*https://oreil.ly/ZwzeU*), that states that distributions of *independently generated random samples* approach a certain distribution as the number of samples gets large.

Central Limit Theorem

The central limit theorem suggests that if you have a sufficiently randomized sample from a given data set with mean μ and standard deviation σ, then the distribution of the sample means will be approximately normally distributed.

The normal distribution, or Gaussian distribution—the famous bell curve everyone is familiar with from statistics class, shown in Figure 4-7—can tell us what normal behavior is for a given data set. Gaussians can be nicely summarized with two variables—their mean, μ, and variance, σ—which makes them powerful and ubiquitous in statistical analysis.

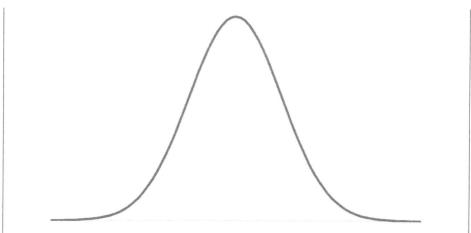

Figure 4-7. A normal (Gaussian) distribution represents the most basic form of anomaly detection (if only it were this easy)

Applying the Gaussian distribution may prompt an initial approach to anomaly detection that's quite naive but surprisingly effective: calculating the standard score (*https://oreil.ly/V618A*) for each observation. That is, subtract μ, and then divide by σ. This score (also called the z-score) gives a quantifiable metric for how "far out" (on the bell curve) each observation is. Anomaly detection: solved! Just draw a line at some point out from the center of the bell and call everything outside that line "anomalous." From a statistical standpoint, you'll be correct. Unfortunately, statistical theory isn't a compelling approach to anomaly detection in the very concrete field of data quality, for two reasons.

First, the central limit theorem states a key characteristic of the data generating process that many people overlook: *independent, random observations* yield normal distributions in the limit. This is a great assumption to make when measuring the volume of wind through grass, or the stride length of the average New Yorker. It's not so great for business intelligence data, where observations tend to be *highly correlated* and confounded with other variables. For example, "daily customers" will not be normally distributed at Chick-Fil-A, which closes on Sundays, since 1/7th of all observations will be 0. These observations are not generated randomly but are instead impacted by the day of the week.

Second, there's a distinction between "anomalous" and "interesting" observations that can't be quite captured with purely statistical thinking. To illustrate this, consider the z-score, as discussed a few paragraphs earlier. We said (in jest) that anomaly detection can be solved with a simple z-score; unfortunately, that's rarely the case.

If we choose to define "anomaly" as anything, say, three standard deviations from the distribution's mean, we can be guaranteed to get that "correct" for any data. But we're *not* just in the business of identifying simply anomalous metrics. For one, our time series contain important contextual information (What day of the week was it? Does the pattern repeat?). More importantly, though, is that not all anomalous observations are interesting—they don't help us identify and correct for data downtime. Example 4-8 queries data with an anomalous distribution.

Example 4-8. Query to pull data about anomalous distributions

```sql
SELECT
  DATE_ADDED,
  CAST(
    SUM(
      CASE
        WHEN DISTANCE IS NULL THEN 1
        ELSE 0
      END
    ) AS FLOAT) / COUNT(*) AS DISTANCE_NULL_RATE,
  CAST(
    SUM(
      CASE
        WHEN G IS NULL THEN 1
        ELSE 0
      END
    ) AS FLOAT) / COUNT(*) AS G_NULL_RATE,
  CAST(
    SUM(
      CASE
        WHEN ORBITAL_PERIOD IS NULL THEN 1
        ELSE 0
      END
    ) AS FLOAT) / COUNT(*) AS ORBITAL_PERIOD_NULL_RATE,
  CAST(
    SUM(
      CASE
        WHEN AVG_TEMP IS NULL THEN 1
        ELSE 0
      END
    ) AS FLOAT) / COUNT(*) AS AVG_TEMP_NULL_RATE
FROM
  EXOPLANETS
GROUP BY
  DATE_ADDED;
```

This query returns a lot of data, as depicted in Example 4-9.

Example 4-9. Data from Example 4-8 query

date_added	DISTANCE_NULL_RATE	G_NULL_RATE	ORBITAL_PERIOD_NULL_RATE
2020-01-01	0.0833333333333333	0.178571428571429	0.214285714285714
2020-01-02	0.0	0.152173913043478	0.326086956521739
2020-01-03	0.0594059405940594	0.188118811881188	0.237623762376238
2020-01-04	0.0490196078431373	0.117647058823529	0.264705882352941
...	...	...	...
2020-07-13	0.0892857142857143	0.160714285714286	0.285714285714286
2020-07-14	0.0673076923076923	0.125	0.269230769230769
2020-07-15	0.0636363636363636	0.118181818181818	0.245454545454545
2020-07-16	0.058252427184466	0.145631067961165	0.262135922330097
2020-07-17	0.101123595505618	0.0898876404494382	0.247191011235955
2020-07-18	0.0673076923076923	0.201923076923077	0.317307692307692

The general formula CAST(SUM(CASE WHEN SOME_METRIC IS NULL THEN 1 ELSE 0 END) AS FLOAT) / COUNT(*), when grouped by the DATE_ADDED column, is telling us the rate of NULL values for SOME_METRIC in the daily batches of new data in EXOPLANETS. It's hard to get a sense by looking at the raw output, but a visual (Figure 4-8) can help illuminate this anomaly.

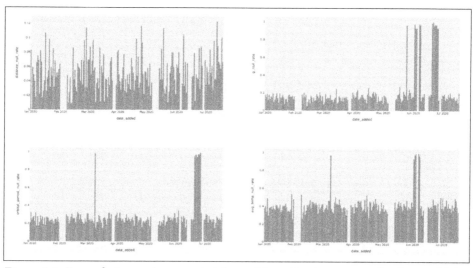

Figure 4-8. By rendering various events triggered by null rates, we can clearly see which dates were anomalous

The visuals make it clear that there are null rate "spike" events we should be detecting. Let's focus on just the last metric, AVG_TEMP, for now. We can detect null spikes most basically with a simple threshold via the query in Example 4-10.

Example 4-10. Detecting null values in the AVG_TEMP column of the EXOPLANETS data set

```
WITH NULL_RATES AS(
  SELECT
    DATE_ADDED,
    CAST(
      SUM(
        CASE
          WHEN AVG_TEMP IS NULL THEN 1
          ELSE 0
        END
      ) AS FLOAT) / COUNT(*) AS AVG_TEMP_NULL_RATE
  FROM
    EXOPLANETS
  GROUP BY
    DATE_ADDED
)

SELECT
  *
FROM
  NULL_RATES
WHERE
  AVG_TEMP_NULL_RATE  > 0.9;
```

In Example 4-11, we share the corresponding data pulled in its raw form, illustrating the rows with null values in the AVG_TEMP column of the data set.

Example 4-11. AVG_TEMP rows with null values

```
DATE_ADDED      AVG_TEMP_NULL_RATE
2020-03-09      0.967391304347826
2020-06-02      0.929411764705882
2020-06-03      0.977011494252874
2020-06-04      0.989690721649485
2020-06-07      0.987804878048781
2020-06-08      0.961904761904762
```

In Figure 4-9, we highlight where the anomalous spikes were, correlating to the rate of null values in the temperature column of our EXOPLANETS data set.

As detection algorithms go, this approach to identifying null values is something of a blunt instrument. Sometimes, patterns in our data will be simple enough for a threshold like this to do the trick. In other cases, though, data will be noisy or have other complications, like seasonality, requiring us to change our approach.

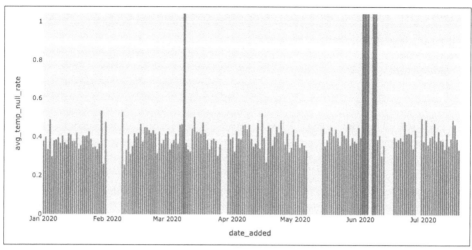

Figure 4-9. Detecting null spikes in the average temperature

Seasonality refers to the tendency of a time series to observe predictable fluctuations over certain intervals. For example, data for "church attendees" might observe a weekly seasonality with a high bias toward Sunday, and data for a department store's coat sales would likely observe yearly seasonality with a high in fall and a low in spring.

For example, detecting 2020–06–02, 2020–06–03, and 2020–06–04 seems redundant. We can filter out dates that occur immediately after other alerts to reduce duplication via the query in Example 4-12.

Example 4-12. Query to filter out dates that occur immediately after other alerts

```
WITH NULL_RATES AS(
  SELECT
    DATE_ADDED,
    CAST(
      SUM(
        CASE
          WHEN AVG_TEMP IS NULL THEN 1
          ELSE 0
        END
      ) AS FLOAT
    ) / COUNT(*) AS AVG_TEMP_NULL_RATE
  FROM
    EXOPLANETS
```

```
  GROUP BY
    DATE_ADDED
),

ALL_DATES AS (
  SELECT
    *,
    JULIANDAY(DATE_ADDED) - JULIANDAY(LAG(DATE_ADDED)
      OVER(
        ORDER BY DATE_ADDED
      )
    ) AS DAYS_SINCE_LAST_ALERT
  FROM
    NULL_RATES
  WHERE
    AVG_TEMP_NULL_RATE > 0.9
)
SELECT
  DATE_ADDED,
  AVG_TEMP_NULL_RATE
FROM
  ALL_DATES
WHERE
  DAYS_SINCE_LAST_ALERT IS NULL OR DAYS_SINCE_LAST_ALERT > 1;
```

The corresponding data set is listed in Example 4-13. These results highlight dates that don't need to be taken into account in our null value anomaly detector, per the query in Example 4-12.

Example 4-13. Results of Example 4-12 query

```
DATE_ADDED    AVG_TEMP_NULL_RATE
2020-03-09    0.967391304347826
2020-06-02    0.929411764705882
2020-06-07    0.987804878048781
```

Note that in both of these queries, the key parameter is 0.9. We're effectively saying, "Any null rate higher than 90% is a problem, and I need to know about it." We visualize these results in Figure 4-10. This helps us reduce white noise and generate more accurate results.

In this instance, we can (and should) be a bit more intelligent by applying the concept of rolling average with a more intelligent parameter using the query in Example 4-14 to improve precision further.

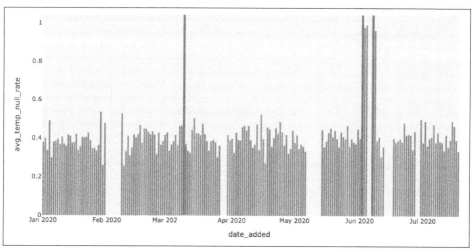

Figure 4-10. Visualizing any null rates higher than 90%

Example 4-14. Query to apply a rolling average to the null rate

```
WITH NULL_RATES AS(
  SELECT
    DATE_ADDED,
    CAST(SUM(CASE WHEN AVG_TEMP IS NULL THEN 1 ELSE 0 END) AS FLOAT) /
      COUNT(*) AS AVG_TEMP_NULL_RATE
  FROM
    EXOPLANETS
  GROUP BY
    DATE_ADDED
),

NULL_WITH_AVG AS(
  SELECT
    *,
    AVG(AVG_TEMP_NULL_RATE) OVER (
      ORDER BY DATE_ADDED ASC
      ROWS BETWEEN 14 PRECEDING AND CURRENT ROW) AS TWO_WEEK_ROLLING_AVG
  FROM
    NULL_RATES
  GROUP BY
    DATE_ADDED
)

SELECT
  *
FROM
  NULL_WITH_AVG
WHERE
  AVG_TEMP_NULL_RATE - TWO_WEEK_ROLLING_AVG > 0.3;
```

The query's results are shown in Example 4-15 and depicted in Figure 4-11. We see null values that might raise bigger alarms (i.e., with a null rate higher than 90%).

Example 4-15. Results from Example 4-14 query

```
DATE_ADDED     AVG_TEMP_NULL_RATE    TWO_WEEK_ROLLING_AVG
2020-03-09     0.967391304347826     0.436077995611105
2020-06-02     0.929411764705882     0.441299602441599
2020-06-03     0.977011494252874     0.47913211475687
2020-06-04     0.989690721649485     0.515566041654715
2020-06-07     0.987804878048781     0.554753033524633
2020-06-08     0.961904761904762     0.594966974173356
```

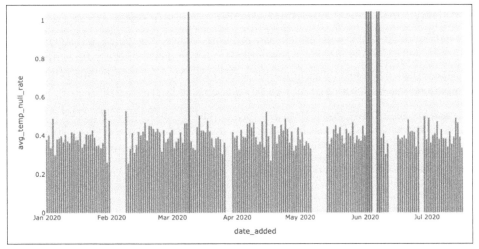

Figure 4-11. Using the query AVG_TEMP_NULL_RATE − TWO_WEEK_ROLLING_AVG to get even more specific when identifying the null value rate

One clarification: notice that we filter using the quantity AVG_TEMP_NULL_RATE − TWO_WEEK_ROLLING_AVG. In other instances, we might want to take the ABS() of this error quantity, but not here—the reason being that a null rate "spike" is much more alarming if it represents an increase from the previous average. It may not be worthwhile to monitor whenever nulls abruptly decrease in frequency, while the value in detecting a null rate increase is clear.

Building Monitors for Schema and Lineage

In the previous section, we looked at the first two pillars of data observability, freshness and distribution, and showed how a little SQL code can operationalize these concepts. These are what I would call more "classic" data anomaly detection problems—given a steady stream of data, does anything look out of whack?

Good anomaly detection is certainly part of the data observability puzzle, but it's not everything. Equally important is context (*https://oreil.ly/bqpxe*). If a data anomaly occurred, great. But where? What upstream pipelines may be the cause? What downstream dashboards will be affected by a data anomaly? And has the formal structure of my data changed? Good data observability hinges on our ability to properly leverage metadata to answer these data anomaly questions.

In our next section, we'll look at the two data observability pillars designed to answer these questions—schema and lineage. Once again, we'll use lightweight tools like Jupyter and SQLite, so you can easily spin up our environment and try these data anomaly exercises yourself. Let's get started.

Anomaly Detection for Schema Changes and Lineage

As before, we'll work with mock astronomical data (*https://oreil.ly/qMpvj*) about habitable exoplanets. It looks like our oldest data is dated 2020-01-01 (note: most databases will not store timestamps for individual records, so our DATE_ADDED column is keeping track for us). Our newest data looks to be from 2020-07-18:

```
sqlite> SELECT DATE_ADDED FROM EXOPLANETS ORDER BY DATE_ADDED DESC LIMIT 1;
    2020-07-18
```

Of course, this is the same table we used in the previous section. If we want to explore the more context-laden pillars of schema and lineage, we'll need to expand our environment.

Now, in addition to EXOPLANETS, we have a table called EXOPLANETS_EXTENDED (*https://oreil.ly/hYqxU*), which is a superset of our past table. It's useful to think of these as the same table at *different moments in time*. In fact, EXOPLANETS_EXTENDED has data dating back to 2020-01-01:

```
sqlite> SELECT DATE_ADDED FROM EXOPLANETS_EXTENDED ORDER BY DATE_ADDED ASC
    LIMIT 1; 2020-01-01
```

But it also contains data up to 2020-09-06, further than EXOPLANETS:

```
sqlite> SELECT DATE_ADDED FROM EXOPLANETS_EXTENDED ORDER BY DATE_ADDED DESC
    LIMIT 1; 2020-09-0
```

Something else is different between these tables, as depicted in Example 4-16. There are two additional fields, making the opportunity for anomalies even higher.

Example 4-16. Two additional fields in EXOPLANETS_EXTENDED data set

```
sqlite> PRAGMA TABLE_INFO(EXOPLANETS_EXTENDED);
_ID             | VARCHAR(16777216)  | 1 |  | 0
DISTANCE        | FLOAT              | 0 |  | 0
G               | FLOAT              | 0 |  | 0
ORBITAL_PERIOD  | FLOAT              | 0 |  | 0
```

```
AVG_TEMP          | FLOAT              | 0 | | 0
DATE_ADDED        | TIMESTAMP_NTZ(6)   | 1 | | 0
ECCENTRICITY      | FLOAT              | 0 | | 0  ❶
ATMOSPHERE        | VARCHAR(16777216)  | 0 | | 0  ❷
```

In addition to the six fields in `EXOPLANETS`, the `EXOPLANETS_EXTENDED` table contains two additional fields:

❶ `ECCENTRICITY`: the orbital eccentricity (*https://oreil.ly/VhNmv*) of the planet around its host star

❷ `ATMOSPHERE`: the dominant chemical makeup of the planet's atmosphere

Note that like `DISTANCE`, `G`, `ORBITAL_PERIOD`, and `AVG_TEMP`, both `ECCENTRICITY` and `ATMOSPHERE` may be NULL for a given planet as a result of missing or erroneous data. For example, rogue planets (*https://oreil.ly/dxcL7*) have undefined orbital eccentricity, and many planets don't have atmospheres at all.

Note also that data is not backfilled, meaning data entries from the beginning of the table (data contained also in the `EXOPLANETS` table) will not have eccentricity and atmosphere information. In Example 4-17, we share a query to highlight that older data is not backfilled; this will hopefully show the schema change that ensued.

Example 4-17. Query highlighting that older data is not backfilled

```
SELECT
 DATE_ADDED,
 ECCENTRICITY,
 ATMOSPHERE
FROM
 EXOPLANETS_EXTENDED
ORDER BY
 DATE_ADDED ASC
LIMIT 10;
```

We can make this file beautiful and searchable (*https://oreil.ly/W0k7V*) if this error is corrected: no commas found in this CSV file (*https://oreil.ly/F8fhc*) in line 0 (depicted in Example 4-18).

Example 4-18. Addition of two new columns, signaling a schema change in our EXOPLANETS data set

```
2020-01-01 | |
2020-01-01 | |
2020-01-01 | |
2020-01-01 | |
2020-01-01 | |
```

```
2020-01-01 | |
2020-01-01 | |
2020-01-01 | |
2020-01-01 | |
2020-01-01 | |
```

The addition of two fields is an example of a schema change—our data's formal blueprint has been modified. Schema changes (*https://oreil.ly/JrcLM*) occur when an alteration is made to the structure of your data, and it's a data anomaly that can be frustrating to manually debug. Schema changes can indicate any number of things about your data, including:

- The addition of new API endpoints
- Supposedly deprecated fields that are not yet deprecated
- The addition or subtraction of columns, rows, or entire tables

In an ideal world, we'd like a record of this change, as it represents a vector for possible issues with our pipeline. Unfortunately, our database is not naturally configured to keep track of such changes. It has no versioning history, as depicted in Example 4-19. A schema change can easily sneak up on us.

Example 4-19. No versioning history in data set

```
sqlite> PRAGMA TABLE_INFO(EXOPLANETS_COLUMNS);

DATE    | TEXT | 0 | | 0

COLUMNS | TEXT | 0 | | 0
```

We ran into this issue when querying for the age of individual records and added the DATE_ADDED column to cope. In this case, we'll do something similar, except with the addition of an entire table.

The EXOPLANETS_COLUMNS table "versions" our schema by recording the columns in EXOPLANETS_EXTENDED at any given date. Looking at the very first and last entries, we see that the columns definitely changed at some point, as highlighted by Example 4-20. The two entries in Example 4-20 highlight that there was an addition of two new columns in our EXOPLANETS data set—in other words, a schema change.

Example 4-20. Two entries highlighting a schema change

```
sqlite> SELECT * FROM EXOPLANETS_COLUMNS ORDER BY DATE ASC LIMIT 1;
2020-01-01 | [
    (0, '_id', 'TEXT', 0, None, 0),
    (1, 'distance', 'REAL', 0, None, 0),
    (2, 'g', 'REAL', 0, None, 0),
```

```
    (3, 'orbital_period', 'REAL', 0, None, 0),
    (4, 'avg_temp', 'REAL', 0, None, 0),
    (5, 'date_added', 'TEXT', 0, None, 0)
]

sqlite> SELECT * FROM EXOPLANETS_COLUMNS ORDER BY DATE DESC LIMIT 1;
2020-09-06 | [
    (0, '_id', 'TEXT', 0, None, 0),
    (1, 'distance', 'REAL', 0, None, 0),
    (2, 'g', 'REAL', 0, None, 0),
    (3, 'orbital_period', 'REAL', 0, None, 0),
    (4, 'avg_temp', 'REAL', 0, None, 0),
    (5, 'date_added', 'TEXT', 0, None, 0),
    (6, 'eccentricity', 'REAL', 0, None, 0),
    (7, 'atmosphere', 'TEXT', 0, None, 0)
]
```

Now, returning to our original question: when, exactly, did the schema change? Since our column lists are indexed by dates, we can find the date of the change and a good clue for where anomalies lie with a quick SQL script, as depicted in Example 4-21.

Example 4-21. A query of the extended EXOPLANETS table to showcase when schema for the data set changed

```
WITH CHANGES AS(
  SELECT
    DATE,
    COLUMNS AS NEW_COLUMNS,
    LAG(COLUMNS) OVER(ORDER BY DATE) AS PAST_COLUMNS
  FROM
    EXOPLANETS_COLUMNS
)

SELECT
  *
FROM
  CHANGES
WHERE
  NEW_COLUMNS != PAST_COLUMNS
ORDER BY
  DATE ASC;
```

Example 4-22 includes the data returned, which we've reformatted for legibility. Looking at the data, we see that the schema changed on 2022-07-19.

Example 4-22. Results pulled from the query in Example 4-21

```
DATE:           2020-07-19
NEW_COLUMNS:    [
                  (0, '_id', 'TEXT', 0, None, 0),
```

```
                (1, 'distance', 'REAL', 0, None, 0),
                (2, 'g', 'REAL', 0, None, 0),
                (3, 'orbital_period', 'REAL', 0, None, 0),
                (4, 'avg_temp', 'REAL', 0, None, 0),
                (5, 'date_added', 'TEXT', 0, None, 0),
                (6, 'eccentricity', 'REAL', 0, None, 0),
                (7, 'atmosphere', 'TEXT', 0, None, 0)
            ]
PAST_COLUMNS: [
                (0, '_id', 'TEXT', 0, None, 0),
                (1, 'distance', 'REAL', 0, None, 0),
                (2, 'g', 'REAL', 0, None, 0),
                (3, 'orbital_period', 'REAL', 0, None, 0),
                (4, 'avg_temp', 'REAL', 0, None, 0),
                (5, 'date_added', 'TEXT', 0, None, 0)
            ]
```

With this query, we return the offending date: 2020–07–19. Like freshness and distribution observability, achieving schema observability follows a pattern: we identify the useful metadata (*https://oreil.ly/sIM86*) that signals pipeline health, track it, and build detectors to alert us of potential issues. Supplying an additional table like EXOPLANETS_COLUMNS is one way to track schema, but there are many others. We encourage you to think about how you could implement a schema change detector for your own data pipeline!

Visualizing Lineage

We've described lineage as the most holistic (*https://oreil.ly/Canj0*) of the five pillars of data observability, and for good reason. Lineage contextualizes incidents by telling us (1) which downstream sources may be impacted, and (2) which upstream sources may be the root cause. While it's not intuitive to "visualize" lineage with SQL code, a quick example may illustrate how it can be useful. (In Chapter 6, we'll teach you how to build your own field-level lineage system from scratch using common open source frameworks.)

To demonstrate how this works, let's add another table to our database. So far, we've been recording data on exoplanets. Here's one fun question to ask: how many of these planets may harbor life?

The HABITABLES table takes data from EXOPLANETS to help us answer that question, among other characteristics, as showcased in Example 4-23.

Example 4-23. HABITABLES provides information on whether the planets listed in EXOPLANETS are habitable

```
sqlite> PRAGMA TABLE_INFO(HABITABLES);
_id            | TEXT | 0 | | 0  ❶
```

```
perihelion    | REAL | 0 | | 0  ❷
aphelion      | REAL | 0 | | 0  ❸
atmosphere    | TEXT | 0 | | 0  ❹
habitability  | REAL | 0 | | 0  ❺
min_temp      | REAL | 0 | | 0  ❻
max_temp      | REAL | 0 | | 0  ❼
date_added    | TEXT | 0 | | 0  ❽
```

An entry in HABITABLES contains the following:

❶ _id: a UUID corresponding to the planet

❷ perihelion: the closest distance (*https://oreil.ly/y3twi*) to the celestial body during an orbital period

❸ aphelion: the furthest distance (*https://oreil.ly/2EdB8*) to the celestial body during an orbital period

❹ atmosphere: the dominant chemical makeup of the planet's atmosphere

❺ habitability: a real number between 0 and 1, indicating how likely the planet is to harbor life

❻ min_temp: the minimum temperature on the planet's surface

❼ max_temp: the maximum temperature on the planet's surface

❽ date_added: the date our system discovered the planet and added it automatically to our databases

Like the columns in EXOPLANETS, values for perihelion, aphelion, atmosphere, min_temp, and max_temp are allowed to be NULL. In fact, perihelion and aphelion will be NULL for any _id in EXOPLANETS where eccentricity is NULL, since you use orbital eccentricity to calculate these metrics. This explains why these two fields are always NULL in our older data entries.

To see which exoplanets are most habitable, we can use the following query to render the output in Example 4-24:

```
sqlite> SELECT * FROM HABITABLES LIMIT 5;
```

Example 4-24. Output of query to get a sense for the most habitable exoplanets

```
_id,perihelion,aphelion,atmosphere,habitability,min_temp,max_temp,date_added
c168b188-ef0c-4d6a-8cb2-f473d4154bdb,,,,0.291439672855434,,,2020-01-01
e7b56e84-41f4-4e62-b078-01b076cea369,,,,0.835647137991933,,,2020-01-01
a27030a0-e4b4-4bd7-8d24-5435ed86b395,,,,0.894000806332343,,,2020-01-01
```

```
54f9cf85-eae9-4f29-b665-855357a14375,,,,0.41590200852556,103.71374885412 ...
4d06ec88-f5c8-4d03-91ef-7493a12cd89e,,,,0.593524201489497,,,2020-01-01
```

So, we know that HABITABLES depends on the values in EXOPLANETS (or, equally, EXOPLANETS_EXTENDED), and EXOPLANETS_COLUMNS does as well. A dependency graph of our database is depicted in Figure 4-12.

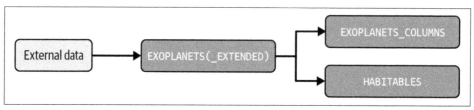

Figure 4-12. Dependency graph depicting the lineage between the source data and downstream "products"

Very simple lineage information, but already useful. Let's look at a data anomaly in HABITABLES in the context of this graph, and see what we can learn.

Investigating a Data Anomaly

When we have a key metric, like habitability in HABITABLES, we can assess the health of that metric in several ways. For a start, what is the average value of habitability for new data on a given day? In Example 4-25, we query the average value of habitability for new exoplanet data.

Example 4-25. Query to pull average habitability value for new exoplanet data

```
SELECT
  DATE_ADDED,
  AVG(HABITABILITY) AS AVG_HABITABILITY
FROM
  HABITABLES
GROUP BY
  DATE_ADDED;
```

Example 4-26 is the CSV file (*https://oreil.ly/o4kZF*) generated by the query.

Example 4-26. Results from Example 4-25 query

```
DATE_ADDED,AVG_HABITABILITY
2020-01-01,0.435641365919993
2020-01-02,0.501288741945045
2020-01-03,0.512285861062438
2020-01-04,0.525461586113648
2020-01-05,0.528935065722722
```

```
...,...
2020-09-02,0.234269938329633
2020-09-03,0.26522042788867
2020-09-04,0.267919611991401
2020-09-05,0.298614978406792
2020-09-06,0.276007150628875
```

Looking at this data, we see that something is wrong. It looks like we have a data anomaly. The average value for habitability is normally around 0.5, but it halves to around 0.25 later in the recorded data (Figure 4-13).

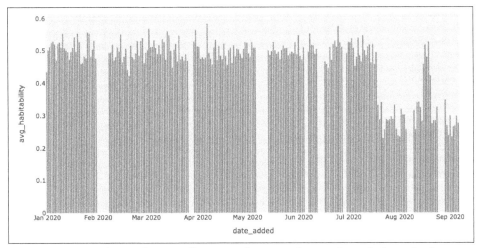

Figure 4-13. Visualizing the CSV file to get a better understanding of where the data anomaly occurred—and why

In Figure 4-13, we can clearly see that this issue is a distributional data anomaly, but what exactly is going on? In other words, what is the *root cause* of this data anomaly?

Why don't we look at the null rate for habitability, like we did when we were detecting distribution anomalies earlier in the chapter? We can do this by leveraging the query in Example 4-27, which pulls the nulls rate for our new, expanded data set, clueing us in to possible data anomalies.

Example 4-27. Null rate query for new data set

```
SELECT
  DATE_ADDED,
  CAST(
    SUM(
      CASE
      WHEN HABITABILITY IS NULL THEN 1
      ELSE 0
      END
```

```
  ) AS FLOAT) / COUNT(*) AS HABITABILITY_NULL_RATE
FROM
 HABITABLES
GROUP BY
 DATE_ADDED;
```

Fortunately, nothing looks out of character here, as you can see in the results, as highlighted in Example 4-28.

Example 4-28. Results of Example 4-27 query

```
DATE_ADDED,HABITABILITY_NULL_RATE
2020-01-01,0.0
2020-01-02,0.0
2020-01-03,0.0
2020-01-04,0.0
2020-01-05,0.0
...,...
2020-09-02,0.0
2020-09-03,0.0
2020-09-04,0.0
2020-09-05,0.0
2020-09-06,0.0
```

As you can see in Example 4-28, this doesn't look promising as the cause of our issue. What if we looked at another distributional health metric, the rate of zero values? This is another potential root cause of a distribution anomaly. Let's run another query, as shown in Example 4-29, to help us do exactly that.

Example 4-29. Query to understand the rate of zero values

```
SELECT
 DATE_ADDED,
 CAST(
   SUM(
     CASE
     WHEN HABITABILITY IS 0 THEN 1
     ELSE 0
     END
   ) AS FLOAT) / COUNT(*) AS HABITABILITY_ZERO_RATE
FROM
 HABITABLES
GROUP BY
 DATE_ADDED;
```

Something seems evidently more amiss here, as evidenced by the CSV file (*https:// oreil.ly/GSOoS*) depicted in Example 4-30. Several exoplanets' habitability have a zero rate, which could be a root cause of a data anomaly.

Example 4-30. Results from our query in Example 4-29

```
DATE_ADDED,HABITABILITY_ZERO_RATE
2020-01-01,0.0
2020-01-02,0.0
2020-01-03,0.0
2020-01-04,0.0
2020-01-05,0.0
...,...
2020-09-02,0.442307692307692
2020-09-03,0.441666666666667
2020-09-04,0.466666666666667
2020-09-05,0.46218487394958
2020-09-06,0.391304347826087
```

In Figure 4-14, we visualize the results of our zero-rate query using `AS FLOAT) / COUNT (*) AS HABITABILITY_ZERO_RATE`; this illustrates the anomalous results in August and September 2020.

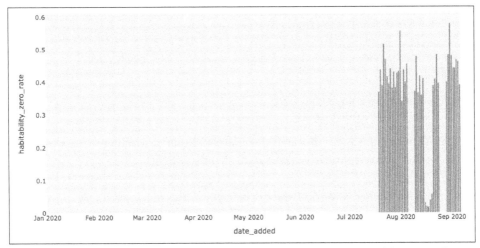

Figure 4-14. Visualizing zero value rates and the probable root cause of the anomaly

We can adapt one of the distribution detectors we built earlier in the chapter to get the first date of appreciable zero rates in the habitability field, as depicted in Example 4-31.

Example 4-31. Query for first date of zero rates in habitability field

```
WITH HABITABILITY_ZERO_RATES AS(
  SELECT
    DATE_ADDED,
    CAST(
      SUM(
```

```
        CASE
          WHEN HABITABILITY IS 0 THEN 1
          ELSE 0
        END
      ) AS FLOAT) / COUNT(*) AS HABITABILITY_ZERO_RATE
  FROM
    HABITABLES
  GROUP BY
    DATE_ADDED
),

CONSECUTIVE_DAYS AS(
SELECT
  DATE_ADDED,
  HABITABILITY_ZERO_RATE,
  LAG(HABITABILITY_ZERO_RATE) OVER(ORDER BY DATE_ADDED)
    AS PREV_HABITABILITY_ZERO_RATE
FROM
  HABITABILITY_ZERO_RATES
)

SELECT
  *
FROM
  CONSECUTIVE_DAYS
WHERE
  PREV_HABITABILITY_ZERO_RATE = 0 AND
  HABITABILITY_ZERO_RATE != 0;
```

We can then run this query through the command line in Example 4-32, which will fetch the first date of appreciable zeros in the habitability field.

Example 4-32. Command-line interface running the query in Example 4-31

```
$ sqlite3 EXOPLANETS.db < queries/lineage/habitability-zero-rate-detector.sql
DATE_ADDED | HABITABILITY_ZERO_RATE | PREV_HABITABILITY_ZERO_RATE
2020-07-19 | 0.369047619047619 | 0.0
```

2020–07–19 was the first date the zero rate began showing anomalous results. Recall that this is the same day as the schema change detection in EXOPLANETS_EXTENDED. EXOPLANETS_EXTENDED is upstream from HABITABLES, so it's very possible that these two incidents are related.

In this way lineage information can help us identify the root cause of incidents and move quicker toward resolving them. Compare the two following explanations for this incident in HABITABLES:

1. On 2020–07–19, the zero rate of the habitability column in the HABITABLES table jumped from 0% to 37%.

2. On 2020–07–19, we began tracking two additional fields, eccentricity and atmosphere, in the EXOPLANETS table. This had an adverse effect on the downstream table HABITABLES, often setting the fields min_temp and max_temp to extreme values whenever eccentricity was not NULL. In turn, this caused the habitability field spike in zero rate, which we detected as an anomalous decrease in the average value.

Let's break these explanations down. Explanation 1 uses just the fact that a data anomaly took place. Explanation 2 uses lineage, in terms of dependencies between both tables and fields, to put the incident in context and determine the root cause. Everything in the second explanation is actually correct, and we encourage you to mess around with the environment to understand for yourself what's going on. While these are just simple examples, an engineer equipped with Explanation 2 would be faster to understand and resolve the underlying issue, and this is all owed to proper observability.

Tracking schema changes and lineage can give you unprecedented visibility into the health and usage patterns of your data, providing vital contextual information about who, what, where, why, and how your data was used. In fact, schema and lineage are the two most important data observability pillars when it comes to understanding the downstream (and often real-world) implications of data downtime.

Scaling Anomaly Detection with Python and Machine Learning

At a high level, machine learning is instrumental for data observability and data monitoring at scale. Detectors outfitted with machine learning can apply more flexibly to larger numbers of tables, eliminating the need for manual checks and rules as your data warehouse or lake grows. Also, machine learning detectors can learn and adapt to data in real time and can capture complicated seasonal patterns that otherwise would be invisible to human eyes. Let's dive in—no prior machine learning experience required.

As you may recall from the previous two sections of this exercise, we're working again with mock astronomical data (*https://oreil.ly/3FLuD*) about habitable exoplanets. Now, we're going to restrict our attention to the EXOPLANETS table again, as we did earlier in the chapter, to better understand how to scale anomaly detection with machine learning, depicted in Example 4-33.

Example 4-33. Our trusty EXOPLANETS data set

```
$ sqlite3 EXOPLANETS.db
sqlite> PRAGMA TABLE_INFO(EXOPLANETS);
_id              | TEXT | 0 | | 0
distance         | REAL | 0 | | 0
g                | REAL | 0 | | 0
orbital_period   | REAL | 0 | | 0
avg_temp         | REAL | 0 | | 0
date_added       | TEXT | 0 | | 0
```

Note that EXOPLANETS is configured to manually track an important piece of meta-data—the date_added column—which records the date our system discovered the planet and added it automatically to our databases. To detect for freshness and distribution anomalies, we used a simple SQL query to visualize the number of new entries added per day, as highlighted in Example 4-34.

Example 4-34. Query to pull the number of new EXOPLANETS entries added per day

```
SELECT
  DATE_ADDED,
  COUNT(*) AS ROWS_ADDED
FROM
  EXOPLANETS
GROUP BY
  DATE_ADDED;
```

This query yields a seemingly healthy set of data, as depicted in Example 4-35. But is there more we should know?

Example 4-35. Results of Example 4-34 (which look entirely standard)

```
date_added,ROWS_ADDED
2020-01-01,84
2020-01-02,92
2020-01-03,101
2020-01-04,102
2020-01-05,100
...,...
2020-07-14,104
2020-07-15,110
2020-07-16,103
2020-07-17,89
2020-07-18,104
```

These results are visualized in Figure 4-15.

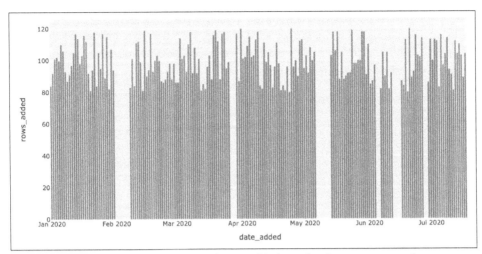

Figure 4-15. Visualizing the number of rows added per day for a given month

In words, the EXOPLANETS table routinely updates with around 100 entries per day, but goes "offline" on some days when no data is entered, as depicted in Figure 4-15. We introduced a metric called DAYS_SINCE_LAST_UPDATE to track this aspect of the table via our anomaly detection query template, as depicted in Example 4-36. This will tell us how many days it has been since the EXOPLANETS data set was updated, between distinct entries.

Example 4-36. Query on how many days since EXOPLANETS data set was updated

```
WITH UPDATES AS(
  SELECT
    DATE_ADDED,
    COUNT(*) AS ROWS_ADDED
  FROM
    EXOPLANETS
  GROUP BY
    DATE_ADDED
)

SELECT
  DATE_ADDED,
  JULIANDAY(DATE_ADDED) - JULIANDAY(LAG(DATE_ADDED) OVER(
    ORDER BY DATE_ADDED
  )) AS DAYS_SINCE_LAST_UPDATE
FROM
  UPDATES;
```

The results are listed in a CSV file (*https://oreil.ly/NI3fz*), depicted in Example 4-37, and visualized in Figure 4-16. We see a list of dates with new data entries.

Example 4-37. Results from Example 4-36

```
DATE_ADDED,DAYS_SINCE_LAST_UPDATE
2020-01-01,
2020-01-02,1
2020-01-03,1
2020-01-04,1
2020-01-05,1
...,...
2020-07-14,1
2020-07-15,1
2020-07-16,1
2020-07-17,1
2020-07-18,1
```

In Figure 4-16, we can clearly see that there were some dates in February, April, May, June, and July 2020 where data was not added to our EXOPLANETS data set, signaling an anomaly.

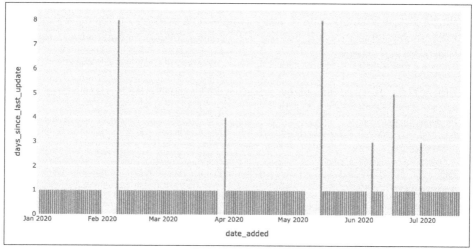

Figure 4-16. Using a freshness anomaly detection query, we can identify when the data goes "offline"

With a small modification, we introduced a threshold parameter to our query to create a freshness detector, which allows us to further refine our anomaly detection. Our detector returns all dates where the newest data in EXOPLANETS was older than one day, as highlighted in Example 4-38.

Example 4-38. Query to identify when a column in our EXOPLANETS data set has not been updated in over one day

```
WITH UPDATES AS(
  SELECT
    DATE_ADDED,
    COUNT(*) AS ROWS_ADDED
  FROM
    EXOPLANETS
  GROUP BY
    DATE_ADDED
),

NUM_DAYS_UPDATES AS (
  SELECT
    DATE_ADDED,
    JULIANDAY(DATE_ADDED) - JULIANDAY(LAG(DATE_ADDED)
      OVER(
        ORDER BY DATE_ADDED
      )
    ) AS DAYS_SINCE_LAST_UPDATE
  FROM
    UPDATES
)

SELECT
  *
FROM
  NUM_DAYS_UPDATES
WHERE
  DAYS_SINCE_LAST_UPDATE > 1;
```

The CSV file (*https://oreil.ly/KDNiX*) generated by this query is depicted in Example 4-39, highlighting freshness anomalies.

Example 4-39. Results of Example 4-38 query

```
DATE_ADDED,DAYS_SINCE_LAST_UPDATE
2020-02-08,8
2020-03-30,4
2020-05-14,8
2020-06-07,3
2020-06-17,5
2020-06-30,3
```

In Figure 4-17, we can clearly visualize the specific dates when our data set was collecting stale data, likely from an exoplanet orbiter or other space probe.

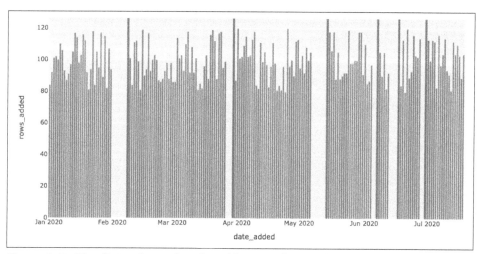

Figure 4-17. Visualizing dates when the table was collecting "stale" data, indicating data downtime

The spikes in Figure 4-17 represent instances where the EXOPLANETS table was working with old or "stale" data. In some cases, such outages may be standard operating procedure—maybe our telescope was due for maintenance, so no data was recorded over a weekend. In other cases, though, an outage may represent a genuine problem with data collection or transformation—maybe we changed our dates to ISO format, and the job that traditionally pushed new data is now failing. We might have the heuristic that longer outages are worse, but beyond that, how do we guarantee that we only detect the genuine issues in our data?

The short answer: you can't. Building a perfect predictor is impossible (for any interesting prediction problem, anyway). But, we can use some concepts from machine learning to frame the problem in a more structured way and, as a result, deliver data observability and trust at scale.

Improving Data Monitoring Alerting with Machine Learning

Whenever we alert about a broken data pipeline, we have to question whether the alert was accurate. Does the alert indicate a genuine problem? We might be worried about two scenarios:

- A data monitoring alert was issued, but there was no genuine issue. We've wasted the user's time responding to the alert.

- There was a genuine issue, but no data monitoring alert was issued. We've let a real problem go undetected.

These two scenarios are described as false positives (predicted anomalous, actually OK) and false negatives (predicted OK, actually anomalous), and we want to avoid them. Issuing a false positive is like crying wolf—we sounded the alarm, but all was OK. Likewise, issuing a false negative is like sleeping on guard duty—something was wrong, but we didn't do anything.

Our goal is to avoid these circumstances as much as possible and focus on maximizing true positives (predicted anomalous, actually a problem) and true negatives (predicted OK, actually OK).

Accounting for False Positives and False Negatives

Anomaly detection is an *unsupervised* task. Unsupervised learning is a machine learning task where the optimal behavior is not knowable at training time. In other words, the data on which you're training doesn't come with labels attached. For this reason, you may be compelled to call anomaly detection unsupervised, since anomalies don't come with a ground truth. Without a ground truth, you can't get an *error signal*, in other words, the difference between what you predicted and what you should have predicted.

While some anomaly detection tasks are best understood as unsupervised learning problems, it *still* makes sense to consider supervised error signal vocabulary like false negative, false positive, precision, etc. Otherwise, we cannot benchmark different detection algorithms against one another or have any metric for improvement and success.

For any given data point, an anomaly detector issues either an "anomalous" or a "not anomalous" prediction. Also, consider that there is some *truth* about the matter—the data point in question is either a genuine problem, or not a problem at all. Consider a measurement reflecting that your key analytics table has not updated once in the last three days. If your table should update hourly, this is a genuine problem!

When a data point is problematic *and* our detector calls it "anomalous," we call this a *true positive*. When a data point is just fine and our detector doesn't detect it (i.e., issues "not anomalous"), we call this a *true negative*. Table 4-1 illustrates this concept.

Table 4-1. Four possible anomaly detection outcomes

		Predicted	
		Negative	Positive
Actual	**Negative**	True Negative	False Positive
	Positive	False Negative	True Positive

False negatives are cases where the data point was genuinely problematic, yet our detector did not detect. A false negative detection is like a sleeping guard dog—your algorithm lets a problem go by undetected. *False positives* are cases where we detected an anomaly, but the point in question was not actually problematic. A false positive detection is like crying wolf—your algorithm issued an "anomalous" result, but the underlying data point was actually fine. False positives and false negatives are realities for even the most well-trained anomaly detection algorithms.

False positives and false negatives both sound bad. It seems like the best anomaly detection techniques ought to avoid them both. Unfortunately, for reasons to do with simple statistics, we can't "just avoid both." In fact, fewer false positives comes at the expense of *more* false negatives—and vice versa.

To understand why, let's think about the boy who cried wolf again—through an anomaly detector lens! The boy who cried wolf detects every data point as an anomaly. As a result, his detection is highly *sensitive* (not likely to let any false negatives slip by) but not at all *specific* (liable to produce lots of false positives). Data professionals dislike boy-who-cried-wolf detectors because their detections aren't *believable*. When an anomaly detector with a high false positive rate detects, you're likely to believe the alert isn't genuine.

The sleeping guard dog is another kind of anomaly detector—actually, the opposite kind. This detector *never* considers data points anomalous. The resulting anomaly detection algorithm is highly *specific* (no false positives will be produced) but not at all sensitive (lots of false negatives will occur). Data professionals dislike sleeping-guard-dog detectors too, because their results aren't *dependable*. Overly conservative detectors will never issue anomalous detections, meaning they're bound to miss when things go really awry.

The trick, as it turns out, is to aim somewhere in the middle between these two detection schemes.

Improving Precision and Recall

For a given collection of data, once you've applied an anomaly detection algorithm, you'll have a collection of true positives (TPs), true negatives (TNs), false positives (FPs), and false negatives (FNs). We typically don't just look at these "scores" by themselves—there are common statistical ways of combining them into meaningful metrics. We focus on precision and recall, accuracy metrics that quantify the anomaly detector's performance.

Precision is defined as the rate of correct predictions made, so:

$$\text{Precision} = \frac{\text{TPs}}{\text{TPs } + \text{ FPs}}$$

In other words: out of all the "positives" (predictions made), how many are correct?

Recall is defined as the rate of actual anomalies detected, so:

$$\text{Recall} = \frac{\text{TPs}}{\text{TPs} + \text{FNs}}$$

In other words: out of all the genuine anomalies, how many did we catch?

These terms are popular accuracy metrics for classification systems, and their names are semantically meaningful. A detector with high precision is "precise" in that when it predicts anomalies, it's more often than not correct. Similarly, a detector with high recall "recalls" well—it catches a high rate of all the actual anomalies.

The problem, of course, is that you can't have the best of both worlds. Notice that there's an explicit trade-off between these two. How do we get perfect precision? Simple: alert for nothing—the guard dog sleeping on duty all the time—forcing us to have a false positive rate of 0%. The problem? Recall will be horrible, since our false negative rate will be huge.

Likewise, how do we get perfect recall? Also simple: alert for everything—crying wolf at every opportunity—forcing a false negative rate of 0%. The issue, as expected, is that our false positive rate will suffer, affecting precision.

Our world of data is run by quantifiable objectives, and in most cases we'll want a singular objective to optimize, not two. We can combine both precision and recall into a single metric called an F-score. The general formula for nonnegative real β is:

$$F_\beta = \frac{\left(1 + \beta^2\right) \cdot (\text{Precision} \cdot \text{Recall})}{\left(\beta^2 \cdot \text{Precision} + \text{Recall}\right)}$$

F_β is called a weighted F-score, since different values for beta weigh precision and recall differently in the calculation. In general, an F_β-score says, "I consider recall to be beta times as important as precision."

When $\beta = 1$, the equation values each equally. Set $\beta > 1$, and recall will be more important for a higher score. In other words, $\beta > 1$ says, "I care more about catching all anomalies than occasionally causing a false alarm." Likewise, set $\beta < 1$, and precision will be more important. $\beta < 1$ says, "I care more about my alarms being genuine than about catching every real issue."

There are many frameworks you can use to apply anomaly detection at scale without having to hand-code your algorithms in Python. See the following for a few of our favorites:

Facebook Prophet

A forecasting model built to handle daily, weekly, monthly, and yearly seasonalities in time series data at scale. Users can load baseline Prophet models and tweak human-interpretable model parameters, adding domain knowledge via feature augmentation. The package ships in both Python and R.

TensorFlow

A popular machine learning library for a variety of tasks, including natural language processing, computer vision, and time series anomaly detection. The package provides useful and well-documented implementations of more advanced anomaly detection algorithms. TensorFlow's Keras package, for example, implements an autoencoder model that can be used for a neural form of autoregression, more powerful than a basic autoregressive-integrated-moving-average (ARIMA) model.

PyTorch

Developed at Facebook, this is another machine learning Python library fulfilling similar use cases to TensorFlow (which is developed by Google). PyTorch typically has higher uptake in the academic side of the industry, while TensorFlow enjoys greater popularity in industry settings.

scikit-learn

Another popular machine learning software package with implementations for all sorts of algorithms. In addition to time series anomaly detection methods like ARIMA, scikit-learn has versions of the *k*-nearest neighbor algorithm and the isolation forest algorithm, two popular methods for clustering. Like TensorFlow, scikit-learn is developed in Python.

MLflow

A popular experiment tracking tool developed as open source by the creators of Databricks. Experiment tracking refers to the process of managing machine learning models in development and production. MLflow is primarily an experiment tracking and reproduction software. MLflow instances have shared model registries where experiments can be backed up and compared side by side. Each model belongs to a project, which is a packaged software environment designed to ensure model reproducibility, as depicted in Figure 4-18. An important aspect of developing anomaly detection software is the guarantee that *the code runs the same on different machines*. You don't want to think you've solved a bug locally just for the fix to fail to apply in production. Likewise, if a colleague reports an accuracy metric for their updated model, you'd like to know that you could replicate their quality results yourself. Also with projects, the MLflow registry assists with deploying models to production environments, including Azure ML and Amazon SageMaker, or to Spark clusters as an Apache Spark UDF.

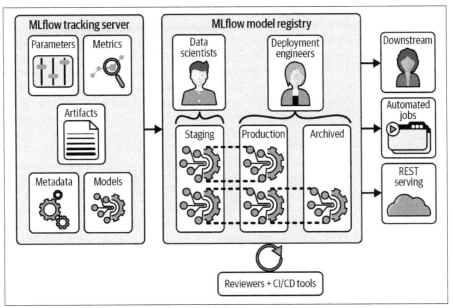

Figure 4-18. MLflow's model registry visualized in the data science workflow

 Experiment tracking, the process of managing machine learning model development and training, involves hyperparameter comparison, dependency checking, managing and orchestrating training jobs, saving model snapshots, and collecting logs —among other tasks! This can in principle be done using some incredibly complicated spreadsheets, though obviously there are better tools for the job.

TensorBoard

This is TensorFlow's visualization toolkit, yet you don't need to model with TensorFlow to take advantage of the software. With TensorBoard, as shown in Figure 4-19, you can visualize common machine learning metrics like loss per epoch of training, confusion matrices, and individual error analysis.

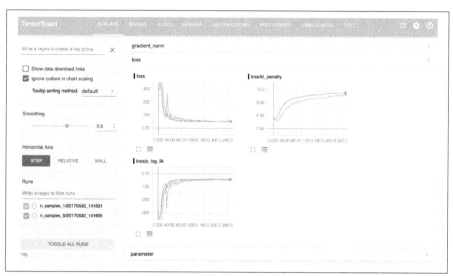

Figure 4-19. A standard TensorBoard view during model training. Source: Tran et al.[1]

These and other frameworks can take your anomaly detectors to the next level, eliminating false negatives and positives and reducing the need for model tuning over time.

Detecting Freshness Incidents with Data Monitoring

With our new vocabulary in hand, let's return to the task of detecting freshness incidents in the EXOPLANETS table. We're using a simple prediction algorithm, since we turned our query into a detector by setting one model parameter X. Our algorithm says, "Any outage longer than X days is an anomaly, and we will issue an alert for it." Even in a case as simple as this, precision, recall, and F-scores can help us!

To showcase, we took the freshness outages in EXOPLANETS and assigned ground truth labels encoding whether each outage is a genuine incident or not. It's impossible to calculate a model's accuracy without some kind of ground truth, so it's always helpful to think about how you'd generate these for your use case. Recall that there are a total of six outages lasting for more than one day in the EXOPLANETS table, as highlighted in the data depicted in Example 4-40.

---

1 Dustin Tran, Alp Kucukelbir, Adji B. Dieng, Maja Rudolph, Dawen Liang, and David M. Blei, "Edward: A Library for Probabilistic Modeling, Inference, and Criticism," arXiv preprint arXiv:1610.09787, 2016, *https://oreil.ly/CvuKL*.

Example 4-40. Results from Example 4-38 query on outages lasting more than one day

```
DATE_ADDED,DAYS_SINCE_LAST_UPDATE
2020-02-08,8
2020-03-30,4
2020-05-14,8
2020-06-07,3
2020-06-17,5
2020-06-30,3
```

Let's say, arbitrarily, that the incidents on 2020-02-08 and 2020-05-14 are genuine. Each is eight days long, so it makes sense that they'd be problematic. On the flip side, suppose that the outages on 2020-03-30 and 2020-06-07 are not actual incidents. These outages are four and three days long, respectively, so this is not outlandish. Finally, let the outages on 2020-06-17 and 2020-06-30, at five and three days, respectively, *also* be genuine incidents, as depicted in Example 4-41.

Example 4-41. Classifying the "true" anomalies

```
INCIDENT,NOT INCIDENT
2020-02-08 (8 days),2020-03-30 (4 days)
2020-05-14 (8 days),2020-06-07 (3 days)
2020-06-17 (5 days),
2020-06-30 (3 days),
```

Having chosen our ground truth in this way, we see that longer outages are more likely to be actual issues, but there's no guarantee. This weak correlation will make a good model effective, but imperfect, just as it would be in more complex, real use cases. To improve model accuracy, we need look no further than one of the most common tools in a data or ML engineer's toolkit: the F-score.

F-Scores

F-scores are classification accuracy metrics designed to optimize jointly for both precision and recall. The "default" of these is the F_1-score, defined (for the statisticians) as the harmonic mean between precision and recall:

$$F_1 = \frac{2}{\frac{1}{\text{Precision}} + \frac{1}{\text{Recall}}}$$

This means that the F_1-score is designed to equally balance precision and recall, which results in meaning we reward gains in one just as much as the other. In some contexts, this kind of evaluation might be appropriate. In other cases, though, either recall or precision might matter a lot more.

A real-world example that drives home the point: on Saturday morning, January 13, 2018 (*https://oreil.ly/aW05x*), Hawaiian islanders received text messages that a ballistic missile was inbound and that they should seek underground shelter immediately. The alert went out at 8:07 a.m. and ended ominously with "This is not a drill."

Thirty-eight minutes later, after the Hawaiian telephone network and 911 emergency line had gone down from overuse, the Hawaiian state government issued that the alert had been a mistake. While one Hawaiian man suffered a heart attack upon hearing the news, there were no immediate fatalities from the event.

The Hawaiian incident had been intended as a test of the island's *actual* alerting system—the problem was, instead, that the system had sent out a *real alert* in error. In this instance, the real alert is an example of anomaly detection gone wrong, in the real world—a false positive. Now, while certainly scary, consider the equivalent *false negative* and the potential repercussions there. When considering real-world impacts, the consequences when things don't work as anticipated could be severe.

What does this mean for product design and what can we do to mitigate it? In terms of what we've been discussing here: a false positive is *better* than a false negative for the missile detection system. Meaning: recall is *more* important than precision. If we're examining the performance of a system such as this, we should use something other than the F_1-score. In particular, a general F_β score lets us say, "recall is *beta* times as important than precision for my detector":

$$F_\beta = \frac{1 + \beta^2}{\frac{\beta^2}{\text{Precision}} + \frac{1}{\text{Recall}}}$$

When $\beta = 1$, note that this equation comes out the same as the F_1-score equation. It would also say "recall is one times as important as precision"—weighing them equally. However, if we were testing something like a missile alert system where recall was twice or three times as important, we might consider evaluating using an F_2 or an F_3.

Does Model Accuracy Matter?

In the past several pages, you may have noticed our sparing use of the word "accuracy." Machine learning algorithms, anomaly detectors included, are supposed to be "accurate"—or so you've heard. Why aren't we then leading with that vocabulary?

Here's part of our answer (an example drawn from a Stanford professor, Mehran Sahami). Suppose you're building a sophisticated, machine learning anomaly detection system to test for acquired immunodeficiency syndrome (AIDS). Here's how our super sophisticated system works: it just predicts "No" anytime you ask it if someone has AIDS. AIDS affects approximately 1.2 million people in the United States today. The US population hovers somewhere about 330 million. Our "accuracy," or how correct we are *on average*, is 1 − (Americans with AIDS / Americans) = 1 − (1.2 million / 330 million) = 99.6%. That's one of the best accuracies we've ever seen—surely, publication worthy, cause for celebration, etc.

I hope this example illustrates the point: accuracy is not as simple as how correct your detector is on average, and moreover it shouldn't be defined the same for different applications. After all, the outcome of relying on accuracy metrics in the preceding example would misdiagnose tens of thousands of individuals—or more. At the end of the day, we want a good detection scheme to minimize both false positives and false negatives. In machine learning practice, it's more common to think about related but more insightful terms, precision and recall, as depicted in Figure 4-20.

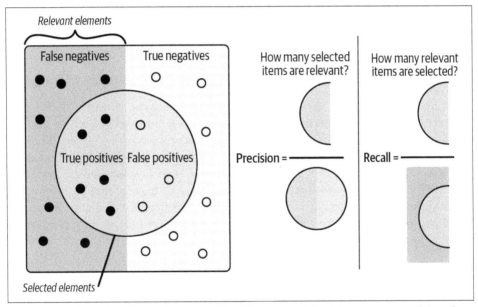

Figure 4-20. Precision (how often your algorithm accurately detects an anomaly) and recall (how many of the total anomalies were caught)

As discussed earlier in the chapter, precision, generally, tells us how often we're right when we issue an alert. Models with good precision output believable alerts, since their high precision guarantees that they cry wolf very infrequently.

Recall, generally, tells us how many issues we actually alert for. Models with good recall are dependable, since their high recall guarantees that they rarely sleep on the job.

Extending our metaphor, a model with good precision is a model that rarely cries wolf—when it issues an alert, you had better believe it. Likewise, a model with good recall is like a good guard dog—you can rest assured that this model will catch all genuine problems.

Now, suppose we begin by setting our threshold to three days—in words, "every outage longer than three days is an anomaly." This means we correctly detect anomalies on 2020-02-08, 2020-05-14, and 2020-06-17, so we have three true positives. But, we unfortunately detected 2020-03-30 as an incident when it isn't one, so we have one false positive. Three true positives / (three true positives + one false positive) means our precision is 0.75. Also, we failed to detect 2020-06-30 as an incident, meaning we have one false negative. Three true positives / (three true positives + one false negative) means our recall is also 0.75. F_1-score, given by the formula:

$$\frac{TP}{TP + \frac{1}{2}(FP + FN)}$$

Inputting the appropriate values, this means that our F_1-score is also 0.75. Not bad!

Now, let's assume we set the threshold higher, at five days. Now, we detect only 2020-02-08 and 2020-05-14, the longest outages. These turn out to both be genuine incidents, so we have no false positives, meaning our precision is 1—perfect! But note that we fail to detect other genuine anomalies, 2020-06-17 and 2020-06-30, meaning we have two false negatives. Two true positives / (two true positives + two false negatives) means our recall is 0.5, worse than before. It makes sense that our recall suffered, because we chose a more conservative classifier with a higher threshold. Our F_1-score can again be calculated with the preceding formula, and turns out to be 0.667.

If we plot our precision, recall, and F_1-score in terms of the threshold we set, we see some important patterns. First, aggressive detectors with low thresholds have the best recall, since they're quicker to alert and thus catch more genuine issues. On the other hand, more passive detectors have better precision, since they only alert for the worst anomalies that are more likely to be genuine. The F_1-score peaks somewhere between these two extremes—in this case, at a threshold of four days. Finding the sweet spot is key to best fine-tune our detectors, as depicted in Figure 4-21.

Finally, let's look at one last comparison (Figure 4-22). Notice that we've looked only at the F_1-score, which weighs precision and recall equally. What happens when we look at other values of beta?

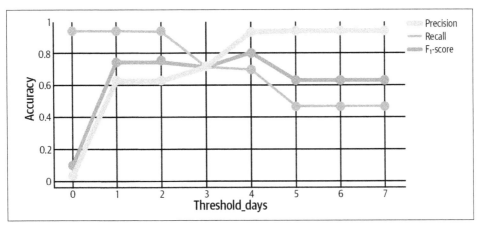

Figure 4-21. Calculating precision, recall, and F₁-score and plotting the results to determine how to tune anomaly detectors

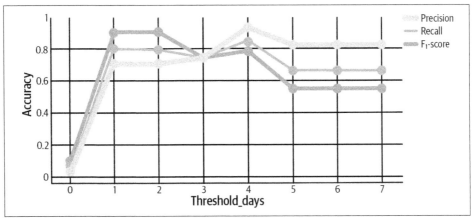

Figure 4-22. Calculating F-score with different values of β

Recall that a general F_β says "recall is β times as important as precision." Thus, we should expect that F_2 is higher than F_1 when recall is prioritized—which is exactly what we see at thresholds less than 4, as depicted in Figure 4-22. At the same time, the $F_{0.5}$-score is higher for larger thresholds, showing more allowance for conservative classifiers with greater precision.

With this F-score in tow and a better-tuned algorithm, you're ready to detect issues across the five pillars of data observability: freshness, volume, distribution, schema, and lineage.

Beyond the Surface: Other Useful Anomaly Detection Approaches

The best anomaly detection algorithms do three things: detect issues in near real time, alert those who need to know, and give you information to help prevent future downtime from occurring. In this chapter, we walked through common approaches and key elements of basic anomaly detection algorithms, but our example only scratches the surface. There are several other best practices, algorithm components, and methodologies that warrant similar, or even more accurate, results depending on the tooling you use:

Rule definitions or hard thresholding

Rule definitions set explicit cutoffs for certain metric values and determine anomalies relative to the threshold. While technically detection, this approach can only properly be called "anomaly" detection if most of the data points lie within the threshold. Rule definitions are incredibly scalable and might work for extremely well-defined SLAs, data uptime guarantees, and so forth.

Autoregressive models

Autoregression works on time-series anomaly detection, where data points are ordered using a timestamp object. Autoregressive models take data from previous timesteps, feed them into a regression (linear) model, and use the output to form a prediction for where the next timestamp's data will be. Data points veering too far from the autoregressive prediction are marked anomalous. Combined with a simple moving average algorithm, autoregression gives us the autoregressive-moving-average and ARIMA detection algorithms. If we had taken our exoplanet example a step further and layered in autoregression, this data set would have worked quite well.

Exponential smoothing

Exponential smoothing methods exist to remove trend and seasonality from time series so that more naive approaches (e.g., ARIMA) can take over. Holt-Winters is a famous seasonal model for time series forecasting, and there is, again, a rich taxonomy (additive, multiplicative, damped, nondamped, and so on).

Clustering

Clustering techniques, like the *k*-nearest neighbor algorithm (*https://oreil.ly/YRRor*) or the isolation forest algorithm (*https://oreil.ly/lY85G*) find anomalies by putting similar data points in buckets, and alerting you to the "odd ones out," e.g., the data fitting into small or even one-off buckets.

Hyperparameter tuning

Machine learning models have lots of *parameters*, which are numerical representations of the data used by the prediction algorithm. Some parameters are learned using the data and training process. For example, with a z-scoring model, μ and σ are parameters set automatically from the input data's distribution. Other parameters, called *hyperparameters*, are not set by the learning process but instead *dictate* the learning and inference processes in certain ways. Some hyperparameters affect the model architecture, for example the size of a neural network, the size of embedding and hidden state matrices, and so on. These are called *model hyperparameters*. Another class, *algorithm hyperparameters*, affects the way training is done, for example the learning rate, number of epochs, or number of data points per training batch.

Ensemble model framework

An ensemble model framework (*https://oreil.ly/Z8oZ8*) takes the best of each method—a bit of clustering, exponential smoothing, and autoregressive nodes combined into a neural feed-forward network (*https://oreil.ly/6CiLU*)—and combines their predictions using a majority-voting ensemble (*https://oreil.ly/oJcR4*) algorithm.

While important, such approaches are outside the scope of this book—for more on building great anomaly detection algorithms, we suggest you check out *Hands-On Machine Learning with Scikit-Learn, Keras, and TensorFlow* (O'Reilly) by Aurélien Géron.

Designing Data Quality Monitors for Warehouses Versus Lakes

When it comes to building data quality monitors for your data system, it's important to distinguish whether you're working with structured, monolithic data from a warehouse or entering the wild west of the modern data lake ecosystem.

The primary differences between designing anomaly detection algorithms for warehouses and lakes boil down to:

- The number of entrypoints you have to account for
- How the metadata is collected and stored
- How you can access that metadata

First, data lake systems tend to have *high numbers of entrypoints*, meaning one should assume *high heterogeneity* in data entering from different sources. In monitoring, say, null rates in tabular data entering from Postgres, application logs, and a web API, a data scientist might notice clusters of table behavior corresponding to the different endpoints. In these cases, be wary of a "one-size-fits-all" modeling approach. More likely than not, different model architectures (e.g., different hyperparameters) may work better at predicting anomalies in each different format. One way to do that is to condition on the endpoint of the data itself, forming a new feature for input into the machine learning model. Another is to use an ensemble model architecture, or simply to have separate models for each of your use cases.

Second, metadata collected straight into a data lake may need varying levels of *prepro-cessing* before you can expect an anomaly detection algorithm to derive anything of value from it. Types may need coercion, schemas may need alignment, and you may find yourself deriving entirely new augmented features in the data before running the detector's training task.

This is fine to do immediately before model training, provided you aren't bottleneck-ing your compute resources by applying "transformations" on large batches of input data. In some cases, it may be advantageous to devise some ELT steps in between the lake data and the machine learning algorithm. "Cleaning Data" on page 43 provides some insight into why this may be valuable.

Summary

In this chapter, we've taken a quick safari through monitoring and anomaly detection as it relates to basic data quality checks. Now, how can these concepts help us apply detectors to our production environments in data warehouses and lakes?

The key lies in understanding that there's no perfect classifier for any anomaly detection problem. There is always a trade-off between false positives and false negatives, or equally precision and recall. You have to ask yourself, "How do I weigh the trade-off between these two? What determines the 'sweet spot' for my model parameters?" Choosing an F_β score to optimize will implicitly decide how you weigh these occurrences, and thereby what matters most in your classification problem.

Also, remember that any discussion of model accuracy isn't complete without some sort of ground truth to compare with the model's predictions. You need to know what makes a good classification before you know that you have one. In Chapter 5, we'll discuss how to apply the technologies highlighted in Chapters 2, 3, and 4 to architecting more reliable data systems, as well as discuss new processes, like SLAs, SLIs, and SLOs, to help them scale.

Architecting for Data Reliability

Airbnb, the global online vacation marketplace, wrote in a 2020 post (*https://oreil.ly/ cfrcJ*) on their engineering blog that "leadership [set] high expectations for data timeliness and quality," leading to the need to make significant investment in their data quality and governance efforts. Meanwhile, Krishna Puttaswamy and Suresh Srinivas, former engineers at Uber, wrote in a 2021 *Uber Engineering* blog article (*https://oreil.ly/2LCeZ*) that high-quality big data is "at the heart of this massive transformation platform."

It's no secret: data quality is top of mind for some of the best data teams. Still, it's one thing to write about it: how do we actually achieve this in practice?

Data reliability—an organization's ability to deliver high data availability and health throughout the entire data life cycle—is the outcome of high data quality. As companies ingest more operational and third-party data than ever before, with employees from across the organization interacting with that data at all stages of its life cycle, it's become increasingly important for that data to be reliable.

Data reliability has to be intentionally built into every level of your organization, from the processes and technologies you leverage to build and manage your data stack to the way you communicate and triage data issues further downstream. In this chapter, we'll explore how to architect for data reliability at each stage of the pipeline—and data engineering experience.

Measuring and Maintaining High Data Reliability at Ingestion

Now that we have a better understanding of the state of data quality, let's look at what all of this means in practice, starting with ingestion. However, we would be remiss not to discuss some of the fundamental best practices that ensure high data quality before ingestion to the data warehouse or lake.

It is common for organizations to ingest data from both internal and external, third-party sources depending on the needs of the business. Your decision making is only as good as the data you are using for insights and analysis: garbage in is garbage out. It's important to make sure your organization has the right set of practices in place to ensure data quality.

To achieve this, organizations have begun to establish rigorous data quality control standards for all data that enters their data ecosystem. While data quality issues can occur at any point in your data pipeline, most organizations will agree that catching and fixing data quality issues at the point of ingestion will help minimize the chances of poor quality data working its way downstream.

Best practices such as data cleaning, data wrangling (the process of structuring and enriching your data into a desired format), and data testing are ways organizations are ensuring data quality is up to their organizations' needs. And with technology advancing over the years in the data industry, an abundance of tools have emerged in the space to automate this process for companies.

Such tools allow organizations to automatically examine aspects of data such as its format, consistency, completeness, freshness, and uniqueness. By automating this process, organizations not only save time and resources when data cleaning but ensure that the quality of incoming data is constantly controlled and managed whenever data enters their ecosystem.

Data cleaning (also commonly referred to as cleansing) involves preparing and modifying data for future analysis by removing incomplete, irrelevant, incorrect, incorrectly formatted, or duplicate data from a data set. While the data cleaning process can be tedious, it often falls to the data engineering team, although with the rise of self-service tooling and more distributed data management approaches, this onus on clean data is increasingly falling to data producers. Regardless of who "owns" data cleaning, it is important to educate the rest of the organization on its importance as everyone in the company plays a key role in ensuring the integrity of data.

When dealing with missing or inaccurate data many companies turn to data enrichment, which is a process where organizations are able to merge and add either first- or third-party data to data sets they already are working with. By enriching data, organizations are able to add more value to their data sets, which in the end makes data more useful and reliable.

After data cleaning, data testing is your best line of defense against data quality before ingestion. Data testing is the process of validating your organization's assumptions about the data, either before or during production. Writing basic tests that check for things such as uniqueness and not_null are ways organizations can test out the basic assumptions they make about their source data. It is also common for organizations to ensure that data is in the correct format for their team to work with and that the data meets their business needs.

There are a few basic types of data quality tests, which we first addressed in Chapter 3:

Unit testing
Unit tests check that a line of code (SQL) does what it is supposed to do; they can be used with very, very small snippets of data. When unit testing data, you must separate the business logic from the "glue code."

Functional testing
Functional tests are used with large data sets and are often separated in data validation, integrity, ingestion, processing, storage, and ETL. This type of testing frequently occurs in the pipeline (pre-analytics layer).

Integration testing
Integration tests are used to ensure that your data pipeline meets your criteria for validity (i.e., within expected ranges); generally, teams will run fake data through the pipeline using these tests before leveraging production data.

As mentioned in Chapter 3, some common data quality checks include:

Null values
Are any values unknown (NULL)?

Freshness
How up-to-date is my data? Was it updated an hour ago or two months ago?

Volume
How much data is represented by this data set? Did two hundred rows turn into two thousand?

Distribution
Is my data within an accepted range? Are my units the same within a given column?

Missing values
Are any values missing from my data set?

How would you write these? In a later chapter, we'll go through a list of common data tests in SQL that can be applied to many open source languages (with varying syntax and glue code, of course), but for explanation's sake, let's walk through an example data set.

Let's assume you're a media distributor working with a data set that tracks your global customer base, including location (City) and how much they're paying for a subscription (Price) of your services. There are 500 entries in this data set, and five columns: City, County, Price, Customers, Product.

If you wanted to test the data to ensure that you're only running a pipeline on customers who live in Berlin, you might run a SQL command that says:

```
SELECT * FROM Customers WHERE City = "Berlin";
```

And if you wanted to understand if there are any null values in City, you might query:

```
SELECT * FROM Customers WHERE City IS NULL;
```

If you wanted to understand if any product is more expensive than $4.50 and less expensive than $8.50, you might run:

```
SELECT * FROM Products WHERE Price > 4.50 AND Price < 8.50;
```

And this just scratches the surface of the types of tests you could run to better understand the health of your data.

Based on the preceding examples, you can tell that data testing can be quite tedious. Before setting your tests, you have to have a clear understanding of the data, what to expect from it, and what "bad data" looks like. We often refer to these expectations as "assertions," derived from the world of unit test-driven development in software engineering.

As a result, data team members often split testing responsibilities over data sets, with individual analysts and engineers responsible for creating and maintaining tests for the data sets they're building pipelines for and interacting with daily. And some companies hire entire Data Quality Assurance teams to handle data testing, with responsibilities including creating tests for business use cases and maintaining existing tests.

In the last few years, tools, including open source solutions like Apache Griffin and Great Expectations, have emerged in the data testing category to help data engineers and analysts automate the data testing process at different stages of the pipeline. dbt (data build tool) is another solution in the data space that has narrow testing capabilities. These tools also help data team members document important information about data sets (in other words, metadata), such as what the data represents and how to use the data in reporting as well as what other data a given asset relies on and feeds into. More on these later.

We cannot emphasize enough the importance of testing your data before production; just as a software engineer would never (purposefully) push code to production without testing it first, a data engineer should never run a pipeline with untested data. But to test your data well, you need a clear understanding of your data health prior to running your pipelines—we'll talk about ensuring data health and observability later.

Keep in mind that data testing catches only expected data quality issues; it does not have the scalability or knowledge to account for "unknown" data quality issues. Data changes a lot, even during production, so it's important to supplement testing with reactive monitoring and anomaly detection, as discussed in Chapter 4.

Measuring and Maintaining Data Quality in the Pipeline

In the 1990s, when your website was down, most people wouldn't notice by the time you were able to get it up and running again given the low volume of users to most websites (after all, not everyone was using the World Wide Web!). Now, in the 2020s, everyone notices when your service or application is down, for instance, Slack's infamous outage (*https://oreil.ly/Yq1JJ*) in January 2021. Slack, a popular enterprise communication management platform with over 12 million daily active users (*https://oreil.ly/xpBQd*) at the time, went down on Monday, January 4, 2021, the first workday after the New Year's holiday, causing many companies to be without their primary means of interoffice communication. Consider the fact that many workers were homebound as a result of the COVID-19 pandemic and you can imagine the frustration that ensued.

Nowadays, nearly every business that hosts software relies on site reliability engineering (SRE) to ensure that applications in production are reliable at all times. As organizations grow and the underlying tech stacks powering them become more complicated (think: moving from a monolith to a microservice architecture), it's important for SRE teams to maintain constant awareness of the health of their systems. Observability, a more recent addition to the engineering lexicon, speaks to this need and refers to the monitoring, tracking, and detection of incidents to prevent downtime.

As a result of this industry-wide shift to distributed systems, SRE has emerged as a fast-growing engineering discipline. At its core, application observability is broken into three major pillars:

- *Metrics* refer to a numeric representation of data measured over time.
- *Logs*, a descriptive, qualitative text record of an event that took place at a given timestamp, also provide valuable context regarding when a specific event occurred.
- *Traces* represent causally related events in a distributed environment.

Increasingly, data teams are coming to rely on similar principles of observability and monitoring to track data quality in production pipelines (see Figure 5-1), with companies developing their own unique methodology for how to measure it, depending on the needs of the business.

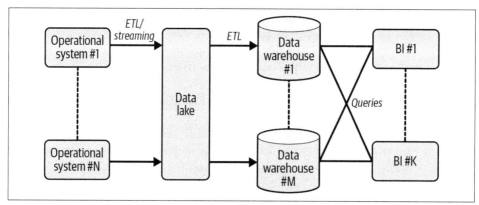

Figure 5-1. A data pipeline refers to "data in production" and is composed of a data warehouse / lake (or both), ETL, and an analytics layer

Similarly, data observability (i.e., ensuring data quality in the pipeline) can be broken down into five major pillars, as shown in Figure 5-2.

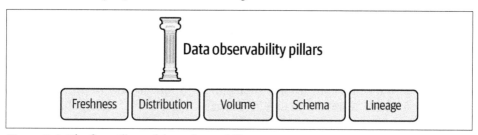

Figure 5-2. The five pillars of data observability

The five pillars of data observability, like the three pillars of application observability, highlight the elements of data health that should be closely monitored as an indicator of high data quality:

Freshness
> Is the data recent? When was the last time it was generated? What upstream data is included/omitted?

Distribution
> Is the data within accepted ranges? Is it properly formatted? Is it complete?

Volume
> Has all the data arrived?

Schema
> What is the schema, and how has it changed? Who has made these changes and for what reasons?

Lineage
> For a given data asset, what are the upstream sources and downstream assets that are impacted by it? Who are the people generating this data, and who is relying on it for decision making?

The five pillars of data observability serve as key measurements for understanding the health of your data at each stage in its life cycle, and provide a fresh (no pun intended) lens with which to view the quality of your data.

As previously mentioned, data downtime refers to periods of time where data is missing, erroneous, or otherwise inaccurate, and often suggests a broken data pipeline. By measuring data downtime, you can determine the reliability of your data and ensure the confidence necessary to use it. While SRE measures application downtime as a function of time, we can similarly measure data downtime.

As data becomes increasingly tied to business outcomes, we're observing a sea change to less subjective, more quantifiable metrics, and for many teams, measuring uptime and downtime for data is broadly applicable and provides a good starting point for understanding data health.

Understanding Data Quality Downstream

Chances are, you won't realize that your data is "bad" until it reaches the analytics layer—or even beyond, when data is piped back to the applications and services you collect it from (i.e., the list of acronyms we shared earlier). As previously mentioned, teams can leverage monitoring and observability tools to catch data quality issues or even set up a sequence of tests based on assumptions about your data.

Once data is in the analytics layer, teams can track, evaluate, and respond to quality and reliability in a few different ways, including:

- A data reliability dashboard that tracks the time to detection (TTD), time to resolution (TTR), and other data quality metrics after data lands in the dashboard. We'll discuss TTD and TTR in more detail later in the chapter.
- Service-level agreements (SLAs) that establish customer promises and punishments for missing service-level objectives (e.g., If we fail, we'll give you a 10% discount next month).
- Service-level indicators (SLIs), in other words, the specific numbers being measured (for instance, Slack's SRE team measures their success rate as the number of 200 responses sent from its servers).
- Service-level objectives (SLOs) are the actual target values you set for your SLIs (for instance, an SLI could be to have a 99% success rate, 95% of the time, for a product functionality).

- A net promoter score measuring how satisfied your stakeholders are with the data (i.e., was it delivered on time and do I trust it?).

However, when understanding data quality in the dashboard (see Figure 5-3), the most important step is to align with your stakeholders around how they intend to use the data and what high-quality, reliable data looks like to them. In many ways, choosing and abiding by an SLI is of grave importance to the success of your data organization and needs to be very specific to what's important to your customers. It's the very score you use to evaluate your performance, so if it's "a bit off" it means your entire strategy for optimizing "uptime" could be flawed. We'll discuss SLAs, SLIs, and SLOs later on in this chapter.

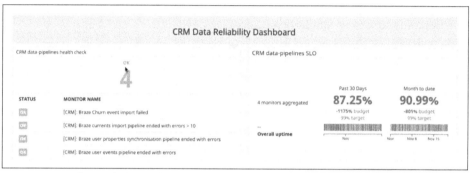

Figure 5-3. A data reliability dashboard (in this case, rendered in Datadog and Grafana) can help your data team and stakeholders keep track of the quality and reliability of your data

An easy way to set SLAs and SLIs is to understand what they'll be using the data for, and which data should be prioritized via testing, observability, and other tooling. It's nearly impossible to write data tests or even monitor for all critical data assets, but aligning on which data matters and to who will cover many of your bases.

Traditionally, data quality is measured by data stewards and data governance leaders by a few defining characteristics. According to the Data Management Association UK (*https://oreil.ly/Mu4OF*), companies have measured data quality based on six key dimensions:

Completeness
How complete is my data?

Timeliness
Did my data arrive on time?

Validity
Does my data meet all syntax requirements (i.e., format, type, or range)?

Accuracy

Does data describe the real-world environment it's trying to represent?

Consistency

Is data consistent against well-understood and accepted definitions?

Uniqueness

Is an individual data point recorded more than once?

In the world of data engineering and data analytics, these measurements are useful, but they aren't always directly applicable (i.e., accuracy). As a data engineer, you're not usually the one working with the end result (clean, reliable data) in the context of the business; you're just notified when something breaks and trusted to apply testing and monitoring at each step of the process.

For data engineers, measuring data quality in the dashboard might boil down to tracking:

- The ratio of data to irrelevant or erroneous data (in other words, if you have 1 TB of data, how much of that data is missing, inaccurate, or stale?)

- The number of null or missing values in a given data set, or the completeness of data (which won't account for "accuracy," given that "inaccurate values" can skew this metric)

- The timeliness of data (in other words, was data late?)

- The percent of duplicated values (which accounts only for uniqueness of data and not any of the other possible ways data can break)

- The consistency of data (i.e., does each value in this row or column have the same format and size?)

- The number of functional teams who consistently access and use your data (this is applicable when applying distributed data architectures, like the data mesh, for which data quality is of the utmost importance)

And the list goes on.

Building Your Data Platform

In addition to monitoring and alerting for data issues at all stages of the data pipeline, delivering reliable data requires a thoughtful data platform—a combination of technologies that enable you to manage data holistically, from ingestion to analytics.

Data platform requirements change with your business. The "right" data platform for a 2,000-person ecommerce company will look quite different from a 20-person FinTech startup, but there are still a few core layers that all data platforms require. We think about the data stack in six layers: ingestion, storage and processing, transformation and modeling, business intelligence (BI) and analytics, discovery and governance, and quality and observability, as shown in Figure 5-4.

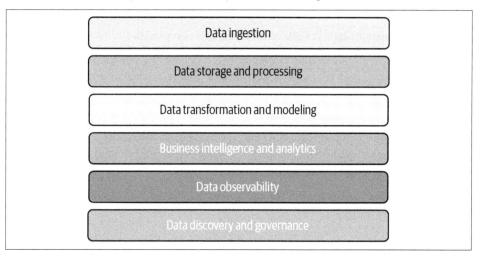

Figure 5-4. Six foundational, interconnected layers needed when building a data platform

It's important to note that "layers" is used in the figurative sense; these elements are interconnected (versus stacked) and are not listed in order of priority or importance. But we've found that best-in-class data teams invest in each of them, sometimes leveraging the same tools or technologies to account for two to three at a time. Of course, as architectures grow to accommodate more advanced use cases, the number of layers will increase depending on the needs of your data team. We'll cover each of these layers in detail as we explore how to build your data stack.

Data Ingestion

Modern data ingestion is complex, usually involving the collection of structured and unstructured data from a wide variety of sources. This is also known as the extraction and loading stages of ETL (extract-transform-load) and ELT (extract-load-transform).

Most ETL tools *extract* data from external sources or internal systems, *transform* it within a staging area into an acceptable (usually relational) format for storage, and *load* it into databases. With the advent of modern cloud-based data warehouses that can store untransformed data, however, data teams can adopt the newer integration architecture of ELT—extracting raw data from a source, loading it directly into a data warehouse, and transforming it at the end of the process.

There are numerous ingestion tools available on today's market—both off-the-shelf and open source—although some data teams choose to use custom code and build custom frameworks to handle ingestion.

Orchestration and workflow automation are often folded into the ingestion layer—taking siloed data, combining it with other sources, and making it available for analysis. However, we would argue that orchestration can, and should, be weaved into the platform after you handle the storage, processing, and business intelligence layers. After all, orchestration requires an orchestra of functioning data!

Keep in mind: it's best practice to test your data at each step of the data pipeline and make the proper assertions to help concretize what data quality at each step looks like. Data tested at ingestion will not necessarily stay reliable as it evolves through the pipeline.

Data Storage and Processing

The storage layer is the workhorse of your data stack—it's where your newly ingested data is stored and processed. Data storage today looks unrecognizable compared to the on-premises computing clusters of a decade ago, thanks to the evolution of cloud-native data storage solutions. These tools make it much more accessible and affordable for companies to store and process massive amounts of data at scale.

There are three primary types of data storage solutions: data warehouses, data lakes, and data lakehouses. *Data warehouses* are fully managed solutions that typically require data to be structured according to specific schema—often forcing stricter data hygiene from the moment of ingestion. *Data lakes*, on the other hand, are often custom-built by data teams with a combination of open source and off-the-shelf technologies, supporting raw, unstructured data and decoupled, distributed computing. *Data lakehouses* are an emerging hybrid, adding warehouse-style features like SQL functionality and schema to data lakes or providing more flexibility to traditional warehouses.

The "right" solution will be different for every company, and even for the same company at different stages—evolving along with the number of data sources you leverage or the skillsets of the primary users of your data platform.

Data Transformation and Modeling

The terms "data transformation" and "data modeling" may be used interchangeably, but they are very distinct processes. Data transformation encompasses preparing raw data for analysis and reporting. Data modeling is the process of identifying the key concepts and relationships in your data that encapsulate your business logic, and then modeling these in the form of tables and the relationships between them.

Data transformation usually includes exploratory data analysis (in other words, profiling data to understand its structure and characteristics), data mapping (defining how individual fields are formatted to produce the final output), code generation (producing executable code based on those defined rules or metadata), code execution (applying the generated code to produce the desired output), and data review (ensuring the transformed data meets requirements).

Traditionally, data transformation has been performed by specialized engineers using scripting languages like Python, R, or SQL and time-consuming work cycles. Today, some data transformation can be accomplished by end users—like business analysts—using cloud-based tools and technologies. This modern, self-service approach allows the business users literate in SQL (and often closest to the data) to maintain more control in setting requirements and speed up the time to actionable insights, and no-code or low-code approaches make this transition possible. That being said, transformation is still very much a data engineer-owned process that incorporates Python and languages outside of SQL.

Data transformation can happen in batch or real-time streaming, the latter of which is a promising and increasingly common approach to handling transformation and modeling in real time (i.e., when having access to fresh data is more important than ensuring that data is accurate). For a more detailed discussion of the trade-offs between the two, revisit Chapter 3.

Business Intelligence and Analytics

Once data is collected, transformed, and stored, it must be made available to business users. After all, the best data in the world won't do any good if your staff can't use it.

This highly visible layer of the data stack is known as business intelligence and analytics. If your data platform is a book, your business intelligence and analytics layer is its cover, complete with a descriptive title, engaging visuals, and a summary of what the data is trying to tell you. The BI layer makes data actionable, and without it, your data lacks meaning.

Analytics tools retrieve, analyze, and surface data through dashboards and data visualizations, allowing users to leverage data for actionable insights. Charts, graphs, maps, and other data visualization tools bring your data to life, giving employees an accessible way to explore and understand patterns and trends in your data. Without visualizations, your data remains virtually inaccessible—millions of rows on a spreadsheet that may be accurate, but aren't easily understood.

Experiencing data through visualizations empowers data storytelling, or the ability to convey data as a narrative that humans can comprehend and, therefore, act on. Data storytelling goes a step beyond visualizations by communicating the context around changes in data and sharing the *why* behind data trends. The discipline of data storytelling must be practiced and honed over time, but your team can't begin to develop those skills without access to self-serve BI and analytics tooling.

Data Discovery and Governance

Data teams need a scalable way to document and understand critical data assets. Historically, this has been accomplished through data catalogs, which serve as an inventory of metadata and provide an understanding of your data's accessibility, health, and location. Data catalogs make it easy to keep track of where personally identifiable information is housed, as well as who within your organization has permission to access it across the pipeline—making them an integral part of data governance and regulatory compliance.

Modern data teams, however, are encountering the limitations of traditional data catalogs. As data ecosystems grow increasingly complex and leverage large amounts of unstructured and schemaless data, traditional catalogs can fall short due to their lack of automation and inability to scale with the growth and diversity of modern data stacks. They tend to require data teams to do the heavy lifting of manual data entry, including updating the catalog as data assets evolve, and often don't support the dynamic nature of unstructured data.

Data discovery is a new approach increasingly applied to data cataloging that provides a domain-specific, dynamic understanding of your data based on how it's being ingested, stored, aggregated, and used by a set of specific consumers. With data discovery, governance standards should remain federated across domains, but unlike more traditional approaches, data discovery enables a real-time understanding of the data's current state—not its ideal or "cataloged" state.

Data discovery can answer these questions not just for the data's ideal state but for the current state of the data across each domain:

- What data set is most recent? Which data sets can be deprecated?
- When was the last time this table was updated?
- What is the meaning of a given field in my domain?
- Who has access to this data? When was the last time this data was used? By whom?
- What are the upstream and downstream dependencies of this data?
- Is this production-quality data?
- What data matters for my domain's business requirements?
- What are my assumptions about this data, and are they being met?

Data discovery makes it possible for data teams to trust that their assumptions about data match reality, empowering dynamic discovery and a high degree of reliability across your data infrastructure.

In our next section, we'll discuss the layer of your data platform we seemingly skipped over: data observability. Don't worry—the method behind our madness will make sense in just a few short paragraphs.

Developing Trust in Your Data

Now that you know what steps to take to ensure data quality pre-, during, and post-production as well as which technologies you need to build a robust data platform, the next step is to develop trust in your data through the right processes and culture. After all, the most advanced data stack in the world is useless unless that data you're using can be trusted to deliver reliable insights to your business. Data for the sake of data is about as useful as a fish riding a bicycle.

When it comes to building reliable and trustworthy data systems, the first step is to understand the health of your data in its current state. In the same way that software engineering teams develop trust in their software applications through observability and DevOps, data teams must embrace similar best practices when it comes to building trust in their data. Data observability is a good first step.

Data Observability

The sixth layer of the modern data stack isn't a final step per se, but rather an interconnected approach that weaves throughout your entire data lifecycle: observability. Over the last two decades, DevOps engineers have developed best practices of observability to ensure applications stay up, running, and reliable. And just as application observability includes monitoring, tracking, and triaging of incidents to prevent downtime, modern data engineers are applying the same principles to data.

Data observability refers to an organization's ability to fully understand the health of the data in their system at every stage of the life cycle. As mentioned in Chapter 1, data observability applies DevOps practices of automated monitoring, alerting, and triaging across five pillars: freshness, distribution, volume, schema, and lineage.

End-to-end data observability is crucial for ensuring data quality. Effective observability tooling will connect to your existing data stack, providing end-to-end lineage that allows you to surface downstream dependencies and automatically monitor your data at rest—without extracting data from your data store and risking your security or compliance. Having observability makes audits, breach investigations, and other possible data disasters much easier to understand and resolve while keeping your CTO from having an ulcer!

Measuring the ROI on Data Quality

Unreliable data can lead to wasted time, lost revenue, compliance risk, and erosion of customer trust. Surveying Monte Carlo's hundreds of customers, we found that data leaders tell us their data scientists and engineers spend 40% or more of their time troubleshooting or firefighting data problems. Gartner estimates companies spend upwards of $15 million annually (*https://oreil.ly/rf54F*) on data downtime, while over 88% of US businesses (*https://oreil.ly/7w0Yb*) have lost money because of data quality issues. And one in five companies (*https://oreil.ly/DbRut*) has lost a customer due to data quality issues.

Before you can improve your data quality, it's important to measure the impact of poor data quality and delineate which data sets matter most to your organization. As you're likely aware, all data is not created equal, but having a sense of the cost of data downtime on your business for key assets will be foundational to communicating the impact of data quality to your stakeholders.

Calculating the cost of data downtime

Quantifying and communicating the value of data quality is a complex endeavor. We've found that the following metrics, borrowed from DevOps practitioners, provide a good start: time to detection and time to resolution.

Time to detection (TTD) describes the length of time it takes for your data team to surface a data quality issue of any kind, from freshness anomalies to schema changes that break entire pipelines. For many teams, TTD is measured in days, weeks, or even months—because, most often, data outages are first detected by downstream consumers when a dashboard or report "looks off."

These periods of time are incredibly costly because the more time that passes, the harder it becomes to recover data through reprocessing or backfilling source data. Additionally, every business decision, marketing campaign, or product roadmap update that relied on the incorrect data needs to be revalidated or communicated to stakeholders.

Time to resolution (TTR) refers to how quickly your team is able to resolve a data incident once alerted. This can be minutes, hours, or days, depending on the complexity of the incident, the availability of your data lineage, the robustness of your data discovery or catalog, and the resources available. TTR metrics allow you to understand the severity of your data issue and track the amount of time it takes to resolve it. By converting to dollars—that is, articulating how much money is spent or saved as a result of TTR—it becomes considerably easier to communicate the impact of this broken data to your stakeholders:

(TTD hours + TTR hours) × Downtime hourly cost = Cost of data downtime

The downtime hourly cost is a generalized metric to represent the engineering time spent per downtime hour and the impact of data downtime on data consumers and business decisions.

Engineering time spent can be calculated as a factor of downtime hours. For example, we can estimate that one data engineer spends one-quarter of every downtime hour monitoring for and investigating issues, which contributes ~$14.75 per downtime hour (avg $59/hr salary + benefits for data engineer, a back-of-the-envelope calculation based on US data engineering salary data from ZipRecruiter (*https://oreil.ly/gih0F*)). Over time and as technical debt accrues, the cost of downtime only grows.

This cost will vary significantly depending on the potential impact of a downtime hour on your business. If, for example, you rely on data to report earnings to Wall Street, a downtime hour resulting in misreporting data is catastrophic, likely contributing $1,000s/hr to the downtime cost. Additionally, you can add the cost of downtime on your analytics team. If, for example, you have 10 analysts, the cost of them sitting idle during a downtime incident is significant (avg $75/hr salary × 10 = $750/hr). Assuming only four of your analysts will be impacted by a downtime hour, we can conservatively reduce this by 60% to $300/hr.

Assuming you have ~100 downtime hours a month split between four analysts, the cost to your business could easily exceed $420,000/year (100 hrs/month × $300/hr × 12 months). And this doesn't even factor in the lost opportunity cost of bad data!

Often, the impact of data quality and reliability goes unnoticed (in fact, many of these issues often go unnoticed until it's too late!), and it can be difficult to proactively justify budget and resources with executives and other stakeholders who aren't on the data team. By calculating baseline TTD and TTR, it becomes much easier to then communicate exactly what impact you expect to generate on the business. Without this baseline, it's much harder to get operational buy-in from the powers that be to grow your team, up-level your tech stack, and scale out the data quality program of your dreams.

Updating your data downtime cost to reflect external factors

Your annual cost of broken data can be approximated by the engineering or resources you must spend to resolve the problem. We believe the right equation factors in the cost of labor to tackle these issues, your compliance risk (we can use average General Data Protection Regulation, or GDPR, fines to quantify this risk), and the opportunity cost of losing stakeholder trust in your data.

Based on available data as well as interviews and surveys conducted with over 150 different data teams across industries, we estimate that data teams spend 30 to 40% of their time handling data quality issues instead of working on revenue-generating activities.

Bringing this together, we can use the following equation to calculate the cost of broken data:[1]

Labor cost + Compliance risk + Opportunity cost = Annual cost of broken data

This framework is a starting point, but measuring the cost is the first step toward fully understanding the implications of broken data at your company—and, ultimately, preventing them altogether.

How to Set SLAs, SLOs, and SLIs for Your Data

Again, we can look to our DevOps counterparts for inspiration on architecting reliability into our data systems. Site reliability engineers use frameworks such as SLAs, SLIs, and SLOs to reduce application downtime and ensure reliability. Several of the data teams interviewed for this book have begun to implement these frameworks across their organizations to prioritize, standardize, and measure data reliability.

Essentially, companies use SLOs to define and measure the SLA a given product, internal team, or vendor will deliver, along with potential remedies if those SLAs are not met. For example, Slack promises its customers (*https://oreil.ly/qU64t*) on Plus plans and above 99.99% uptime every quarter—and if they fall short, Slack will provide service credits on their accounts for future use.

Many software teams develop internal SLOs to help engineering, product, and business teams align on what matters most about their applications and prioritize incoming requests. The very practice of codifying SLOs—rather than counting on everyone to do their best and shoot for as close to 100% uptime as possible—helps set clear expectations. With these SLOs in place, engineering teams and their stakeholders can be confident they're paying attention to the same metrics and speaking the same language.

And setting those non-100% expectations leaves space for growth. Without some tolerance for minimal downtime, there's zero room for innovation—and seasoned engineers know that even with all the best practices in place, systems will still break occasionally. But with solid SLAs in place, engineers know exactly how and when to intervene once something does go wrong.

Similarly, SLAs can help data teams and their consumers define, measure, and track data reliability across its life cycle. Setting data reliability SLAs builds trust between

---

1 In making this calculation, we take labor cost to equal the number of data engineers multiplied by their annual salary multiplied by 30%. Compliance risk is estimated at 4% of annual revenue. Opportunity cost is the revenue you could have generated if you moved faster, releasing X new products and acquiring Y new customers.

your data, your data team, and downstream consumers. Without agreed-upon SLIs, consumers can make inaccurate assumptions or look to anecdotal evidence about the reliability of your data. With SLOs in place, your organization can become more "data-driven" about data.

Additionally, by formalizing communication and prioritization processes, data reliability SLAs help your data team have a clearer grasp on business priorities and make it easier to respond swiftly when incidents occur. Still, setting SLAs in and of themselves is meaningless: you need alignment from data producers, engineers, analysts, and consumers on what these SLAs should be and how much attention and resources should be devoted to maintaining them.

Setting data SLAs requires specificity and collaboration, and clear, up-front alignment with everyone this SLA affects (data producers, data engineers, data analysts, business developers, data consumers, etc.). In fact, just setting SLAs for the sake of setting them can often leave your team in a poor position if there's no investment or accountability in meeting them. Instead, teams should create and evangelize SLAs the same way they set key performance indicators (KPIs) to larger strategic projects:

1. Take stock of business priorities.
2. Assess how these business priorities are enabled or tied to data analytics.
3. Understand your consumer's need for high data quality / tolerance for poor data quality.
4. Set SLOs accordingly, and seek stakeholder feedback and alignment.
5. Measure SLOs.

So, how do we get started? For data teams, setting reliability goals usually includes three steps: defining, measuring, and tracking.

Step 1: Defining data reliability with SLAs

Setting SLAs first requires agreeing upon and clearly defining what reliable data means to your business. We recommend starting this process by conducting an inventory of your data, how it's being used, and by whom—assessing the historical performance of your data to get a baseline metric of reliability.

Data teams should also gather feedback from their consumers on what reliability looks like to them. Data engineers can be removed from their colleagues' daily workflows, but it's crucial to understand how consumers interact with data, what data matters most, and which potential issues require immediate attention. All relevant stakeholders, including data leaders or business consumers, should weigh in—and buy in—on the definitions of reliability you're developing. For instance, 99% of users might not care about TABLE X, but for 1% of users, that table is their lifeblood to the rest of the business. Consumer interviews are critical to understand your business's data needs and what "reliable" data looks like.

After all, powerful technologies and workflows can facilitate proper incident response, but they can't replace a poor culture. Data teams, partners, and consumers must align on SLAs before they are useful to the business.

Step 2: Measuring data reliability with SLIs

With a baseline in place and thorough understanding of your data consumers' needs, you can begin to target the metrics that will become your service-level indicators of reliability. Generally speaking, data SLIs should reflect the agreed-upon state of data you defined in the first step, providing boundaries of how data is and isn't used and describing what data downtime looks like. Scenarios here could include missing, duplicative, or stale data.

SLIs will vary based on your specific use case, but here are a few examples of metrics often used to quantify data health:

The number of data incidents for a particular data asset (N)
This may be beyond your control for external data sources, but it is still a key driver of data downtime and typically worth measuring.

The frequency with which a critical table is updated
If an important table should be updated every 10 hours or less, you—and your data consumers—should know.

The expected distribution for a given data set
If your distribution falls outside the standard range, this could indicate an issue outside of your control (maybe sales were just really high that day?), but it's likely worth looking into.

Step 3: Tracking data reliability with SLOs

Once SLIs are identified, you can set objectives, or ranges of acceptable downtime for your data. These SLOs should be based on your real-world circumstances—for example, if you decide to track TTD but don't use automated monitoring tools, your SLO should be more generous than a mature organization with robust data observability tooling.

Setting these ranges makes it possible to create a uniform framework that rates incidents by level of severity and makes it easy to respond swiftly when issues occur. With these objectives set and incorporated into your SLAs, you can build dashboards that track and report on progress—either custom, ad hoc solutions or using dedicated data observability tools.

These measurements can be quite useful for data teams when understanding the health of their data at an operational level, but when it comes to measuring the impact of data quality on the business, we suggest revisiting data downtime.

Setting SLAs, SLOs, and SLIs for data is only the first piece of the puzzle. When data incidents occur, we also need a way to triage and manage incidents before they become a massive headache for downstream consumers.

For this, we can again turn to our friends in DevOps for inspiration. Most engineering organizations allocate entire site reliability teams to identifying, resolving, and preventing downtime. In today's modern data organization, data engineers often bear the brunt of the pain when pipelines break and dashboards turn wonky. To make the incident resolution process easier and more seamless, we can take a page out of the SRE handbook to effectively communicate and triage data issues as they arise.

For example, let's say one of your executive's critical reports is surfacing stale data. From the outset, you're not sure how this pipeline broke, but you need to communicate that it *has* broken and that your team is on the case. And as you're resolving this issue, you need to consistently update not just your fellow data downtime sleuths but also your key stakeholders on the incident resolution process. While what it takes to achieve reliable data is ultimately up to the needs of your business, having a great communications strategy in place will make it that much easier to execute on your SLAs.

Let's shift gears from talking about principles and take a look at how all of these concepts were applied when an ebook subscription service was struggling with a lack of real-time data.

Case Study: Blinkist

With over 16 million users worldwide, Blinkist helps time-strapped readers fit learning into their lives through their ebook subscription service. Gopi Krishnamurthy, Director of Engineering, led the team responsible for data engineering, infrastructure, cloud center of excellence, growth, and monetization. For Blinkist, having trustworthy and reliable data is foundational to the success of their business.

Lack of real-time data tracking caused marketing spend to decrease across critical distribution channels. As a high-growth company, Blinkist leveraged paid performance marketing to fuel customer acquisition. Their 2020 strategy—with a 40% growth target—included a significant investment in channels like Facebook and Google, which would auto-optimize campaigns based on behavioral data shared between the Blinkist app and the channels themselves.

Of course, like so many companies in 2020, the COVID-19 pandemic changed everything. Now, historic data didn't reflect the current reality of their audience's daily lives, and real-time data became essential—not just for determining advertising spend, but also for understanding the current state of how users were interacting with the Blinkist app and content across the web.

Any inaccuracies in this data could impact decision making, from campaign spending to updating the product roadmap. It was crucial that no opportunities to innovate were missed—from adding new features to simplifying onboarding to testing new advertisements—because a campaign around "improving your commute" just wasn't relevant anymore. As C-level execs and campaign managers grew increasingly dependent on real-time insights to drive marketing strategy, budget spend, and ROI, Gopi and his team were struggling with data downtime—issues with data quality, dashboard update delays, and broken pipelines.

In our interview with Gopi, he said, "Every Monday, we had executive calls. And almost every Monday, I was on this call trying to answer why we are not able to scale, what were the issues, how many problems we face in terms of tracking data…trying to explain the severity of the problem and trying to boost confidence with executive stakeholders." Gopi estimates his team was spending 50% of their working hours firefighting data drills, trying to resolve data downtime issues while rebuilding trust with the rest of the organization. It wasn't sustainable and something had to change.

Foundational to achieving data reliability was a focus on data governance, data quality, and refactoring systems. Gopi and his team implemented a regimented approach to data testing and observability that tracked key data SLAs and SLIs. "At the core of this framework is data reliability engineering—that we treat data reliability as a first-class citizen, the same way engineering teams in the last decade have started to treat DevOps and site reliability engineering," said Gopi.

By investing in testing and data observability and setting clear data reliability SLAs to measure data reliability, Blinkist was able to remediate data downtime before it affected downstream consumers. As Gopi and his team worked to rebuild broken trust along with broken pipelines, they partnered with company leaders to build a shared understanding of data reliability principles and set concrete data SLAs.

Outcome: Time savings of 120 hours per week for a team of 6 data engineers through testing, observability, and SLA alignment.

"The scale of growth that we've seen this year is overwhelming," Gopi said. "Although the data teams can't take full credit, I definitely think the things we were able to do—in terms of data observability and bringing transparency into data operations—improved how we target our audience and channels."

Still, it's important to remember that setting SLOs and measuring SLIs don't *themselves* improve anything. The key to Gopi's success is that his team evaluated what was most important, set SLIs to measure it and SLOs to judge their progress, and then were able to properly prioritize and evaluate the success of the projects they executed to improve those metrics. Often data teams get caught up in setting their metrics but don't give the proper value to actually *executing* against them and identifying what negative features of their environment contribute to each of their missing SLOs.

Summary

For those beginning their data quality journeys, architecting for data reliability requires a three-pronged approach:

- Invest in DevOps-inspired processes (testing and observability) up front—and across functional domains.
- Build a resilient and performant data platform.
- Set and align on cross-organizational data SLAs, SLIs, and SLOs.

Without these steps, data teams will have a challenging time achieving any semblance of reliable, high-quality data. Still, taking your data quality strategy from a siloed experience managed solely by data engineers and other upstream roles to something prioritized by your broader company is a gradual process. At the risk of sounding cliche: Rome wasn't built in a day, and neither is your data quality strategy.

In the next chapter, we'll dive into a critical component of the data reliability workflow: incident management and resolution, an end-to-end approach to fixing data quality at scale.

CHAPTER 6

Fixing Data Quality Issues at Scale

Picture this: it's Friday at 5 p.m., and you're about to log off for the day. You start closing your tabs, packing up your bag, and settling into your weekend state of mind. Just as you're about to turn off your laptop, you get an urgent Slack message from your CFO about a broken dashboard.

"The numbers are wrong in our quarterly results report," she Slacks you. "I didn't sign off on this!"

Assuming the issue is about the data itself and not rooted in your company's shoddy financials, you have a serious case of data downtime on your hands. You frantically open Looker to find she's right—the report looks way off and you have no idea why. You validated the numbers yesterday with her. Your charts and graphs were absolutely glowing with accuracy.

You pull up the source data (an Excel spreadsheet living on your desktop, "Financial Report V. 212 GOOD_I_ PROMISE_YES_GOOD"), but that confuses you even more. Dozens of emails, two phone calls, a few Zoom meetings, and seven hours later, you determined the culprit of the errant dashboard: a schema change upstream with a source table.

Great, you figured out what happened—now what?

For most data teams, pausing the pipeline and identifying the root cause of the issue at hand is just the tip of the iceberg when it comes to restoring data reliability and trust in your data.

Fixing Quality Issues in Software Development

Fortunately, analysts and engineers don't need to reinvent the wheel when it comes to managing these types of "data downtime" incidents in individual pipelines and even larger data systems. Instead, we can look to DevOps and site reliability engineering (SRE) yet again for inspiration when it comes to handling incident management and resolution at scale. To build and release more performant software, DevOps teams apply a feedback loop, called the DevOps life cycle (as depicted in Figure 6-1), that helps teams reliably deliver features aligned with business objectives at scale.

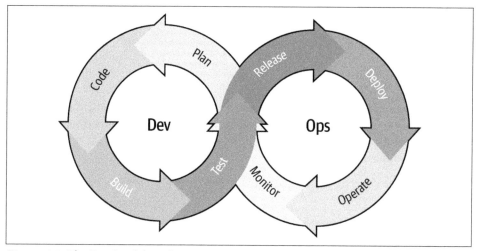

Figure 6-1. The DevOps life cycle gives engineers a framework with which to manage the reliability and performance of software applications

The DevOps life cycle incorporates eight sections, or continuous stages, including:

Plan
   The dev team aligns with product and business teams to understand the goals and SLAs for your software.

Code
   Write new software.

Build
   Release your software into a test environment.

Test
   Test your software.

Release
   Release the software to production.

Deploy
> Integrate and deploy the software with your existing applications.

Operate
> Run the software, adjust as necessary.

Monitor
> Monitor and alert for issues in the software.

And the cycle repeats itself. While many of our data technologies and frameworks (i.e., data testing, data SLAs [service-level agreements], distributed architectures, etc.) have adapted to meet the standards and best practices set by our software engineering counterparts, our tendency to handle data quality reactively has prevented us from driving the adoption of analytics in a meaningful and scalable way. By leveraging the best practices of incident management from software engineering to data environments, we can approach data quality with a proactive and scalable approach that can meet the analytical demands of your business.

According to Andrew Stribblehill and Kavite Guiliana, two authors who collaborated on Google's canonical *SRE Handbook* (*https://oreil.ly/Jon0X*), "Effective incident management is key to limiting the disruption caused by a [software] incident and restoring normal business operations as quickly as possible. If you haven't gamed out your response to potential incidents in advance, principled incident management can go out the window in real-life situations."

In short, incident management is the process of identifying, root causing, resolving, analyzing, and preventing issues that arise in your day-to-day engineering workflows. DevOps and SRE teams leverage incident management to programmatically discover and address buggy software, outages, and other performance issues in real time.

In this chapter, we'll discuss how data teams can fix data incidents at scale by applying principles of software incident management to their data systems, from investing in the right technology and tooling to implementing DevOps-inspired processes and organizational structures.

Data Incident Management

Francisco Alberini, a former Data Product Manager at Segment, a leading customer data platform, was responsible for building their data governance tool, Protocols. In this role, Francisco was no stranger to tackling broken data pipelines. In our discussion with Francisco, he said:

> Data systems can break for a million different reasons, and there isn't a one-size-fits-all approach to understanding how or why. As the PM for Protocols, I spent a lot of time thinking about and building dashboards to evaluate the quality of data our customers were receiving. When issues occurred, my approach consisted of two steps:

(1) frantically ping that one data engineer who had been on our team for 4+ years (decades of historical knowledge in engineering time) to ask for urgent help, and (2) if she wasn't available, spend hours debugging this pipeline by spot-checking thousands of tables. Neither was particularly scalable.

Francisco's experience is not unique.

As data systems become increasingly distributed and companies ingest more and more data, the opportunity for error (and incidents) only increases. For decades, software engineering teams have relied on a multistep process to detect, resolve, and prevent issues from taking down their applications. As data operations mature, it's time we treat our data systems with the same diligence, particularly when it comes to building more reliable pipelines.

While not a ton of literature exists about how data teams can handle incident management for their data, there are already great resources and best practices we can leverage from our friends in software development. We recommend data teams apply a similar, but modified approach to incident management: the data reliability life cycle (Figure 6-2), which is inspired by the DevOps life cycle and helps data teams manage the performance and reliability of data pipelines.

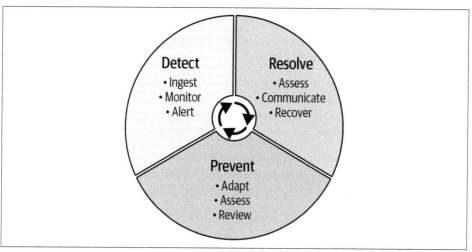

Figure 6-2. The data reliability life cycle

By applying the data reliability life cycle to data pipelines, data engineering teams can more seamlessly detect, resolve, and, ultimately, prevent data quality issues before they impact the business. And when it comes to building a data incident management workflow for your pipelines, critical steps include incident detection, response, root cause analysis (RCA), resolution, and a blameless postmortem.

Incident Detection

With the right tooling and processes, incident detection (Figure 6-3) can easily be integrated into data engineering and analytics workflows, ensuring that all data stakeholders and end users are alerted when issues arise across the proper communication channels (i.e., Slack, Microsoft Teams, email, SMS, PagerDuty, or carrier pigeon).

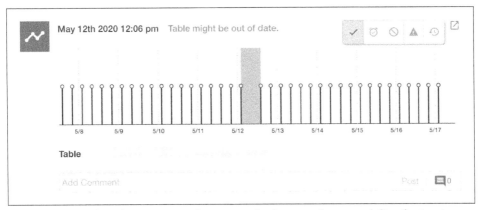

Figure 6-3. Incident detection can alert you to freshness, volume, and distribution issues across your data pipelines

It goes without saying that you should, first and foremost, test your data before it enters production. Still, even with the most robust tests and checks in place, bad data will fall through the cracks and be pushed to prod before you can say "broken data pipeline." When data pipelines break or dashboards go haywire, the first step is incident detection. Incidents can be detected through data monitoring and alerting, which can be both implemented manually on your data pipelines and triggered based on specific thresholds. Incident detection can also be layered as part of an anomaly detection or data observability solution and triggered automatically at regular intervals based on historical data patterns and custom rules.

One critical component of incident detection is anomaly detection (Figure 6-4) or the ability to identify when pillars of data health (i.e., volume, freshness, schema, and distribution) veer from the norm. Anomaly detection is most valuable when implemented end to end (across your warehouses, lakes, ETL, and BI tools) as opposed to only in a specific silo of your data ecosystem. Good anomaly detection will also tune algorithms to reduce white noise and false positives, leveraging precision and recall. We went into detail about how to build your own anomaly detectors and data quality monitors in Chapter 4, but let's recap and walk through a high-level view here.

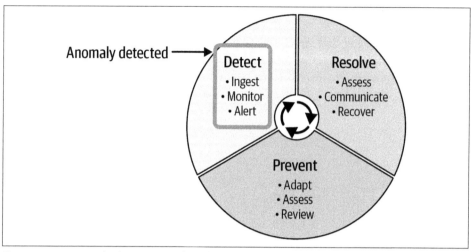

Figure 6-4. Anomaly detection within the data reliability life cycle

Over the years, we've found that there is a predilection for data teams to rely on anomaly detection alone to "solve" incident management. There are a few issues with this statement. First and foremost, incident management is never truly "solved." As long as companies continue to leverage data to power their digital services and drive decision making, data incidents will continue to happen. Pipelines will break, schema changes will disrupt downstream dashboards, and null values will crop up at the least opportune times. Second, relying on anomaly detection alone is a single point of failure; incident detection is a multilayered process that relies not just on the ability to detect incidents, but also respond to, resolve, and prevent them in an iterative and repeatable way.

Don't get us wrong: anomaly detection is an extremely important part of the data reliability life cycle and a key tool for the "detect" stage of your data incident management protocol. But relying on anomaly detection without the additional support of testing, versioning, observability, lineage, and the various other technologies and processes available to automation-inclined data teams is problematic at best and a recipe for frustration and long data downtime recovery times at worst. Anomaly detection is a tool, not a silver bullet.

To articulate our point, imagine for a moment that you're a car mechanic. A sedan drives into your garage, engine sputtering. "What's wrong?" you ask, lifting your eyes from your desk. The driver rolls down their window. "Something's wrong with my car," they respond. Very descriptive, you think, wiping the sweat from your brow. Your sarcasm makes you chuckle. "Something is wrong with my car," they repeat, this time without the contraction.

After a few hours of poking around, you figure out that the car has a loose spark plug. Sure, their lack of information isn't the end of the world, but imagine how much quicker this process could have been if they had been proactive and said, "I have trouble getting my engine to start, my car won't accelerate, and my battery keeps dying."

What does this story have to do with data? Well, on the surface, not much. But we can learn a thing or two from our friendly mechanic when it comes to not relying on anomaly detection alone to resolve data quality issues.

Nowadays, most data teams employ some measure of anomaly detection to solve for data quality. Anomaly detection is great for organizations that are looking to identify when the key pillars of data health (i.e., volume, freshness, schema, and distribution) are not meeting an organization's expectations in production. Moreover, anomaly detection is extremely valuable to businesses when implemented end to end (such as across your data warehouse, lake, ETL, and BI tools), as opposed to only living within one or two layers of your data platform.

As most data teams are learning, however, anomaly detection alone is not cutting it when it comes to building the trust, accountability, and transparency demanded by insight-driven organizations. Recently, Barr was having (virtual) coffee with the VP of Analytics at a Fortune 500 software company who summarized this problem almost too perfectly:

> I want things that are tied to impact so I can take action on them. Anomaly detection is necessary as a starting point, but we need to do a lot more work to understand the root cause and assess the impact. Knowing there's a problem is great, but it's really hard to understand what to do with it. Instead, we need to understand exactly what broke, who's impacted by it, why and where it broke, and what the root cause might be.

Here's where the rest of the data incident management life cycle comes in.

Response

Good incident response starts—and ends—with effective communication, and fortunately, much of it can be prepared in advance and automated through a workflow via PagerDuty and Slack when the time comes. Data teams should spend time writing runbooks and playbooks that walk through standard incident response. While runbooks give you instructions for how to use different services and common issues they encounter, playbooks provide step-by-step processes for handling incidents. Both will provide links to code, documentation, and other materials that can help teams understand what to do when critical pipelines break. One important part of a good runbook? Delegating roles when outages or breakages occur. (Read on for more best practices regarding role delegation during incident management.)

In traditional site reliability engineering programs, there is an on-call process that delegates specific roles depending on service, often segmented by hour, day, or week. In addition to an "incident responder," there is often an "incident commander" responsible for assigning tasks and synthesizing information as the responder and other stakeholders troubleshoot the issue. The incident commander is also tasked with spearheading communication to upstream and downstream consumers that might be affected, i.e., those that work with the data products powered by the broken pipeline.

With business context, metadata is a powerful tool for understanding which teams are affected by a given data downtime incident; coupled with end-to-end lineage, as depicted in Figure 6-5, communicating the upstream and downstream relationships between these affected assets can be a painless and quick process, saving teams hours of manual graphing and ensuring the appropriate parties can be notified before bad data affects the business.

Figure 6-5. End-to-end lineage is a valuable tool for understanding upstream and downstream dependencies when data pipelines break

Once data downtime occurs, it's important to communicate its impact to upstream and downstream consumers, both those that work with the data and those that use it. With the right approach, much of this can be baked into automated workflows using PagerDuty, Slack, and other communication tools.

Root Cause Analysis

In theory, RCA sounds as easy as running a few SQL queries to segment the data, but in practice, this process can be quite challenging. Incidents can manifest in nonobvious ways across an entire pipeline and impact multiple, sometimes hundreds, of tables.

For instance, one common cause of poor data quality is freshness–i.e., when data is unusually out-of-date. Such an incident can be a result of any number of causes, including a job stuck in a queue, a timeout, a partner that did not deliver its data set timely, an error, or an accidental scheduling change that removed jobs from your directed acyclic graph (DAG).

In our experience, we've found that most data problems can be attributed to one or more of these events:

- An unexpected change in the data feeding into the job, pipeline or system, as depicted in Figure 6-6
- A change in the logic (ETL, SQL, Spark jobs, etc.) transforming the data
- An operational issue, such as runtime errors, permission issues, infrastructure failures, schedule changes, etc.

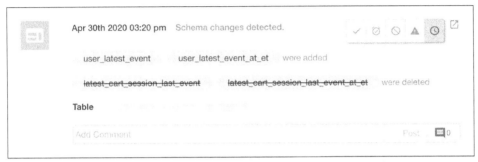

Figure 6-6. Schema change alert delivered via a data observability platform

Quickly pinpointing the issue at hand requires not just the proper tooling but also a holistic approach that considers how and why each of these three sources could break. It's also important to note that incidents rarely have a single root cause; rather, they're often a confluence of "causes" that can be turned into valuable learnings for process optimization and technical fine-tuning.

As software (and data) systems become increasingly complex, it becomes more and more difficult to pinpoint one exact cause (or root) of an outage or incident. Amazon's five whys approach (*https://oreil.ly/IuBzc*) provides a helpful framework through which to contextualize RCA:

- Identify the problem.
- Ask *why* the problem happened, and record the *reason*.
- Decide if the reason is the root cause.
  - — Could the reason have been prevented?
  - — Could the reason have been detected before it happened?
  - — If the reason is human error, why was it possible?
- Repeat the process using the reason as the problem. Stop when you are confident that you have found the root causes.

There is very rarely a single reason why your system broke. As data engineers work to reduce manual toil, smarter processes, tests, data freshness checks, and other solutions should be able to identify the issue before it surfaces downstream, as depicted via the data observability schema change alert in Figure 6-6. When they don't, it's a strong indication that these fail-safes are inadequate.

To get started, we've identified the five steps data teams must take when conducting RCA on their data pipelines:

1. *Look at your lineage.* To understand what's broken, you need to find the most upstream nodes of your system that exhibit the issue—that's where things started and that's where the answer lies. If you're lucky, the root of all evil occurs in the dashboard in question and you will quickly identify the problem.

2. *Look at the code.* A peek into the logic that created the table, or even the particular field or fields that are impacting the incident, will help you come up with plausible hypotheses about what's wrong.

3. *Look at your data.* After steps 1 and 2, it's time to look at the data in the table more closely for hints of what might be wrong. One promising approach here is to explore how other fields in a table with anomalous records may provide clues as to where the data anomaly is occurring (Figure 6-6).

4. *Look at your operational environment.* Many data issues are a direct result of the operational environment that runs your ETL/ELT jobs. A look at logs and error traces from your ETL engines can provide some answers.

5. *Leverage your peers.* More often than not, your teammates will have some knowledge of or insights into the data causing you problems. Never hurts to ask!

Let's look at this in practice. In the following sections, we'll walk through the five steps necessary to conduct root cause analysis for a broken customer dashboard.

Step 1: Look at your lineage

You know the customer dashboard is broken. You also know this dashboard is built on top of a long chain of transformations, feeding off several (or maybe several dozen) data sources. To understand what's broken, you will need to find the most upstream nodes of your system that exhibit the issue—that's where things started and that's where the answer lies. If you're lucky, the root of all evil occurs in the dashboard in question and you will quickly identify the problem. On a bad day, the problem happened in one of the most upstream sources of your system, many transformation steps away from the broken dashboard—which would require a long day of tracing the issue up the DAG, and then backfilling all broken data.

Make sure everyone (data engineers, data analysts, analytics engineers, and data scientists) troubleshooting data problems has access to the most up-to-date lineage. To be useful, your lineage should include data products like BI reports, ML models, or reverse-ETL sinks. Field-level lineage is a plus (Figure 6-7). Often automated, field-level lineage is an important investment for data engineering teams seeking to easily and quickly understand which data assets are broken and how these breakages have impacted downstream data products and dashboards.

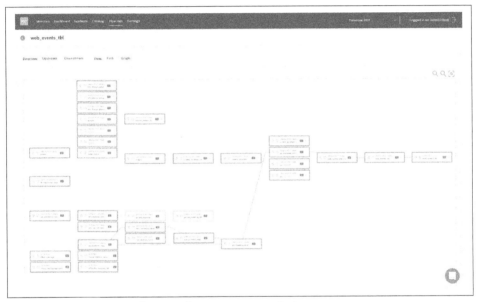

Figure 6-7. Lineage visualization for root cause analysis

Step 2: Look at the code

You found the most upstream table that's experiencing the issue. Congratulations, you're one step closer to understanding the root cause! Now, you need to understand how that particular table was generated by your ETL or ELT processes (Figure 6-8).

A peek into the logic that created the table, or even the particular field or fields that are impacting the incident, as well as the metadata associated with that table, will help you come up with plausible hypotheses about what's wrong.

Ask yourself:

- What code most recently updated the table? And when?
- How are the relevant fields calculated? What could possibly have created the "wrong" data given this logic?

- Have there been any recent changes to the logic, potentially introducing an issue?
- Have there been any ad hoc writes to the table? Has it been backfilled recently?

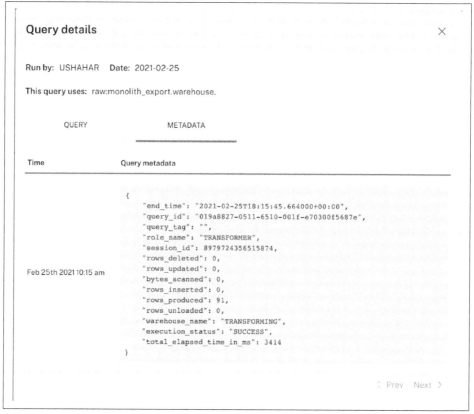

Figure 6-8. Looking at the code and how the query was generated during root cause analysis

 Make sure everyone troubleshooting data problems can quickly trace back tables to the logic (SQL, Spark, or otherwise) that created them (Figure 6-9). To get to the bottom of things, you need to know not only what the code currently looks like, but also what it looked like when the table was last updated and ideally when that happened. While we all try to avoid them, backfills and ad hoc writes should be accounted for.

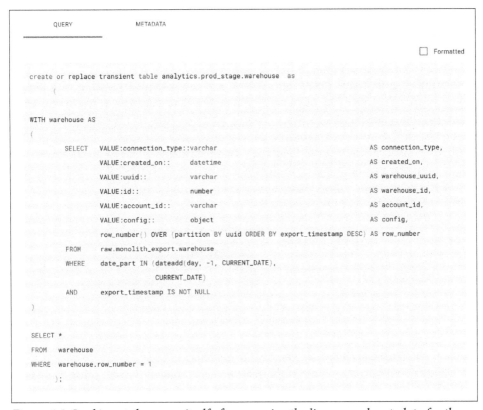

```
QUERY                METADATA

                                                                            ☐ Formatted

create or replace transient table analytics.prod_stage.warehouse  as

        (

WITH warehouse AS
(
        SELECT   VALUE:connection_type::varchar                      AS connection_type,
                 VALUE:created_on::      datetime                    AS created_on,
                 VALUE:uuid::            varchar                      AS warehouse_uuid,
                 VALUE:id::              number                       AS warehouse_id,
                 VALUE:account_id::      varchar                      AS account_id,
                 VALUE:config::          object                       AS config,
                 row_number() OVER (partition BY uuid ORDER BY export_timestamp DESC) AS row_number
        FROM     raw.monolith_export.warehouse
        WHERE    date_part IN (dateadd(day, -1, CURRENT_DATE),
                        CURRENT_DATE)
        AND      export_timestamp IS NOT NULL
)

SELECT *
FROM    warehouse
WHERE   warehouse.row_number = 1
        );
```

Figure 6-9. Looking at the query itself after assessing the lineage and metadata for the data asset in question

Step 3: Look at your data

You now know how the data was calculated and how that might have contributed to the incident. If you still haven't spotted the root cause, it's time to look at the data in the table more closely for hints of what might be wrong.

Ask yourself:

- Is the data wrong for all records? For some records?
- Is the data wrong for a particular time period?
- Is the data wrong for a particular subset or segment of the data, e.g., only your Android users or only orders from France?
- Are there new segments of the data (that your code doesn't account for yet) or missing segments (that your code relies on)?
- Has the schema changed recently in a way that might explain the problem?

- Have your numbers changed from dollars to cents? Your timestamps from PST to EST?

- And the list goes on.

One promising approach here is to explore how other fields in a table with anomalous records may provide clues as to where the data anomaly is occurring (Figure 6-10). For example, Lior's team recently surfaced that an important Users table for one of our customers experienced a jump in the null rate for the user_interests field. We looked at the source field (i.e., Twitter, Facebook, or Google) to see if a relational pattern could point us in the right direction. This type of analysis provides two key insights; both would explain the increase of null records, but each ultimately drives very different actions.

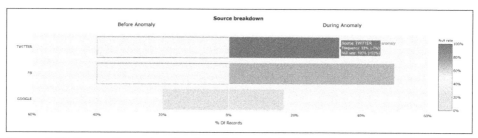

Figure 6-10. Generating a visualization of the statistical prevalence of anomalies like null values relative to other issues in the data can help pinpoint the root cause of a data problem

The proportion of records associated with source="Twitter" increased significantly, which normally has more records where user_interests="null" than other sources. The proportion of records where user_interests="null" increased for records with source="Twitter", while the proportion of records with source="Twitter" did not change.

For the first insight, we may just be experiencing a seasonality issue or the result of an effective marketing campaign. For the second insight, we likely have a data processing issue with user data coming from our Twitter source and can focus our investigation on the data coming from Twitter.

Make sure everyone troubleshooting data problems can handily slice and dice data to find how the issue correlates with various segments, time periods, and other cuts of the data. Visibility into recent changes to the data or its schema is a lifesaver. Keep in mind that while these statistical approaches are helpful, they are just one piece of the larger RCA process.

Step 4: Look at your operational environment

OK, the data checks out. What now? Many data issues are a direct result of the operational environment that runs your ETL/ELT jobs (as depicted in Figure 6-11). One powerful open source tool for handling these runs is dbt.

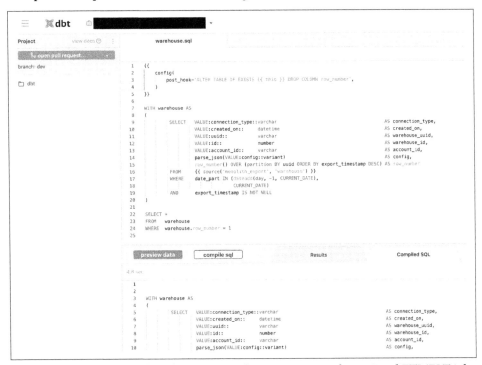

Figure 6-11. Taking a peek at the operational environment and associated ETL/ELT job runs, often one of the final steps in root cause analysis

A look at logs and error traces from your ETL engines can help answer some of the following questions:

- Have relevant jobs had any errors?
- Were there unusual delays in starting jobs?
- Have any long running queries or low performing jobs caused delays?
- Have there been any permissions, networking, or infrastructure issues impacting execution? Have there been any changes made to these recently?
- Have there been any changes to the job schedule to accidentally drop a job or misplace it in the dependency tree?

Make sure everyone troubleshooting data problems understands how ETL jobs are performed and have access to the relevant logs and scheduling configuration. Airflow, an open source data orchestration tool, allows teams to dive into job logs to better understand what might have gone wrong in the process (Figure 6-12). Understanding infrastructure, security, and networking can help as well.

Figure 6-12. Using Airflow to analyze job logs can help troubleshoot data problems

Step 5: Leverage your peers

You did everything you can (or maybe you're looking for shortcuts)—what's next? You need to get guidance from your data team. Before you start bombarding Slack with questions, ask yourself:

- What similar issues have happened in the past with this data set? What has the team done to investigate and then resolve those issues?

- Who owns the data set that's experiencing the issue right now? Who can I reach out to for more context?

- Who uses the data set that's experiencing the issue right now? Who can I reach out to for more context?

Make sure everyone troubleshooting data problems has access to metadata about data set ownership and usage, so they know who to ask. A history of data incidents with helpful documentation can be useful as well.

Root cause analysis can be a powerful tool when it comes to addressing—and preventing—data quality issues in near real time, but it's important to remember a broken pipeline can rarely be traced to one specific issue. Like any distributed architecture, your data ecosystem is composed of a series of complex logic, events, and of course, pipelines that, like a science experiment, react in a multitude of ways.

That being said, we've found that this five-step approach can help turn root cause analysis from a stress-inducing wake-up call into a scalable and sustainable practice for your entire data organization. And in the process, you'll give that one data engineer (you know, the human data pipeline encyclopedia on your data engineering team) a bit of a break.

Resolution

Once you identify that something has gone awry and understand its initial impact, the next step (sometimes even before root cause analysis) is to fix the issue and communicate next steps to the proper stakeholders. This could be as easy as pausing your data pipelines or models and rerunning them, but since data can break for millions of reasons, this often involves a fair amount of troubleshooting.

In many cases, there may be an "initial resolution" (i.e., pause or "circuit break" a pipeline—recall we looked at circuit breaking in Chapter 3) and a "final resolution," in other words, implement a more permanent solution that addresses the underlying cause of the data downtime incident. Throughout this process, it's important to communicate the status of the incident in a dedicated Slack channel, email chain, Wiki site, Google Document, JIRA workflow, or other collaboration tool that makes it easy for various stakeholders to keep track of the current state of affairs.

After the incident is fixed, whether through changes to the code, data, or operational environment, teams should communicate next steps to the affected parties and in the coming days, schedule a postmortem.

Blameless Postmortem

Our friend, a site reliability engineer with over a decade of experience firefighting outages at Box, Slack, and other Silicon Valley companies, told us that I couldn't write a chapter about incident management without making this abundantly clear: "For every incident, the system is what's at fault, not the person who wrote the code. Good systems are built to be fault and human tolerant. It's the system's job to allow you to make mistakes."

When it comes to data reliability and DataOps, the same ethos rings true. Pipelines should be fault-tolerant, with processes and frameworks in place to account for both known unknowns and unknown unknowns in your data pipeline.

Regardless of the type of incident that occurred or what caused it, the data engineering team should conduct a thorough, cross-functional postmortem after they've fixed the problem and conducted root cause analysis. A postmortem (which, literally, means after death) is a meeting, and corresponding document, created after an incident is resolved that highlights the key information, sequence of events, affiliated parties, associated technologies, and other relevant facts about the issue. A postmortem is useful not just as a way to communicate the effects and outcome of an incident but also to chronicle what happened so you can act more proactively to prevent similar issues from happening again.

Here are a few best practices for conducting great postmortems on your data pipelines:

Frame everything as a learning experience.
> To be constructive, postmortems must be blameless (or if not, blame aware). It's natural to try and assign "blame" for incidents, but it's rarely helpful when it comes to instilling trust in your colleagues or fostering a collaborative culture. By reframing this experience around the goal of "learning and improvement," it's easier to proactively take the organizational (creating better workflows and processes) and technological steps (making a case for investing in new tools) necessary to eliminate data downtime.

Use this as an opportunity to assess your readiness for future incidents.
> Update runbooks and make adjustments to your monitoring, alerting, and workflow management tools. In short, runbooks are detailed how-to guides for completing a common task or procedure widely used by DevOps and IT teams. When applied to data, runbooks might include information about who owns what tooling or data assets at your company, as well as when jobs are regularly run or dashboards updated. As your data ecosystem evolves (adding new, third-party data sources, APIs, and even consumers), this step will become critical when it comes to incident prevention.

Document each postmortem and share with the broader data team.
> As in software engineering, documenting what went wrong, how systems were affected, and what the root cause is often comes as an afterthought. But documentation is just as important as any other step in the incident management process because it prevents knowledge gaps from accruing if engineers with tacit knowledge leave the team or aren't available to help.

Revisit service-level agreements (SLAs).
> This isn't the first (or last!) time we'll be discussing SLAs in this book. Broadly speaking, SLAs are a method many companies use to define and measure the level of service a given vendor, product, or internal team will deliver—as well as potential remedies if they fail. As data systems mature or change over time, it's

important to consistently revisit your SLAs, service-level indicators (SLIs), and service-level objectives (SLOs). SLAs that made sense six months ago probably don't any more; your team should be the first to know and communicate these changes with downstream consumers.

At the end of the day, postmortems are just as important for data teams as they are for software engineers. As our field continues to advance (we're in the decade of data, after all), understanding how and why data downtime occurs is the only way we can make continued improvements to the resiliency of our systems and processes.

Incident Response and Mitigation

Understanding how to instrument an effective incident management workflow is the first step when it comes to preventing data anomalies and other data downtime issues, but it only scratches the surface of what it takes to deliver comprehensive data reliability. After all, testing only covers your "known unknown" data quality issues; what about your "unknown unknowns"? Testing, a data engineer's first line of defense against data downtime, which usually accounts only for about 20% of "unknown unknown" issues. Without proactive incident prevention measures in place, however, the other 80% are often identified through disgruntled stakeholders downstream messaging them about "broken reports and dashboards" (Figure 6-13).

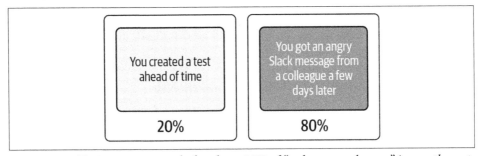

Figure 6-13. Testing accounts only for about 20% of "unknown unknown" issues; the rest may be identified by colleagues without proactive incident prevention measures

It helps to think of the first two sections of the data reliability life cycle (Detect and Resolve in Figure 6-2) as the "reactive" stages of this process, and Prevent as the "proactive" stage, ideally reducing the amount of time spent firefighting. Now that you've identified, root-caused, resolved, and conducted a postmortem on your incident, the next step is to prevent similar incidents from occurring again by implementing a data reliability stack that layers testing, CI/CD, discovery, and observability for a more proactive approach to incident management, as depicted by Figure 6-14.

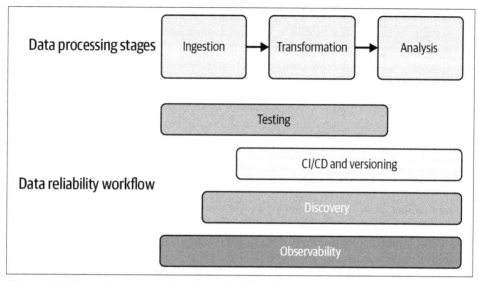

Figure 6-14. Proactive approach to data reliability that incorporates testing, CI/CD, discovery, and observability, necessary components of managing and preventing data incidents

The best part? These four elements are applicable to nearly any data architecture. In fact, layering these discrete processes will enable you to build more resilient data pipelines regardless of whether you're building a centralized, distributed, or hybrid data stack.

Establishing a Routine of Incident Management

Too often, data engineers are burdened not just with fixing data issues but also with prioritizing what to fix, how to fix it, and communicating status as the incident evolves. For many companies, data team responsibilities underlying this firefighting are often ambiguous, especially when it relates to answering the question "Who is managing this incident?" Sure, data reliability SLAs should be managed by entire teams, but when the rubber hits the road, we need a dedicated person to help call the shots and make sure SLAs are met should data break. In software engineering, this role is often defined as an incident commander, and its core responsibilities include:

- Flagging incidents to the broader data team and stakeholders early and often
- Maintaining a working record of affected data assets or anomalies
- Coordinating efforts and assigning responsibilities for a given incident
- Circulating runbooks and playbooks as necessary
- Assessing the severity and impact of the incident

Data teams should assign rotating incident commanders on a weekly or daily basis, or for specific data sets owned by specific functional teams. Establishing a good, repeatable practice of incident management (that delegates clear incident commanders) is primarily a cultural process, but investing in automation and maintaining a constant check on data health gets you much of the way there. The rest is education.

Here are four key steps every incident manager must take when triaging and assessing the severity of a data issue.

Step 1: Route notifications to the appropriate team members

When responding to data incidents, the way your data organization is structured will impact your incident management workflow, and as a result, the incident commander process. If you sit on an embedded data team, it's much easier to delegate incident response (i.e., the marketing data and analytics team owns all marketing analytics pipelines), as depicted in Figure 6-15. Team members are spread across different business units and data team members in each domain are responsible for fielding incidents for their stakeholders. In this structure, data team members typically report to the head of a business unit or in some cases the chief data officer (CDO) or head of data.

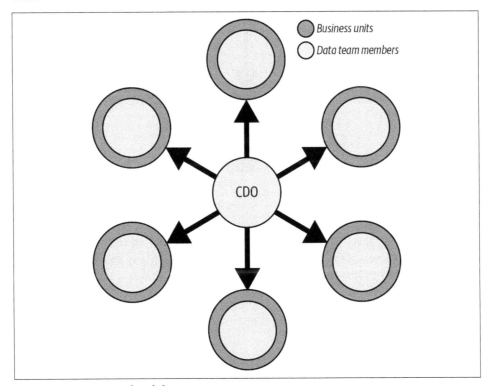

Figure 6-15. Decentralized data team structure

If you sit on a centralized data team (Figure 6-16), fielding and routing these incident alerts to the appropriate owners requires a bit more foresight and planning. A centralized data team reports directly to the CDO or head of data and simultaneously fields queries and incidents from data corresponding to different business units. Unless otherwise specified, several business units are its stakeholders. There are pros and cons to both data team structures when it comes to ensuring data reliability, but more on this in Chapter 8.

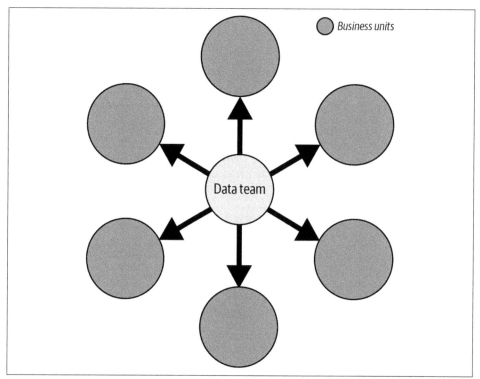

Figure 6-16. Centralized data team structure

Either way, we suggest you set up dedicated Slack channels for data pipelines owned and maintained by specific members of your data team, inviting relevant stakeholders so they're in the know if critical data they rely on is down. Many teams we work with set up PagerDuty or Opsgenie workflows to ensure that no bases are left uncovered.

Step 2: Assess the severity of the incident

Once the pipeline owner is notified that something is wrong with the data, the first step they should take is to assess the severity of the incident. Because data ecosystems are constantly evolving, there are an abundance of changes that can be introduced into your data pipelines at any given time. While some are harmless (i.e., expected schema change), some are much more lethal, causing impact to downstream stakeholders (i.e., rows in a critical table dropping from 10,000 to 1,000).

Once your team starts troubleshooting the issue, it is a best practice to tag the issue based on its status, whether fixed, expected, investigating, no action needed, or false positive. Tagging the issue helps users with assessing the severity of the incident and also plays a key role in communicating the updates to relevant stakeholders in channels that are specific to the data that was affected so they can take appropriate action.

What if a data asset breaks that isn't important to your company? In fact, what if this data is deprecated?

Phantom data haunts even the best data teams, and we can't tell you how many times we have been on the receiving end of an alert for a data issue that, after all of the incident resolution was said and done, did not matter to the business; in fact, the data hadn't been used in months! So, instead of tackling high priority problems, we spent hours or even days firefighting broken data only to discover we were wasting our time.

So, how do you determine what data matters most to your organization? One increasingly common way teams have been able to discover their most critical data sets is by utilizing tools that help them visualize their lineage and understand how data is being used by the business (Figure 6-17). Operational analytics help data teams understand how data is being used across the company, what data pipelines are more susceptible to data downtime, how much cloud storage costs per data asset, and other valuable insights about data health. This allows them to have visibility into how all of their data sets are related when an incident does arise, and to be able to trace data ownership to alert the right people that might be affected by the issue. In many respects, data observability solutions fill these gaps by providing rich lineage and a way to explore the operational analytics of your data platform.

Once your team can figure out if the incident affected critical data, they will have a better understanding of the severity of the downtime. If it affects data that is directly powering financial insights, it's likely a super high priority issue; if it's not, it's time to move on.

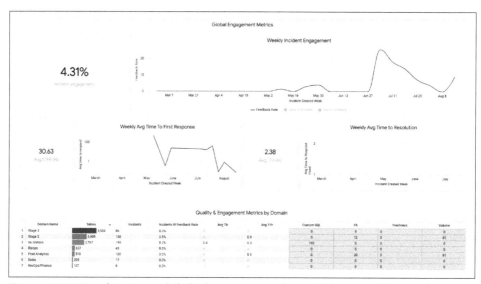

Figure 6-17. Visualization tools help data teams understand the use of data in the business

Step 3: Communicate status updates as often as possible

Good communication goes a long way in the heat of responding to a data incident, which is why we have already discussed how and why data teams should create a runbook that walks step by step through how to handle a given type of incident. Following a runbook is crucial to maintain correct lines of responsibility and reduce duplication of effort.

Once you have "who does what" down, your team can then start updating a status page where stakeholders can follow along for updates in real time. A central status page also allows team members to see what others are working on and the current status of those incidents.

In talks with fellow data leaders, we have seen incident command delegation handled in one of two ways:

Assign a team member to be on call to handle any incidents during a given time period.
    While on call, that person is responsible for handling all types of data incidents. Some teams have someone full time that does this for all incidents their team manages, while others have a schedule in place that rotates team members every week to cover.

Team members are responsible for covering certain tables.
    This is the most common structure we see. With this structure, team members handle all incidents related to their assigned tables or reports while doing their

normal daily activities. Table assignment is generally aligned based on the data or pipelines a given member works with most closely.

Either approach works; it's just a matter of figuring out what works *best* for your team structure, resources, and priorities.

Step 4: Define and align on data SLOs and SLIs to prevent future incidents and downtime

While the incident commander is not accountable for setting SLOs, they are often held responsible for meeting them. Simply put, SLOs are a method many companies use to define and measure the level of service a given vendor, product, or internal team will deliver—as well as potential remedies if they fail to deliver.

For example, Slack's customer-facing SLA promises 99.99% uptime every fiscal quarter, and no more than 10 hours of scheduled downtime, for customers on Plus plans and above. If they fall short, affected customers will receive service credits on their accounts for future use.

Your SLIs, quantitative measures of your SLAs, will depend on your specific use case, but here are a few metrics used to quantify incident response and data quality, as previously discussed in Chapter 5:

The number of data incidents for a particular data asset (N)
Although this may be beyond your control, given that you likely rely on external data sources, it's still an important driver of data downtime and usually worth measuring.

Time to detection (TTD)
When an issue arises, this metric quantifies how quickly your team is alerted. If you don't have proper detection and alerting methods in place, this could be measured in weeks or even months. "Silent errors" made by bad data can result in costly decisions, with repercussions for both your company and your customers.

Time to resolution (TTR)
When your team is alerted to an issue, this measures how quickly you were able to resolve it.

By keeping track of these, data teams can work to reduce TTD and TTR, and in turn, build more reliable data systems.

Why Data Incident Commanders Matter

When it comes to responding to data incidents, time is of the essence, and as the incident commander, time is both your enemy and your best friend. In an ideal world, companies want data issues to be resolved as quickly as possible. However, that is not always the case and some teams often find themselves investigating data issues more frequently than they would like. In fact, while data teams invest a large amount of their time writing and updating custom data tests, they still experience broken pipelines. An incident commander, armed with the right processes, a pinch of automation, and organizational support, can work wonders for the reliability of your data pipelines.

Case Study: Data Incident Management at PagerDuty

PagerDuty helps over 16,800 businesses across 90 countries hit their uptime SLAs through their digital operations management platform, powering on-call management, event intelligence, analytics, and incident response. So how does PagerDuty approach data-specific incident management within their own organization? We sat down with Manu Raj, Senior Director of Data Platform and Analytics (aptly named the DataDuty team), to learn more about his team's strategy for preventing "data downtime" and achieving more reliable data pipelines at scale.

The DataOps Landscape at PagerDuty

PagerDuty's business data platform team has a clear mandate: to provide its customers with trusted data anytime, anywhere, that is easy to understand and enables efficient decision making. "The most critical part of that is data governance, data quality, security, and infrastructure operations," said Manu. The team's customers include "pretty much all the departments in PagerDuty, including finance, executives, customer success, engineering, sales, and marketing."

In terms of the platform itself, the DataDuty team uses PagerDuty—"we absolutely have to eat our own dog food"—as well as Snowflake for data warehousing, Fivetran, Segment, Mulesoft, AWS, Monte Carlo, and Databricks. The team also recently integrated ML-powered data observability, giving them the ability to fully understand the health of data systems by monitoring, tracking, and troubleshooting data incidents at each stage of the pipeline.

Data Challenges at PagerDuty

Like most SaaS companies, PagerDuty uses a lot of SaaS cloud applications (think Salesforce, Marketo, and Netsuite) and ingests a lot of internal and third-party data. Structured data, unstructured data, data coming in at different cadences, and real-time batches across different granularities are all part of the overall data ecosystem at PagerDuty.

The DataDuty team's primary challenge is making sure the quality of the data meets end-user expectations by enabling them to make faster decisions based on accurate data. "The dynamic nature of the business is what drives data challenges," said Manu. "The business data needs are changing continuously, quarter by quarter, and accurate decisions have to be made quickly. Everything is data driven, so we have to be agile."

Using DevOps Best Practices to Scale Data Incident Management

To fulfill their ambitious mandate, the DataDuty team implemented a number of DevOps incident management best practices to their data pipelines.

Best practice #1: Ensure your incident management covers the entire data life cycle

At PagerDuty, incident management for data engineers falls under what they call data operations, which is an extension of DevOps. It includes tracking, responding, and triaging for both data and pipeline issues. Once the data is in the warehouse and all the way until it appears in customer-facing reports, there is potential for various types of data downtime, from missing data to errant models. The DataDuty team monitors for data quality issues including anomalies, freshness, schema changes, metric trends, and more.

Data observability is especially important to monitor and ensure data quality in your data warehouse. You could intervene at a data pipeline level through custom data quality checks via ETL tools, but over time the management of the logic, scripts, and other elements of your data ecosystem becomes cumbersome. Moreover, as Manu notes, issues with data trends cannot be identified by pipeline quality checks.

Best practice #2: Incident management should include noise suppression

Data noise is a major issue when it comes to implementing data monitoring and anomaly detection, and at the enterprise scale, you will have a variety of "alerts" coming in daily, many of which will indicate changes in your data but not necessarily net-new "issues." One can even judge the operability of an alerting system on its signal-to-noise ratio, striving to bring this ratio as close to zero as possible.

Data teams need to be able to triage between customers and business owners and respond to these alerts in a timely fashion while delegating clear ownership over the data products themselves. Manu's DataDuty team uses PagerDuty to identify similar data incident alerts, suppressing multiple alerts for one incident that contains multiple data issues. This way, his team members aren't overwhelmed with alerts and can focus on fixing the root cause(s) of the data issue at hand.

Best practice #3: Group data assets and incidents to intelligently route alerts

According to Manu, data observability is the first step before any data incident management steps, including incident response and escalation, can happen. After all, "my data is not refreshed" is an entirely different issue compared to an abnormal trend or metric. Teams need to be able to identify that this data issue exists over time.

When the DataDuty team began to integrate data observability with PagerDuty across their own data platform, they followed best practices from DataOps, including grouping together data issues to enable easier routing and alerting based on that

360-degree view. By grouping similar data pipeline issues with data observability and implementing triaging and alerting on top of this workflow, they were able to ensure that these alerts were properly routed to the DataDuty team.

Since they use Airflow for scheduling, the team receives Airflow alerts via PagerDuty, too. Additionally, by identifying the company's most critical data assets, including executive-level reporting and financial reporting-level data, through data observability, they can ensure that alerts related to those assets come via PagerDuty with an escalation policy and automatically go to additional stakeholders and the Business Intelligence team.

By monitoring and alerting on the health of BI metrics, such as the number of customers, customer churn rate, the number of accounts, and the number of data incidents, Manu and his team can gain a better sense of the reliability of their data. These alerts are then routed to the business intelligence team so they can monitor and take action as needed.

With these best practices, PagerDuty's platform team lives up to their mandate by approaching data incident management from a DevOps perspective—which aligns perfectly with the principles of data observability.

Summary

When it comes to fixing broken data pipelines at scale, data teams should invest in repeatable incident management, root cause analysis, and data reliability workflows. To recap, we suggest taking these four important steps:

- Roll out an incident management program for critical data pipelines.
- Leverage anomaly detection as part of a larger incident detection strategy.
- Conduct thorough root cause analysis and impact analysis when incidents occur.
- Tackle data quality proactively through testing, CI/CD, data observability, and data.

Without these steps, data engineers and analysts will have a challenging time handling data quality issues in near real time, particularly as data systems evolve and companies ingest more and more data. In Chapter 7, we'll take incident management and resolution a step further by walking through how to build your own lineage system—a critical tool for resolution and prevention in your quest against data downtime.

Building End-to-End Lineage

On July 27, 2004, a five-year-old startup by the name of Google was faced with a serious problem: their application was down (*https://oreil.ly/R7fqg*).

For several hours, users across the United States, France, and Great Britain were unable to access the popular search engine. The then-700-person company and their millions of users were left in the dark as engineers struggled to fix the problem and discover the root cause of the issue. By midday, a tedious and intensive process conducted by a few panicked engineers determined that the MyDoom virus (*https://oreil.ly/N01Ks*) was to blame.

In 2021, an outage of that length and scale was considered rather anomalous, but 15 years ago, these types of software outages weren't uncommon. After leading teams through several of these experiences over the years, Benjamin Treynor Sloss, a Google engineering manager at the time, determined there had to be a better way to manage and prevent these dizzying fire drills, not just at Google but across the industry.

Inspired by his early career building data and IT infrastructure, Sloss codified his learnings as an entirely new discipline—site reliability engineering (SRE) (*https://oreil.ly/THjBi*)—dedicated to optimizing the maintenance and operations of software systems (like Google's search engine) with reliability in mind.

According to Sloss and others paving the way forward for the discipline (*https://oreil.ly/bdoRU*), SRE was about automating away the need to worry about edge cases and unknown unknowns (like buggy code, server failures, and viruses). Ultimately, Sloss and his team wanted a way for engineers to automate away the manual toil of maintaining the company's rapidly growing codebase while ensuring that their bases were covered when systems broke.

"SRE is a way of thinking and approaching production. Most engineers developing a system can also be an SRE for that system," he said (*https://oreil.ly/Uw8a8*). "The question is: can they take a complex, maybe not well-defined problem and come up with a scalable, technically reasonable solution?" If Google had the processes and systems in place to anticipate and prevent downstream issues, not only could outages be easily fixed with minimal impact on users, but they could even be prevented.

Nearly 20 years later, data teams are faced with a similar situation. Like software, data systems are becoming increasingly complex, with multiple upstream and downstream dependencies. Ten or even five years ago, it was normal and accepted to manage your data in silos, but now, teams and even entire companies are working with data, facilitating a more collaborative and fault-resistant approach to data management.

Over the past few years, we've witnessed the widespread adoption of software engineering best practices by data engineering and analytics teams to address this gap, from adopting open source tools like dbt and Apache Airflow for easier data transformation and orchestration to cloud-based data warehouses and lakes like Snowflake and Databricks (*https://oreil.ly/srqDm*).

Fundamentally, this shift toward agile principles relates to how we conceptualize, design, build, and maintain data systems. Long gone are the days of siloed dashboards and reports that are generated once, rarely used, and never updated; now, to be useful at scale, data must also be productized, maintained, and managed for consumption by end users across the company. And in order to do this reliably, we need some sort of map connecting the dots between disparate systems—in other words, lineage.

And in order for data to be treated like a software product, it has to be as reliable as one, too. In this chapter, we'll walk through how to build one of the most critical features of this workflow (lineage!) and review a real-world case study from a data platform product manager.

Building End-to-End Field-Level Lineage for Modern Data Systems

Data engineers are no strangers to the schema changes, null values, and distribution errors that plague even the healthiest data systems. In fact, as data pipelines become increasingly complex and teams adopt more distributed architectures, such data quality issues only multiply.

While data testing is an important first step when it comes to preventing these issues, data lineage has emerged as a critical component of the data pipeline root cause and impact analysis workflow. Akin to how site reliability engineers or DevOps practitioners might leverage commands like `git blame` to understand where software broke in the context of larger systems, data lineage gives data engineering and analytics teams visibility into the health of their data at each stage in its life cycle, from ingestion in the warehouse or lake to eventual analysis in the business intelligence layer. As part of a larger approach to data reliability, lineage is critical when it comes to understanding the ins and outs of broken data.

Data lineage refers to a map of the data set's journey throughout its life cycle, from ingestion in the warehouse or lake to visualization in the analytics layer. In short, data lineage is a record of how data got from point A to point B. In the context of data pipelines, lineage traces the relationships across and between upstream source systems (i.e., data warehouses and data lakes) and downstream dependencies (e.g., analytics reports and dashboards), providing a holistic view of data as it evolves. As depicted in Figure 7-1, modern lineage tools also highlight the effects of system changes on associated assets, down to individual columns.

Figure 7-1. Table-level lineage with upstream and downstream connections between objects in the data warehouse and tables

Due to the complexity of even the most basic SQL queries, however, building data lineage from scratch is no easy feat. Historically, lineage is parsed manually, requiring an almost encyclopedic knowledge of a company's data environment and how each component interacts with each other.

Adding further complexity to the equation, keeping manual lineage up-to-date becomes more challenging as companies ingest more data, layer on new solutions, and make data analysis more accessible to additional users through codeless analytics tools and other reporting software. In the next few sections, we will walk through what it takes to build field-level lineage, focusing on the backend architecture, key use cases, and best practices for data engineering teams planning to build field-level lineage for their own data systems.

Basic Lineage Requirements

For the past several years, data teams across industries have relied on table-level lineage (*https://oreil.ly/8zf8w*) to improve their data reliability workflows by generating a map of upstream and downstream dependencies. While useful at the macro level, table-level lineage doesn't provide teams with the granularity they need to understand exactly why or how their data pipelines break.

As with building any new product functionality, the first step is to understand user requirements, and from there, scope out what could actually be delivered in a reasonable timeframe. Here are a few key features to consider when building lineage:

Fast time to value
Data teams want to quickly understand the impact of code, operational, and data changes on downstream fields and reports. You will need to abstract the relationships between data objects down to the field level; the table level may be too broad for quick remediation.

Secure architecture
Generally speaking, you don't want lineage to access user data or personally identifiable information (PII) directly. We recommend an approach that accesses metadata, logs, and queries but keeps the data in the customer's environment.

Automation
Field-level lineage products often take a manual approach (*https://oreil.ly/iwjnF*), which puts more responsibility in the lap of the customer; we advocate for investing in an automated approach that updates data assets based on changes in the data life cycle.

Integration with popular data tools
We needed a knowledge graph that could automatically generate nodes across an entire data pipeline, from ingestion in the data warehouse or lake down to the business intelligence or analytics layer. Many data teams require integration with data warehouse and lake technologies like Snowflake (*https://oreil.ly/yQvJO*), Redshift (*https://oreil.ly/mjqzV*), Databricks (*https://oreil.ly/BGzjw*), and Apache Spark (*https://oreil.ly/S7C1M*); transformation tools like dbt (*https://oreil.ly/9nHct*), Apache Airflow (*https://oreil.ly/Vmb8O*), and Prefect (*https://oreil.ly/XOvSE*); and business intelligence tools like Looker (*https://oreil.ly/tbKN7*), Tableau (*https://oreil.ly/Yi1iq*), and Mode (*https://oreil.ly/9RxbQ*), which requires that your solution account for every possible join and connection between every table in their data system.

Extraction of column-level information
Many table-level lineage solutions are mainly derived from parsing query logs, which can't extract parsed column information—the metadata necessary to help

users understand anomalies and other issues in their data. For field-level lineage, we suggest going down to the column level, a difficult task that we'll discuss later in the chapter.

Based on this basic field-level lineage, users can also aggregate the metadata in further steps to serve different use cases, such as operational analytics. For example, you could precalculate for a given table and each of its fields how many downstream tables are using the field. This would be particularly useful when it comes to identifying the impact of data quality issues on downstream reports and dashboards in the business intelligence layer. After all, who doesn't want a painless root cause analysis?

At its most basic, field-level lineage can be used to massively reduce time to detection and time to resolution of data quality issues, with the goal of bringing down the total amount of time it takes data teams to root-cause their data pipelines. In an analytics capacity, data lineage can be used for a variety of applications, including:

Reviewing suspicious numbers in a revenue report
One data team at a 400-person FinTech company generates monthly revenue forecasts using data collected and stored in Snowflake and visualized by Looker. They can use field-level lineage to trace which table in their warehouse has the source field for the "suspicious" numbers in this report, and through this process, realize that the culprit for the data issue was a dbt model that failed to run.

Reducing data debt
Many data teams leverage data observability to deprecate columns in frequently used data sets to ensure that outdated objects aren't being used to generate reports. Field-level lineage makes it easy for them to identify if a given column is linked to downstream reports.

Managing personally identifiable information
Several of our customers deal with sensitive data and need to know which columns with PII are linked to destination tables in downstream dashboards. By being able to quickly connect the dots between columns with PII and user-facing dashboards, customers can remove the information or take precautions to deprecate or hide the dashboard from relevant parties.

These use cases just scratch the surface of how leading data teams leverage field-level lineage. By integrating it with their existing root cause analysis workflows, getting to the bottom of these questions can save time and resources for analysts and engineers across their companies.

Data Lineage Design

When it comes to actually building field-level data lineage, the first thing you need to do is architect a way to understand which columns belong to which source tables, as depicted in Figure 7-2. This is a challenging task given that most data transformations leverage more than one data source. Further complicating matters, you need to recursively resolve the original sources and columns in the event that some of the source tables are aliases of existing subqueries derived from other subqueries.

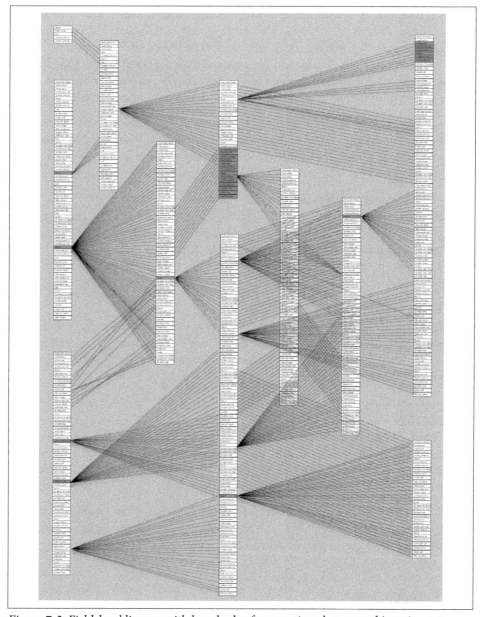

Figure 7-2. Field-level lineage with hundreds of connections between objects in upstream and downstream tables

The sheer number of possible SQL clause combinations makes it extremely difficult to cover every possible use case. In fact, when our team was building field-level lineage for Monte Carlo's customers, the original prototype covered only about 70% of possible combinations. So, to cover every possible clause and clause combination across all possible data warehouse, data lake, ETL, and business intelligence integrations across your stack (often dozens of tools!), you must individually test each clause with one another and ensure that the solution still works as intended before moving on to the next use case.

At a foundational level, the structure of most lineages incorporates three elements (Figure 7-3):

- The destination table, stored in the downstream report
- The destination fields, stored in the destination table
- The source tables, stored in the data warehouse

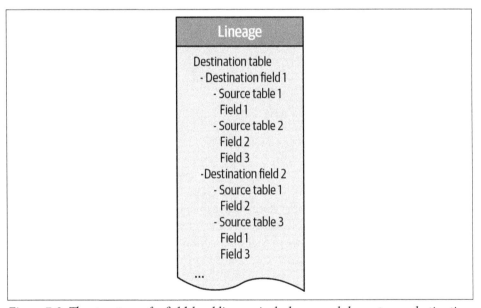

Figure 7-3. The structure of a field-level lineage includes several downstream destination fields per upstream table

As previously mentioned, there are infinite relationships between destination and source objects, which required us to leverage a data model that was flexible enough to capture multiple queries at once.

We suggest using a logical data model, a `table_mcon` ID, and hashed field-level lineage objects together as the ID for the document. For the same destination table, there could be several different queries to update it. Using the destination table mcon and a hashed field-level lineage object, you can capture all the different lineage combinations for a given destination table. Example 7-1 shows an example of an index schema.

Example 7-1. Lineage query between a destination (analytics report) and one or more source tables in the warehouse

```
{
  "edge_id": "37d65dc5c943cab124398b2c43f0d8f2c0ff5e76a2ba3052",
  "account_id": "ee7c21ae-9af9-4ce0-ac51-fa953065d6f7",
  "version": "normalized_v0.25",
  "job_ts": "2021-08-06 18:51:02.439000",
  "expire_at": "2021-08-13 18:51:02.439000",
  "destination_table_mcon": "", // destination table mcon
  "source_table_mcons": [
    "", // mcon 1
    "", // mcon 2
  ], // adding the destination table mcon, and source table ...
  "sources": [
    {
      "table_mcon": "", // mcon of the table
      "field_name": ""
    },
    ...
  ],
  "destination_field": "new field name",
  "created_time": "2021-08-06 06:29:44.341000",
  "last_update_time": "2021-08-06 18:51:02.439000",
  "last_update_user_id": null,
  "parsed_query": ""
}
```

In this lineage model, we have one destination table. For each of the fields in the destination table, there is a list of source tables and source columns that define the field, referred to as *selected fields*. This model also contains another list of source tables and columns containing the nonselected fields. In this case, our model (Figure 7-4) incorporates one denormalized data structure that contains edges between fields in a destination table and their source fields in some source tables.

In Example 7-2, we offer a real example of how field-level lineage can "simplify" a complex query. The WITH clause contains nine temporary tables, with some of the tables using other temporary tables defined before them. Additionally, in the main query, there could be joins between real tables, temporary tables declared in the WITH clause, and subqueries.

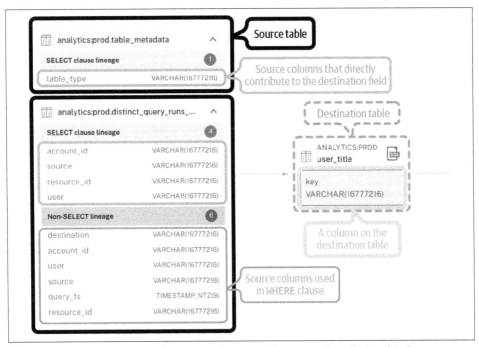

Figure 7-4. In this example, the lineage data model exposes the relationship between source tables and destination tables

Example 7-2. JSON query that simplifies a complex WHERE query to identify the root cause of a data quality issue, down to the field level

```
CREATE OR REPLACE TABLE decom.usage_timelines.pdt_usage_activities AS (
WITH usage_stuck_to_be_processed AS (
  SELECT s.usage_id,
    s.created_date
  FROM 'decom.processed.subscriptions' s
  JOIN 'decom.processed.usages' u
  ON s.usage_id = u.id
  WHERE (s.state = 'to_be_processed' AND u.activated_at IS NOT NULL)  ❶
),
usage_subscription_state_updated as (
  SELECT *,
    rank() OVER (PARTITION BY usage_id ORDER BY created_at desc
      AS sub_update_no_desc
  FROM 'decom.usage_timelines.usage_subscription_states' al_s
),
usages_batch_removeled as (
  select distinct u.id as usage_id
  from 'decom.processed.usages' u
  join 'decom.processed.subscriptions' s on u.id = s.usage_id
  left join usage_subscription_state_updated ussu on ussu.usage_id
```

```
        = u.id and ussu.sub_update_no_desc = 1  ❶
      where s.state = 'in_question' and ussu.to_value = 'active'  ❶
      ),
  usage_subscription_state_change_actions AS (
    SELECT ussu.usage_id AS usage_id,
      CASE
        WHEN (
          ussu.from_value = 'to_be_processed' AND
          ussu.to_value = 'active' AND
          sub_update_no = 1
        ) THEN 'activate subscription'
        WHEN (
          ussu.from_value = 'to_be_processed' AND
          ussu.to_value IN ('in_question', 'disabled') AND
          sub_update_no = 1
        ) THEN 'remove from to_be_processed'
        WHEN (
          ussu.to_value IN ('in_question', 'disabled')
        ) THEN 'remove'
        WHEN (
          ussu.to_value = 'active' AND (
            ussu.from_value IN ('in_question', 'disabled') OR
            (from_value = 'to_be_processed' AND sub_update_no >= 3))
        ) THEN 're-activate'
        WHEN (
          ussu.to_value = 'to_be_processed'
        ) THEN 'other - to to_be_processed'
        WHEN (
          ussu.to_value = 'active'
        ) THEN 'other - to active'
        ELSE 'other change'
      END AS action
      ussu.created_at AS action_at
    FROM decom.usage_timelines.usage_subscription_states ussu
  ),
  lead_subscription_orders AS (
    SELECT usage_id AS usage_id,
      CASE
        WHEN order_type = 'lead'
          THEN CAST('lead_order' AS string)
        WHEN order_type = 'regular'
          THEN CAST('regular_order' AS string)
      END AS action,
      MIN(order_placed_at) AS action_at
    FROM 'decom.cart.usages_orders_process'
    WHERE usage_legit_order_no = 1 AND order_placed_at IS NOT NULL  ❶
    GROUP BY
      1, 2
  ),
  lead_subscription_order_send_dates AS
  (
    SELECT usage_id                                    AS usage_id,
```

```
    CASE
      WHEN order_type = 'lead'
        THEN CAST('send lead order' AS string)
      WHEN order_type = 'regular'
        THEN CAST('send regular order' AS string)
    END                                          AS action,
    MIN(timestamp_add(send_date, interval 10 hour)) AS action_at
  FROM 'decom.cart.usages_orders_process'
  WHERE usage_legit_order_no = 1 AND send_date IS NOT NULL   ❶
  GROUP BY
    1, 2
),
submit_email AS
(
  SELECT id                                      AS usage_id,
    CAST('submit email' AS string)               AS action,
    created_at                                   AS action_at
  FROM 'decom.processed.usages'
  WHERE created_at IS NOT NULL   ❶
),
activations AS
(
  SELECT id                                      AS usage_id,
    CAST('activate' AS string)                   AS action,
    created_at                                   AS action_at
  FROM 'decom.processed.usages'
  WHERE activated_at IS NOT NULL   ❶
),
unioned AS
(
  SELECT * FROM activations
    UNION ALL
  SELECT * FROM usage_subscription_state_change_actions
    UNION ALL
  SELECT * FROM lead_subscription_orders
    UNION ALL
  SELECT * FROM lead_subscription_order_send_dates
    UNION ALL
  SELECT * FROM submit_email
)
SELECT
  u.*,   ❷
  COALESCE(usa.action_general_order, -1 AS action_general_order,   ❷
  usa.subscription_phase_change_to      AS subscription_phase_change_to   ❷
FROM unioned u
INNER JOIN (
  select usage_id,
    max(created_time) as max_created_date
  from usage_stuck_to_be_processed
  group by usage_id
) as usage_created_date
  on usage_created_date.usage_id = u.usage.id   ❶
```

```
LEFT JOIN tfddatawarehouse.cart.usage_subscription_actions usa
  ON u.action = usa.action  ❶
WHERE
  NOT (u.usage_id IN ((SELECT usage_id FROM usages_stuck_to_be_processed)) )  ❶
  and NOT (u.usage_id IN ((SELECT usage_id FROM usages_batch_removeled)) )  ❶
);
...
```

❶ Nonselected fields

❷ Selected fields

In each query or subquery's SELECT clause, there are fields that apply additional functions, expressions, and subqueries. In even more complex examples, lineage can reflect queries that have many nested layers of subqueries, and even more complex expressions.

The ❷ shows the selected fields in the lineage that derived from this query. The selected fields are the fields that define the result table. The fields flagged with ❶ are extracted as nonselected fields. Nonselected fields have an impact on the rows to be fetched from source tables, but they don't contribute to the field values in the result table, which offers a more intuitive UI and quick root cause analysis process because unaffected lineage is obscured.

Parsing the Data

To "interpret" the data and build lineage, you need to parse it with a tool like ANother Tool for Language Recognition (ANTLR) (*https://oreil.ly/SbtO5*), an open source queryparser generator that reads, processes, executes, and translates structured text or binary files. Using the queryparser to extract the columns that were defining grammars, you can access the field-level relationships for more basic SELECT clause use cases. From there, we were confident that we could build a fully functional backend.

A common problem that arises during query parsing relates to performance issues, particularly when working with more complex queries. In some cases, the queries are too long to be easily parsed: some use WITH clauses that define some subqueries, and those subqueries are referenced in the main queries themselves. For example, if a column doesn't have quotes around it, it's parsed as a column, and if it has quotes, it's parsed as a string. To fix this, you can modify the grammar of our query log parser to better support your data warehouse or lake, which will each have its own parsing nuances and complexities.

This SQL query complexity often manifests itself in another design challenge: architecting a user interface. To build useful lineage, you need to ensure that it provides rich context and metadata about the represented tables and fields without burdening the user with superfluous information. Essentially, you need to abstract away this spider web of relationships and possible interactions in order to deliver on the vision of offering a truly powerful product experience for your customers. You need to architect a tree with only the most relevant blossoms, leaves, and roots showing.

Building the User Interface

When it comes to building the frontend interface, you need to decide which technologies to use and determine the most useful and intuitive way to display field-level lineage. You also need to augment lineage as opposed to just automating it to allow for quick incident resolution and a more scalable data reliability workflow. In other words, you need a way of highlighting what connections are likely to be relevant to a given use case or issue. After all, the most effective lineage doesn't just surface information—it surfaces *the right* information at the right time.

Generally speaking, data teams care most about either the most downstream layer (business intelligence objects in tools like Looker or Tableau), or the most upstream layer (the source table or field stored in the warehouse or lake, which is frequently the root cause of the issue). As depicted in Figure 7-5, these layers aren't often as critical when it comes to conducting root cause analysis or understanding the health of your data.

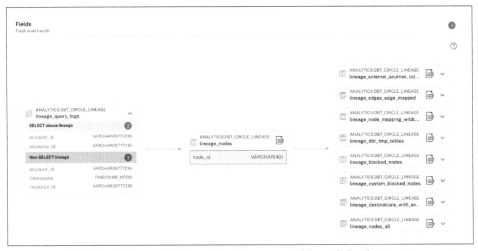

Figure 7-5. Field-level lineage UI featuring the source table and the destination reports that indicate which source data impact downstream dashboards and reports, down to the column level

The most downstream layer, BI reports and dashboards, is the end products that data consumers use for their day-to-day work. This is important because data teams want to know the direct impact on the consumer-facing data products, so they know how to communicate with end users, i.e., "Hey finance analyst, don't use this number, it's outdated."

The most relevant upstream layer, the source table in the warehouse or lake, is leveraged when users trace the lineage layer by layer and find that one upstream layer with the table/field has a data quality issue. Once they find it, then they can fix the issue in that table/field and solve the problem.

To write the field-level lineage UI, you can create a reusable component using an open source framework like JavaScript or TypeScript to easily port the field lineage UI to other parts of your data platform. Since fields can potentially have tens of upstream or downstream tables, which in turn could have hundreds or thousands of fields, rendering all of those components without affecting the performance of the app is crucial. Using lightweight visualization frameworks like Apache Preset or React Virtuoso, a React framework makes it easy to visualize large data sets.

Currently, lineage should display at least two types of field relationships:

SELECT *clause lineage*
Field relationships defined by the SQL clause SELECT; these are field-to-field relationships where a change in an upstream field directly changes the downstream field.

*Non-*SELECT *lineage*
Field relationships defined by all other SQL clauses, e.g., WHERE; these are field-to-table relationships, where the downstream fields are often shaped by a filtering or ordering logic defined by upstream fields.

A chosen field's upstream non-SELECT lineage fields (as depicted via the query in Example 7-3) display as the filtering/ordering fields that result in the chosen field. Its downstream non-SELECT lineage fields are the resulting fields from the filtering/ordering logic defined by the chosen field.

Example 7-3. Lineage query that helps users understand table-to-field relationships

```
create or replace transient table
  analytics.prod_lineage.looker_explore_to_dashboard_edges as
  (with tile_with_upstream_explores as (
select
  a.account_id,
  a.resource_id,
  b.value::varchar as upstream_explore,
  a.name,
  a.metadata:dashboard:dashboard_id as dashboard_id
from analytics.prod_lineage.looker_dashboard_tile_nodes a,
  lateral flatten(input => a.extra:upstream_explores) as b
```

Like any agile development process, building field-level lineage is an exercise in prioritization, listening, and quick iteration. Here are some best practices when building lineage—or really, any other part of your data platform:

Listen to your teammates and take everyone's advice into consideration.
When we began to work with our team's own queryparser, we underestimated how challenging it would be to parse queries. One of our teammates had previous experience working with the parser, warned us of its quirks, and suggested we might build a different one to complete the task. If we had listened to our teammate early on, we would have saved a good chunk of time.

Invest in prototyping.
As startup founders, our customers are our north star. Whenever we create new product features, we take care to consider their opinions and preferences. Doing so effectively requires sharing a product prototype. To speed up the feedback cycle and make these interactions more useful for both parties, we shipped an early prototype to some of our most enthusiastic champions within weeks of development. While this first iteration was not perfect, it allowed us to demonstrate our commitment to meeting customer demands and gave us some early guidance as we further refined the product.

Ship and iterate.
This is a common practice in the software engineering world and something we take very seriously. Time is of the essence, and when we prioritize one project we have to ensure we are optimizing the time of everyone who is involved in that project. When we began working on this feature, we didn't have time to make our product "perfect" before showing our prototype to customers—and moving forward without perfection allowed us to expedite development. Our repeatable process included building out the functionality of the feature, showing it off to our customers, asking for feedback, then making improvements and/or changes where needed.

We predict that more and more data teams will start adopting automatic lineage and other knowledge graphs to identify the source of data quality issues as the market matures and data engineering teams look to increase efficiencies and reduce downtime.

In our next section, we highlight how a data leader at Fox, the global entertainment and media company, leverages lineage as part of a broader data observability solution to achieve DevOps processes at scale for this data organization.

Case Study: Architecting for Data Reliability at Fox

Companies are ingesting and storing an incredible amount of data—but not every organization knows how to realize its full value. Data often gets stuck in silos, with requests backing up in ticket queues that never reach overworked data engineers and analysts struggling to serve the needs of their entire organization.

As VP of Data Services at media giant Fox Networks, Alex Tverdohleb (*https:// oreil.ly/tQxhn*) has spent the last several years focusing on this problem. He intentionally built out the teams, the technology, and the trust necessary to give internal stakeholders across the digital organization the freedom to conduct ad hoc analytics without getting centralized data engineers and analysts involved. At least as much as this is possible.

As distributed architectures continue to become a new gold standard for data-driven organizations, this kind of self-serve motion would be a dream come true for many data leaders. So when we got the chance to sit down with Alex, we took a deep dive into how he made it happen. Figure 7-6 depicts how his team architected a hybrid data architecture that prioritizes democratization and access, while ensuring reliability and trust at every turn.

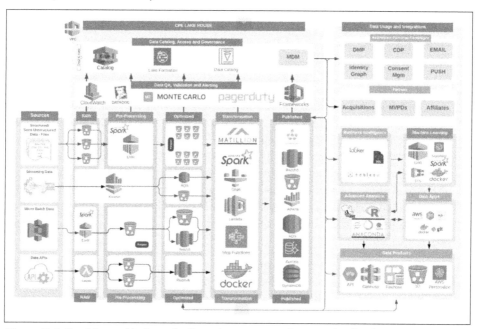

Figure 7-6. Fox Network's data platform incorporates dozens of technologies across even more data use cases. Source: Monte Carlo

Exercise "Controlled Freedom" When Dealing with Stakeholders

Alex has built decentralized access to data at Fox on a foundation he calls "controlled freedom." In fact, he believes using your data team as the single source of truth within an organization actually creates the biggest silo. So instead of becoming a guardian and bottleneck, Alex and his data team focus on setting certain parameters around how data is ingested and supplied to stakeholders. Within the framework, internal data consumers at Fox have the freedom to create and use data products as needed to meet their business goals.

"If you think about a centralized data reporting structure, where you used to come in, open a ticket, and wait for your turn, by the time you get an answer, it's often too late," Alex said. "Businesses are evolving and growing at a pace I've never seen before, and decisions are being made at a blazing speed. You have to have data at your fingertips to make the correct decision."

To accomplish this at scale, Alex and his centralized data team control a few key areas: how data is ingested, how data is kept secure, and how data is optimized in the best format to then be published to standard executive reports. When his team can ensure data sources are trustworthy, data is secure, and the company is using consistent metrics and definitions for high-level reporting, it gives data consumers the confidence to freely access and leverage data within that framework. Alex said:

> Everything else, especially within data discovery and your ad-hoc analytics, should be free. We give you the source of the data and guarantee it's trustworthy. We know that we're watching those pipelines multiple times every day, and we know that the data inside can be used for X, Y, and Z—so just go ahead and use it how you want. I believe this is the way forward: striving toward giving people trust in the data platforms while supplying them with the tools and skill sets they need to be self-sufficient.

Invest in a Decentralized Data Team

Under Alex's leadership, five teams oversee data for the Fox digital organization: data tagging and collections, data engineering, data analytics, data science, and data architecture. Each team has its own responsibilities, but everyone works together to solve problems for the entire business.

"I strongly believe in the fact that you have to engage the team in the decision-making process and have a collaborative approach," said Alex. "We don't have a single person leading architecture—it's a team chapter approach. The power of the company is, in essence, the data. But people are the power of that data. People are what makes that data available."

While members of different data teams collaborate to deliver value to the business, there's a clear delineation between analysts and engineers within the Fox data organization. Analysts sit close to the business units, understanding pain points and working to find and validate new data sources. This knowledge informs what Alex and his teams call an STM, or Source to Target Mapping—a spec that essentially allows engineers to operate from a well-defined playbook to build the pipelines and architecture necessary to support the data needs of the business. According to Alex:

[The division of labor between analysts and engineers] allows people to focus on their specific areas instead of being spread thin. Some people may disagree with me, but quite frankly, having developers attend a lot of business meetings can be a waste of their time—because collecting and understanding business requirements often is a strenuous and time-consuming effort. By installing the analytics before engineering gets involved, we can bridge that gap and then allow the developers to do what they do best—building the most reliable, resilient and optimized jobs.

By giving engineers a problem to solve as opposed to an analytics strategy to assemble, practitioners on Alex's team can stay focused and work on projects that support the goals of the business. When it comes to building your data stack, alignment is key.

 It's worth noting that this decentralized approach won't work for every organization, and the needs of your team structure will vary based on the SLAs your company sets for data.

Avoid Shiny New Toys in Favor of Problem-Solving Tech

Cumulatively, Barr, Lior, and Molly have been in data for half of a century, and we can say in no uncertain terms that Fox has one of the most robust and elegant data tech stacks that we've ever seen. But Alex is adamant that data leaders shouldn't pursue shiny new tech for its own sake.

"First and foremost, in order to be successful at delivering the right underlying architecture, you need to understand the business," said Alex. "Don't chase the latest and greatest technology, because then you're never going to stop. And sometimes the stack you have right now is good enough—all you have to do is optimize it."

The Fox data team built their tech stack to meet a specific need: enabling self-service analytics. "We embarked on the journey of adopting a lakehouse architecture because it would give us both the beauty and control of a data lake, as well as the cleanliness and structure of a data warehouse."

Several types of data flow into the Fox digital ecosystem, including batched, micro-batched, streaming, structured, and unstructured. After ingestion, data goes through what Alex refers to as a "three-layer cake":

First, we have the data exposed at its raw state, exactly how we ingest it. But that raw data is often not usable for people who want to do discovery and exploration. That's why we're building the optimized layer, where data gets sorted, sliced-and-diced, and optimized in different file formats for the speed of reading, writing, and usability. After that, when we know something needs to be defined as a data model or included in a data set, we engage in that within the publishing layer and then build it out for broader consumption within the company. Inside of the published layer, data can be exposed via our tool stack.

The optimized layer makes up the pool of data that Alex and his team provide to internal stakeholders under the "controlled freedom" model. With self-serve analytics, data users can discover and work with data assets that they already know are trustworthy and secure.

"If you don't approach your data from the angle that it's easy to discover, easy to search, and easy to observe, it becomes more like a swamp," said Alex. "We need to instill and enforce some formats and strict regulations to make sure the data is getting properly indexed and properly stored so that people can find and make sense of the data."

To Make Analytics Self-Serve, Invest in Data Trust

For this self-serve model to work, the organization needs to have trust that the data is accurate, reliable, and trustworthy. To help achieve this goal, the entire data stack is wrapped in QA, validation, and alerting—in other words, observability. "Data observability has become a necessity, not a luxury, for us," said Alex. "As the business has become more and more data driven, nothing is worse than allowing leadership to make a decision based upon data that you don't have trust in. That has tremendous costs and repercussions."

Alex estimates that the Fox digital organization receives data multiple times a day from over two hundred sources. They process nearly ten thousand schemas and tens of billions of records per week:

> You can't scale the team to maintain and support and validate and observe that amount of data. You have to have at least a few tools at your disposal. For us to make sure that we have trust in the data's timeliness, completeness, and cleanliness, tools like Monte Carlo are "must-have." It's been a great addition to allow us to build an AI-powered overview of what's happening in our data stack.

The continual monitoring and alerting (*https://oreil.ly/Y4PUz*), along with automated data lineage, helps Alex's team to be more proactive about data incidents when they do occur:

> We can catch the issues before they hit production and if they do, we know the level of impact by using reverse-engineering to see how many and what kind of objects have been involved, and we can stop it in-flight before it causes a massive impact downstream. It all comes with trust—the moment you drop transparency or start hiding things, people lose trust and it's really hard to regain it back. I've learned that no matter what happens, if you're being honest and you're owning the problem, people tend to understand and give you another chance to fix it.

By keeping open lines of communication and being transparent about data health, Alex and his teams have earned the trust required to build a self-serve data platform that powers decisions on a daily basis.

Summary

In this chapter, we discussed what it takes to build more reliable data workflows, zeroing in on one of the key technologies: lineage. As you work toward more reliable data, it's hard to understand where you're going if you don't know where you're starting from. Data lineage is the "map" of your data that tells you just that, no matter what stage of the data pipeline is affected by data downtime. When automated and providing end-to-end coverage (which, we'll admit, isn't easy to achieve), lineage is even more powerful.

Combined with detection and alerting, lineage forms the basis of true data reliability and is an increasingly critical part of modern data stacks. Still, it doesn't matter how advanced your lineage is if it's not scalable and easily understood by data analysts, data scientists, and other stakeholders in your organization. This accessibility allows you to give consumers a level of "controlled freedom" that turns data quality from a siloed entity scattered among few visibility tables to something actually achievable on a wide plane.

In our next chapter, we'll dive deeper into some of the processes and techniques leading data organizations are adopting to democratize data quality across their organizations.

CHAPTER 8

Democratizing Data Quality

"Hey—is this good data?"

"Can I trust this dashboard?"

"Who owns this data set?"

If you've heard these questions—and many others like them—from business analysts and other data consumers at your company, congratulations! The onus of data trust falls on your shoulders.

As companies ingest more and more data and analytics becomes part and parcel of every organizational strategy, the need for high-quality data only increases, putting pressure on data engineers, analytics engineers, and even data analysts to take ownership of this important, but challenging task.

Still, it doesn't matter how many data quality tests you run—data trust can only be achieved when the entire company buys into it. Despite the data-driven nature of nearly all teams, data organizations often shoulder the brunt of the work when it comes to tracking, enforcing, and scaling data quality initiatives.

After all, data quality isn't just about building more reliable data pipelines and setting service-level agreements (SLAs) for data freshness. It's also about education and communication. In fact, data quality is just as much a technical process as it is a cultural one. And very often, it's not about having fully accurate data—it's about understanding to what extent we can trust it.

In an interview with the authors, Cindi Howson, Chief Data Strategy Officer at ThoughtSpot and former VP at Gartner, summarized it best:

> You build trust when people understand where the data comes from, and when they understand that even high-quality data will never be perfectly clean. I like how one of our data analytics leaders talks about "Is the data directionally accurate—accurate

enough to make decisions on it?' Now there are some things that have to be perfect. You have to get your blood type right, for instance. But if I'm looking at campaign analytics and customer experience trends, we can make decisions with accurate-enough data.

When it comes to democratizing data quality, it helps to make working with data as easy and iterative as possible, much in the same way as software engineers work with code.

As previously discussed, DevOps and software engineering teams have been applying this "agile" approach to building applications for several years. To really give data quality the diligence it deserves, we can learn a thing or two from these processes and systems. The first step? Treating your data with the same diligence as production software.

Treating Your "Data" Like a Product

For the past few decades, most companies have kept data in an organizational silo. Analytics teams served business units, and even as data became more crucial to decision making and product roadmaps, the teams in charge of data pipelines were treated more like plumbers and less like partners.

Data is no longer a second-class citizen. With better tooling, more diverse roles, and a clearer understanding of data's full potential, many businesses have come to view the entire ecosystem as a fully formed element of the company tech stack.

And the most forward-thinking teams are adopting a new paradigm: treating data like a product. This is a hot topic in the data community right now, and in recent months, we've had the privilege of discussing data-as-a-product with several industry leaders—and uncovering their real-world takeaways on what it looks like to bring this new approach to life on a daily basis.

But defining a data product is surprisingly difficult. The truth is, many things can be considered a data product, from a Looker dashboard or Tableau report, to an A/B testing platform or even a multilayered data platform (*https://oreil.ly/h7vmF*).

So let's get specific. Regardless of what data the product visualizes / crunches / puts to work, there are specific outcomes it should *deliver*:

- Increased data accessibility (surface data where people need it when they need it)
- Increased data democratization (make it easier for people to manipulate the data)
- Faster ROI on data (quicker insights)
- Time savings for the data team / data consumers
- More precise insights (i.e., experimentation platforms)

Similarly, there are important characteristics or qualities a data product should have:

Reliability and observability
Acceptable downtime for a SaaS product is a discussion of "How many 9s?" as in 99.9% or 99.999% availability. Just as software engineers use products such as Datadog or New Relic to track SaaS product performance, data product managers need solutions to identify and solve data product performance issues in near real time.

Scalability
The data product should scale elasticity as the organization and demand grow.

Extensibility
While the data product has likely been built from an integration of different solutions, it needs to maintain the ability to easily integrate with APIs and be versatile enough to be ingested in all the different ways end users like to consume data.

Usability
Great SaaS products focus on providing a great user experience. They are easy to learn, fun to use, and quick to get work done.

Security and compliance
Data leaks are costly and painful, as are regulatory fines.

Release discipline and roadmap
SaaS products continually evolve and improve. Roadmaps are built at least a year into the future with a strong quality assurance process for updates.

In the next section, we share how some of today's most innovative data leaders describe what it means to "treat data like a product."

Perspectives on Treating Data Like a Product

In the early 2000s, companies like LinkedIn, Netflix, and Uber had a problem. Teams across the organization were working with data, and lots of it, at scale. Data was powering their product roadmap, fueling executive-level decision making, and informing their paid marketing campaigns.

Internal and external data was flowing in and out of the company. There were regulations, guidelines, and restrictions for how this data could be used and by whom. But nobody was in charge of developing data solutions to make analytics operational, scalable, and accessible.

A new generation of data engineers, technical architects, managers, and even directors has started applying best practices of software engineering and site reliability to data systems, learning a few lessons along the way. As described in the following sections, we spoke with data leaders at companies of various industries and sizes, including Convoy and Uber. While working with vastly different volumes and types of data, these three companies have one critical thing in common: data quality is a topline priority, and the means to this end, by and large, starts with treating data like a product.

Convoy Case Study: Data as a Service or Output

Until recently, disparate operational and analytical data was often managed in silos, with functional teams and associated analysts responsible for ensuring quality, availability, and performance. As data sharing and more distributed architectures like the data fabric or data mesh come to prominence, processes and workflows that treat data like an evolving, cross-disciplinary entity will become the industry standard.

At Convoy, a Seattle-based freight marketplace, data is treated like a product in two discrete ways: as a service or an output. We talked to Head of Product, Data Platform, Chad Sanderson, and he suggested that:

> There are two schools of thought that are still developing around what it means to treat data as a product: in the first, you have an external or internal product or service that generates data, meaning that the data—including the entire pipeline—is part of the product. In the second approach, you think of the output of any codebase that's serving a customer as a product.

Chad suggests that in the first scenario, data must be subject to the same level of rigor as application code. Generally speaking, this product is a service, whether that service deploys ML models, queries the warehouse to gather insights, or something else entirely.

In the second approach, data teams treat the output of the data (a report, dashboard, a platform, etc.) as a product. Chad uses the data warehouse as an example: "When you think about a data warehouse, it's really just a codebase—primarily composed of SQL—that's serving internal customers like other analysts, data scientists, and product managers who are using that data to go and make business decisions."

Anything that's pushed to a "production data environment" that the company can access is a product. So if you're using a dashboarding tool like Mode or Metabase, and you're writing SQL and pushing that dashboard to a public environment where other people can access it, that is also a product.

In both scenarios, data is less of a siloed entity and more of a microservice, with discrete business functions leveraging the same data across multiple use cases, and more consumers beyond the data team actually accessing the data. Moreover, the data is often being applied to use cases outside corporate decision making: powering financial products, surfacing relevant advertisements to users, and even generating lists upon lists of movies and TV shows to watch online.

In either case, Chad says, teams need good data testing, clear SLAs, SLIs, and SLOs, and extensive documentation and monitoring. In other words, data should be expected to be reliable, and if it's not, data teams and stakeholders should know and be given the tools to fix the issue at hand.

We couldn't agree more.

Uber Case Study: The Rise of the Data Product Manager

Since its inception in 2009 as Ubercab, Uber, the global ridesharing company, has prioritized data as a competitive advantage and means of building more reliable and custom-tailored experiences for their users. Like LinkedIn, Netflix, Google, and other Silicon Valley giants, Uber employs a team of thousands to manage their data and analytics operations, from data scientists building real-time pricing models to operations analysts putting together forecasts to predict driver demand.

To truly operationalize data at scale, Uber needed to treat data not like a discrete set of services for a discrete set of use cases but instead like production software that can be leveraged by multiple teams at the company. At a traditional software company, software solutions are managed from ideation to fruition by product managers. If data needs to be given the same attention as reliability, fulfilling multiple use cases at once, and as accessibility, does it need a product manager, too?

For Uber, the answer was yes. According to Atul Gupte, a former data product manager at the company (*https://oreil.ly/FxuCb*), data product managers were responsible for data democratization and increasing the time to value for the data itself. They design, build, and manage the cross-functional development of a data platform, or a suite of specific data tools, to serve multiple customers.

At Uber, the data product manager was a role solely dedicated to answering questions like:

- What data exists?
- Who needs this data?
- Where is this data flowing to/from?
- What purpose does this data serve?
- Is there a way to make it easier to work with/access this data?
- Is this data compliant and/or actionable?
- How can we make data more useful to more people at the company, faster?

Data product managers answer these questions by building internal tooling and platforms for employees.

Like a product management role, data product managers are beholden to the needs of their stakeholders (data analysts, data scientists, and operations teams, to name a few) and executives. Their primary purpose is to ensure that the preceding questions are answered, and as a result, reliable, fresh, and usable data is generated and delivered to those who need it.

Because the role is nascent, data product managers like Atul usually come from backgrounds like traditional B2B product management, internal tooling product management, data analysis, or backend engineering.

Applying the Data-as-a-Product Approach

From our conversations with these leaders and several others, we've identified five key ways modern data teams can apply this approach to their own organizations.

Gain stakeholder alignment early—and often

When data is your product, your internal customers are also your stakeholders. Make it a priority to partner with your key data consumers as you map out your own data product roadmap, develop SLAs, and begin treating data as a product.

This means putting on your product manager hat—or, as Atul suggested earlier, having a role dedicated to data product management—to fully understand the needs, concerns, and motivations of your internal customers. You'll want to have a clear grasp on who uses your data and how, and for what purposes. This will help you understand what types of data products you need to build to meet those needs.

This understanding also helps you adopt data storytelling. Software, product, and UX teams use storytelling to share the context of their work through different perspectives that will help stakeholders understand its value based on what matters most to them. You'll also be working to convince your stakeholders that data should be prioritized and to justify the investments required to treat data as a product.

Data storytelling is an invaluable tool when it comes to persuading stakeholders to invest in data infrastructure over flashier machine learning models or new features that promise to generate millions of dollars. By clearly communicating the "So what?" behind why the given data initiative will further business goals—and in turn, your company's bottom line—it can be easier to justify budget, headcount, and resources, including those allocated to data quality.

For years, the connection between data quality and revenue wasn't always obvious. Data was managed in silos, and stakeholders accepted what little data they had access to; while the seasoned eye could probably tell if data was wrong or inaccurate, it was often a blurry line, eroding trust in the data itself. As technologies advanced and more employees across the enterprise became data literate, the appetite for data increased, as did the onus on data quality.

Necessity is the mother of invention; as data needs grow, so do the ways in which we justify spending behind it. For example, sharing a tight narrative about how data reliability can lead to more accurate machine learning models that forecast revenue is a more compelling story than "data quality is good for the business."

Apply a product management mindset

Another key step is to apply a product management mindset to how you build, monitor, and measure data products. When it comes to building pipelines and systems, use the same proven processes as you would with production software, like creating scope documents and breaking projects down into sprints.

In our interview with Jessica Cherny, Lead Data Analyst at Ironclad, she described her company's agile-inspired workflow:

> We're treating data internally as a product, and that means applying product management principles to data and the data team. So when we have a big strategic project that requires data, we create data scoping documents, just like a product manager would create a spec, with the right stakeholders. And we keep iterating with engineers and the product managers to make sure it's a cross-functional, stakeholder-aligned output—as opposed to just having data people working in a silo and not interacting with anyone.

And similar to engineering processes, data teams should be factoring in scalability and future use cases when building pipelines. According to Chad, this can represent a significant shift from how data teams have approached their work in the past:

> Oftentimes, the data that actually lands in a production database is really just service-level events that get thrown in by engineers without really thinking about it. So one of the big reasons why data models get so messy as a company evolves is that we're usually focused on rapidly building services first and thinking critically about data second. And this idea of data as a product is kind of a continuum shift to start to change that.

Kyle Shannon, Senior Data and Analytics Engineer at SeatGeek, shared in the same webinar (*https://oreil.ly/YpV7U*) that his company is focusing on scalability due to the rapid growth of their data team:

> We're really trying to understand how we can better onboard new people coming in and making better processes to make data more discoverable and accessible. People that have been at a company for a long time know where to go to find information, but if you're hiring 20 or 30 data team members over the year, it's really hard to say, "Oh, just go into the Slack channels and ask questions." It's not going to scale. So as you are building your data products, you have to document everything and make sure it's very clear—that you're removing redundancies or any issues you might find along the way.

Another product mindset to adopt is setting up KPIs aligned with your business goals before you begin building any new data product. As Chad described earlier, storytelling can help illustrate the potential benefits of investments in data quality, but most organizations will still expect mature teams to measure the financial impact of their initiatives.

Many data teams are adopting KPIs related to data quality, such as calculating the cost of data downtime—times when data is partial, erroneous, missing, or otherwise inaccurate—or by measuring the amount of time data team members spend troubleshooting or fixing data quality issues, rather than focusing on innovations or building new data products.

Setting baseline metrics for your data will help quantify the impact of your data initiatives over time. Just ensure these metrics are applied consistently across use cases, particularly if you have a central data platform.

Invest in self-serve tooling

In order for data to be brought out of silos and treated as a valued product in its own right, business users need to have the ability to self-serve and meet their own data needs. Self-serve tooling that empowers nontechnical teams to access data allows your data team to focus on innovative projects that add value, rather than functioning as an on-demand service to fulfill ad hoc requests.

Self-serve tooling is also one of the main principles of the data mesh concept—a new approach to decentralized data architecture. Mammad Zadeh, the former VP of Engineering at Intuit for their Data Platform team, is an enthusiastic advocate of the data mesh and believes self-serve tooling is integral to data architecture and data products. To measure the impact of their self-serve approach, the team even implemented a metric that assesses whether a specific self-serve tool has reduced the time it takes a user to complete a task, such as data discovery or access.

In our discussion with Mammad, he suggested, "We, in the central data teams, should make sure the right self-serve infrastructure and tooling is available to both producers and consumers of data so that they can do their jobs easily. Equip them with the right tools, let them interact directly, and get out of the way."

Prioritize data quality and reliability

One key component of approaching data as a product is applying standards of rigor to the entire ecosystem, from ingestion to consumer-facing data deliverables. As we discussed in the context of storytelling earlier, this means prioritizing data quality and reliability throughout the data life cycle. Companies can assess their current state of data quality by mapping their progress against the data reliability maturity curve (*https://oreil.ly/CsX3x*). Briefly, this model (see Figure 8-1) suggests there are four main stages of data reliability:

Reactive

Teams spend a majority of their time responding to fire drills and triaging data issues—resulting in a lack of progress on important initiatives, an organizational struggle to use data effectively in their product, machine learning algorithms, or business decision making.

Proactive

Teams collaborate actively between engineering, data engineering, data analysts, and data scientists to develop manual checks and custom QA queries to validate their work. Examples might include validating row counts in critical stages of the pipelines or tracking timestamps to ensure data freshness. Slack messages or email alerts still pop up when things go wrong, but these teams do catch many issues through their proactive testing.

Automated

At this level, teams prioritize reliable, accurate data through scheduled validation queries that deliver broader coverage of pipelines. Teams use data health dashboards to view issues, troubleshoot, and provide status updates to others in the organization. Examples include tracking and storing metrics about dimensions and measures to observe trends and changes, or monitoring and enforcing schema at the ingestion stage.

Scalable

These teams draw on proven DevOps concepts to institute a staging environment, reusable components for validation, and/or hard and soft alerts for data errors. With substantial coverage of mission-critical data, the team can resolve most issues before they impact downstream users. Examples include anomaly detection across all key metrics and tooling that allows every job and table to be monitored and tracked for quality.

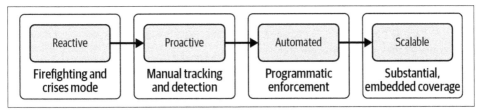

Figure 8-1. The data reliability maturity curve buckets common approaches to data quality in four distinct camps: reactive, proactive, automated, and scalable

Find the right team structure for your data organization

Of course, team structure makes a huge impact on how your organization interacts with data on a daily basis. Do you have a centralized data team that handles every aspect of data management and application? Or analysts embedded across business units, meeting specific needs and gaining domain expertise—but suffering from silos and lack of cohesive governance?

Different companies will require distinct approaches depending on their size and business needs, but many data leaders we've talked to have found the best outcomes with a hub and spoke model. In this structure, a centralized data platform team handles infrastructure and data quality, while decentralized, embedded analysts and engineers deal with semantic layers and apply data to the business. This model works well if your organization is growing fast and needs to move quickly, but it can lead to duplication and repeated efforts on the embedded analysts' part without solid alignment with the centralized data team.

Greg Waldman, Senior Director of Business Intelligence at restaurant POS software Toast, led his team through a five-year organizational evolution that included switches from centralized to decentralized to hub and spoke models. In our discussions with Greg, he advised data leaders at growth companies to follow a key tenet of product management—stay agile:

> The way I think about data teams, in a nutshell, is that you want everyone to add as much business value as possible. We've been very open to change and trying different things and understanding that what works with 200 people versus 500 people versus a thousand is not the same answer, and that's okay. It can be somewhat obvious when you've reached those inflection points and need to try something new.

For Jessica Cherny, the advantage of decentralized analysts and engineers is their ability to understand the real business need behind data requests:

> I want to understand how to design a deliverable that actually serves their needs. It happened recently when I was asked by someone on a strategic initiative to get a specific set of data right away. And I was able to say, "Wait, hold on. Do I really need to use this complex clustering method to answer this question? What is the actual need for this—so I don't have to drop everything I'm working on, and can actually serve you in a timely and useful way?" And we ended up completely reorganizing what her ask was, because I got to better understand the business need behind her question and how to answer that in a simple, easily understood way.

Again, every company will have its own cultural landscape and challenges to address, but a hub and spoke model can help growing teams move fast to meet business needs without giving up ownership of data quality and governance.

Treating data like a product isn't just a buzzworthy trend. It's an intentional shift in mindset that leads to meaningful outcomes: increasing data democratization and the ability to self-serve, improving data quality so decisions can be made accurately and confidently, and scaling the overall impact of data throughout the organization.

Building Trust in Your Data Platform

Now that we have a better understanding of what it means to treat data like a product, how do we actually implement this approach in practice?

In Chapter 2, we discussed what it takes to build a data platform, but how can we set the groundwork in place to ensure that (1) your team uses it and (2) stakeholders trust its outputs? In other words, how can we ensure they treat your data platform like a product? Whether you're just getting started or are in the process of scaling your platform, the following best practices will help you avoid common pitfalls while building trust in your data platform.

Align Your Product's Goals with the Goals of the Business

For several decades, data platforms were viewed as a means to an end versus "the end," as in, the core product you're building. In fact, although data platforms powered many services, fueling rich insights into the applications that power our lives, they weren't given the respect and attention they truly deserve until very recently.

When you're building or scaling your data platform, the first question you should ask is: *how does data map to your company's goals?* To answer this question, you have to put on your data platform product manager hat. Unlike specific product managers, a data platform product manager must understand the big picture versus area-specific goals since data feeds into the needs of every other functional team, from marketing and recruiting to business development and sales.

For instance, if your business's goal is to increase revenue (go big or go home!), how does data help you achieve these goals? For the sake of this experiment, consider the following questions:

- What services or products drive revenue growth?
- What data do these services or products collect?
- What do we need to do with the data before we can use it?
- Which teams need this data? What will they do with it?
- Who will have access to this data or the analytics it generates?
- How quickly do these users need access to this data?
- What, if any, compliance or governance checks does the platform need to address?

By answering these questions, you'll have a better understanding of how to prioritize your product roadmap, as well as who you need to build for (often, the engineers) versus design for (the day-to-day platform users, including analysts). Moreover, this holistic approach to KPI development and execution strategy sets your platform up for a more scalable impact across teams.

Gain Feedback and Buy-in from the Right Stakeholders

It goes without saying that receiving buy-in up front and getting iterative feedback throughout the product development process are necessary components of the data platform journey. What isn't as widely understood is whose voice you should care about.

Yes, you need the ultimate sign-off from your CTO or VP of Data on the finished product, but their decisions are often informed by their trusted advisors: staff engineers, technical program managers, and other day-to-day data practitioners. While developing a new data cataloging system for her company, one product manager we spoke with at a leading transportation company spent three months trying to sell her VP of Engineering on her team's idea, only to be shut down in a single email by his chief of staff.

Consider different tactics based on the DNA of your company. We suggest following these three concurrent steps:

1. Sell leadership on the vision.
2. Sell the brass tacks and day-to-day use case to your actual users.
3. Apply a customer-centric approach, no matter who you're talking to. Position the platform as a means of empowering different types of personas in your data ecosystem, including both your data team (data engineers, data scientists, analysts, and researchers) and data consumers (program managers, executives, business development, and sales, to name a few categories).

A great data platform will enable the technical users to do their work easily and efficiently, while also allowing less technical personas to leverage rich insights or put together visualizations based on data without much assistance from engineers and analysts.

There are a variety of data personas (Figure 8-2) you have to consider when you're building a data platform for your company, from engineers to data scientists, product managers, business function users, and general managers.

At the end of the day, it's important that this experience nurtures a community of data enthusiasts that build, share, and learn together. Since your platform has the potential to serve the entire company, everyone should feel invested in its success, even if that means making some compromises along the way.

Figure 8-2. When you're gaining buy-in to build your data platform—or simply scaling it—it helps to have input from core users and stakeholders across the company. Source: Image courtesy of Atul Gupte

Prioritize Long-Term Growth and Sustainability Versus Short-Term Gains

Unlike other types of products, data platforms are not successful simply because they benefit from being "first to market." Since data platforms are almost exclusively internal tools, we've found that the best data platforms are built with sustainability in mind versus feature-specific wins.

Remember: your customer is your company, and your company's success is your success. This is not to say that your roadmap won't change several times over (it will), but when you do make changes, do it with growth and maturation in mind.

For instance, Uber's big data platform (*https://oreil.ly/Cb5AG*) was built over the course of five years, constantly evolving with the needs of the business; Pinterest (*https://oreil.ly/Rh9QV*) has gone through several iterations of their core data analytics product; and leading the pack, LinkedIn (*https://oreil.ly/UFXhk*) has been building and iterating on its data platform since 2008!

Our suggestion: choose solutions that make sense in the context of your organization over time (Figure 8-3) and align your plan with these expectations and deadlines. Data solutions with short-term usability in mind are often easier to get off the ground but, over time, end up being more costly than platforms built with sustainability in mind. Sometimes, quick wins as part of a larger product development strategy can help with achieving internal buy-in—as long as it's not shortsighted. Rome wasn't built in a day, and neither was your data platform.

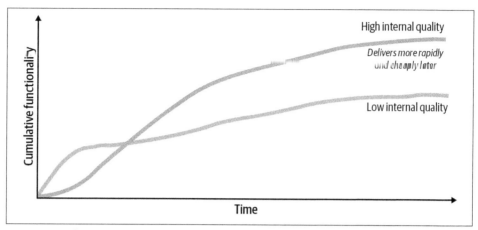

Figure 8-3. Short-term usability often comes at the expense of sustainability over time

Sign Off on Baseline Metrics for Your Data and How You Measure Them

It doesn't matter how great your data platform is if you can't trust your data, but data quality means different things to different stakeholders. Consequently, your data platform won't be successful if you and your stakeholders aren't aligned on this definition.

To address this, it's important to set baseline expectations for your data reliability, in other words, your organization's ability to deliver high data availability and health throughout the entire data life cycle. Setting clear service-level objectives (SLOs) and service-level indicators (SLIs) for software application reliability is a no-brainer. Data teams should do the same for their data pipelines.

This isn't to say that different stakeholders will have the same vision for what "good data" looks like; in fact, they probably won't, and that's OK. Instead of fitting square pegs into round holes, it's important to create a baseline metric of data reliability and, as with building a new platform feature, gain sign-off on the lowest common denominator.

We suggest choosing a novel measurement like specific SLAs for hours of data downtime (as discussed in Chapter 6) or number of data quality issues per week that will help data practitioners across the company align on baseline quality metrics.

Know When to Build Versus Buy

One of the first decisions you have to make is whether or not to build the platform from scratch or purchase the technology (or several supporting technologies) from a vendor.

While companies like—you guessed it—Uber, LinkedIn, and Facebook have opted to build their own data platforms, often on top of open source solutions, it doesn't always make sense for your needs. While there isn't a magic formula that will tell you whether to build versus buy, we've found that there is value in buying until you're convinced that:

- The product needs to operate using sensitive/classified information (e.g., financial or health records) that cannot be shared with external vendors for regulatory reasons.

- Specific customizations are required for it to work well with other internal tools/systems and are niche enough that a vendor may not prioritize them.

- There is some other strategic value to building versus buying (i.e., competitive advantage for the business or beneficial for hiring talent).

For larger, more universal technical challenges (i.e., data warehouses, lakes, or data visualization tools), it often makes more sense to buy. When it comes to solving niche but critical problems for the business (for instance, aggregating GPS data on highways), you'll probably need to build it.

The good news for data teams? Data engineering is going through a renaissance reminiscent of software engineering's rise to prominence in the early 2010s, meaning greater innovation and investment in tools that solve more complex and granular needs. (Reverse ETL, data science workbooks, behavioral analytics, and even ML feature stores come to mind as formerly niche technologies that are gaining widespread adoption. We discussed these tools and others in Chapter 7).

Building your data platform as a product will help you ensure greater consensus around data priorities, standardize on data quality and other key KPIs, foster greater collaboration, and, as a result, bring value to your company.

In addition to serving as a vehicle for effective data management, reliability, and democratization, the benefits of building a data platform as a product include:

- Guiding sales efforts (giving you insights on where to focus your efforts based on how prospective customers are responding)

- Driving application product roadmaps

- Improving the customer experience (helps teams learn what your service pain points are, what's working, and what's not)

- Standardizing data governance and compliance measures across the company (General Data Protection Regulation [GDPR], California Consumer Privacy Act [CCPA], etc.)

Building a data platform might seem overwhelming, but with the right approach to ensuring and scaling data quality, your solution has the potential to become a force multiplier for your entire organization.

Now that we've highlighted the "what" for building a data quality-first culture, it's only fitting to discuss the "who." Next, we dive into some of the data personas responsible for ensuring data quality at the cross-functional level and share best practices for assigning ownership along the way.

Assigning Ownership for Data Quality

In the modern data organization, there are so many answers to the question of ownership of data quality, and it really varies depending on the size of the company and the needs of the business. While many data professionals are quick to assign blame when data quality issues arise and data downtime strikes, few are set up for success when it comes to resolving the issues and communicating the impact downstream.

In data, this growing sphere of impact is often called the blast radius (as shown in Figure 8-4) and refers to the extent of downtime experienced by downstream stakeholders when data breaks. Across your organization, there are several stakeholders involved when data breaks, from your chief data officer to your resident data engineer. Data downtime affects everyone that relies on data and analytics at your company, with the impact of poor data quality only growing as data migrates down the pipeline.

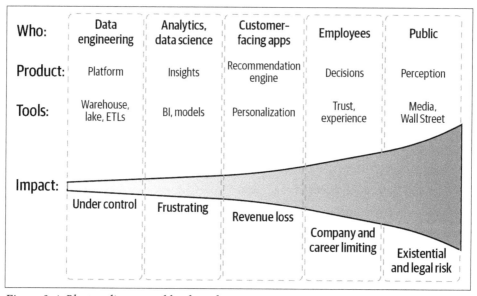

Figure 8-4. Blast radius caused by data downtime

We'll walk you through what data reliability looks like to a fictional data organization and highlight key roles when it comes to ensuring data quality for the rest of the company. We'll introduce these roles, zero in on their hopes, dreams, and fears, and share our approach to conquering data reliability at your company.

Chief Data Officer

Meet Ophelia, your CDO. Although she's probably not (wo)manning your company's data pipelines or Looker dashboards, Ophelia's impact is tied to the consistency, accuracy, relevance, interpretability, and reliability of the data her team provides.

Ophelia wakes up every day and asks herself two things. First, are different departments getting the data they need to be effective? And second, are we managing risk around that data effectively?

She would sleep much easier with a clear, bird's-eye view showing that her data ecosystem is operating as it should. At the end of the day, if bad data gets in front of the CEO, out to the public, or to any other data consumer, she's on the line.

Business Intelligence Analyst

Betty, the business intelligence lead or data analyst, wants a punchy and insightful dashboard she can share with her stakeholders in marketing, sales, and operations to answer their multifarious questions about how their business functions are performing. When things go wrong at the practitioner level, Betty is the first one called.

To ensure reliable data, she needs to answer these questions:

- Are we translating data into metrics and insights that are meaningful to the business?
- Are we confident that the data is reliable and means what we think it means?
- Is it easy for others to access and understand these insights?

Null values and duplicated entries are Betty's archnemeses, and she's a fan of anything that can prevent data downtime from compromising her peace of mind. She's fatigued by business stakeholders that ask her to investigate a funny value in a report—it's a long process to chase the data upstream and validate if it's right!

Analytics Engineer

Meet Anna, the analytics engineer. She sits at the intersection of business teams, data analytics, and data engineering, and is primarily responsible for ensuring that stakeholders can access and use the data required for their specific needs. Anna is fluent in dbt, the data build tool, and prides herself on being able to model her way out of nearly anything.

That is, until an errant schema change causes her transformations to nosedive. When downtime strikes, Anna is on the hook for explaining why and how the data broke, often partnering with the data engineering and data platform teams to get to the root cause. As a result, data observability is her best friend.

Data Scientist

Sam, the data scientist, studied Forestry in undergrad, but decided to make the jump to industry to pay off his student loans. Somewhere between a line of Python code and a data visualization, he fell in love with data science. And the rest was history.

To do his job well, Sam needs to know (1) where the data comes from and (2) that it's reliable, because if it's not, his team's A/B tests won't work and all downstream consumers (analysts, managers, executives, and customers) will suffer. Sam's team spends roughly 80% of their time scrubbing, cleaning, and understanding the context of the data, so they need tools and solutions that can make their lives easier.

Data Governance Lead

Proud owner of a seven-month-old puppy, Gerald is the company's very first data governance specialist. He started off on the legal team, and then, when GDPR and CCPA entered the picture, eventually focused his efforts exclusively on data compliance. It's a novel role that is becoming increasingly important as the organization grows.

When it comes to data reliability, Gerald cares about (1) unified definitions of data and metrics across the company and (2) understanding who has access and visibility to what data. For Gerald, bad data can mean costly fines, erosion of customer trust, and lawsuits. Despite the criticality of his role, he sometimes jests that it's like accounting: "You're only front and center if something has gone wrong!"

Data Engineer

When it comes to data reliability, Emerson, the data engineer, is at the crux of the equation. Emerson started out as a full-stack developer at a small ecommerce startup, but then as the company grew, so too did their data needs. Before she knew it, she was responsible not just for building their data product but also integrating the data sources the team relies on to make decisions about the business. Now, she's a Snowflake expert, PowerBI guru, and general data tooling whiz.

Emerson and her team are the glue that holds the company's data ecosystem together. They implement technologies that monitor the reliability of their company's data, and if something goes awry, she's the one who is paged by the analytics team at 3 a.m. to fix it. Like Betty, she's lost countless hours of sleep because of this.

To be successful at her job, Emerson must tackle a lot of things, including:

- Designing a data platform solution that scales
- Ensuring that data ingestion is reliable
- Making the platform accessible to other teams
- Being able to fix data downtime quickly when it happens
- Above all else, making analytics sustainable for the entire data organization

Data Product Manager

Meet Peter, the data product manager. Peter got his start as a backend developer but made the jump to product management a few years ago. Like Gerald, he's the company's first-ever hire in this role, which is simultaneously exciting and challenging.

He's up-to-date on all the latest data engineering and data analytics solutions, and is often called upon to make decisions on what offerings his organization needs to invest in to be successful. He knows firsthand how automation and self-serve tooling make all the difference when it comes to delivering an accessible, scalable data product.

All other data stakeholders, from analysts to social media managers, are dependent on him for building a platform that ingests, unifies, and makes accessible data from a myriad of sources to consumers all over the business. Oh, and did we mention that this data must be compliant with GDPR, CCPA, and other industry regulations? It's a challenging role and it's difficult to keep everyone happy—it seems like his platform is always one transformation away from what BI *actually* wanted.

Who Is Responsible for Data Reliability?

So, who in your data organization owns the reliability piece of your data ecosystem?

As you can imagine, the answer isn't simple. From your company's CDO to your data engineers, it's ultimately everyone's responsibility to ensure data reliability. And although nearly every arm of every organization at every company relies on data, not every data team has the same structure, and various industries have different requirements. For instance, it's the norm for financial institutions to hire entire teams of data governance experts, but at a small startup, not so much. And for those startups that do—we commend you!

In Table 8-1, we outline our approach to mapping data responsibilities, from accessibility to reliability, across your data organization using the RACI (Responsible, Accountable, Consulted, and Informed) matrix guidelines (*https://oreil.ly/waboH*). The RACI matrix for data personas offers a clear way of understanding who owns what in the modern data organization.

Table 8-1. RACI matrix for ownership in a modern data organization

	CDO	Business Intelligence	Analytics Engineer	Data Science	Data Engineering	Data Governance	Product Manager
Facilitate Data Accessibility	A[a]	R	A	C	R	C	R
Make It Easy to Interpret Data	A	R	C	R	C	I	C
Drive Insights and Recommendations Based on Data	A	R	R	R	C	C	C
Ensure Data Compliance	A	I	I	I	I	R	C
Maintain High Data Quality	A	C/I	A	R	R	C	R
Deliver on Data Reliability	A	C/I	R	C	R	I	R

[a] R = Responsible, A = Accountable, C = Consulted, and I = Informed

At companies that ingest and transform terabytes of data—like Netflix (*https://oreil.ly/7kuDl*) or Uber (*https://oreil.ly/oG0pW*)—we've found that it's common for data engineers and data product managers to tackle the responsibility of monitoring and alerting for data reliability issues. Barring these behemoths, the responsibility often falls on data engineers and product managers. They must balance the organization's demand for data with what can be provided reliably.

Notably, the brunt of any bad choices made here is often borne by the BI analysts, whose dashboards may wind up containing bad information or break from uncommunicated changes. In very early data organizations, these roles are often combined into a jack-of-all-trades data person or a product manager.

Creating Accountability for Data Quality

Say it with me: data engineers are not data catalogs. You would be hard pressed to find "answering multiple Slack messages every week about which tables are good to use for this report," in their job description, but it happens nonetheless. Data analysts aren't psychic. Yet, they are often placed in the position of having to intuit if the data being piped is trustworthy. This misalignment has arisen as data teams are pushed to move faster, weave themselves across the data mesh (*https://oreil.ly/446YT*), and enable increasingly self-service data platforms.

It's the data team's equivalent of the classic document version control issues that have plagued knowledge workers for decades. What starts as a tight pitch deck evolves into:

- A million people making and sharing ad hoc slides
- Massaging content on those slides until it becomes an echo of its original intent
- Creating copies labeled *V6_Final_RealFinal*

The same thing happens across the data team. Everyone is trying to do the right thing (i.e., support your stakeholders, generate insights, pipe more data, etc.), but everyone is also moving fast. One day you look up and notice you have six different models with slight variations essentially doing the same thing, and no one knows which one is most up-to-date or even which field to use.

This creates real operational problems downstream including:

- Inefficient cycles of redundant "traffic control"
- Lower data quality
- Time spent resolving problems created from analysts using improper/problematic data
- Lower data trust across the organization
- Increased data downtime

When you don't trust your data or you have lower data reliability, organizations often pad the margins of error in their forecasts. As highlighted by Peleton's recent production halt (*https://oreil.ly/0EnK1*), poor forecasting can be especially problematic during a pandemic when uncertainty across demand, supply chains and the overall business environment is at an all-time high.

Balancing Data Accessibility with Trust

As discussed in Chapter 2, data discovery is a new and important approach to understanding the health of your distributed data assets in real time, and it's an essential part of the modern data stack. Data discovery (depicted in Figure 8-5) provides a domain-specific, dynamic understanding of your data based on how it's being ingested, stored, aggregated, and used by a set of specific consumers. It can replace the modern data catalog by providing distributed, real-time insights about data across different domains, all while abiding by a central set of governance standards.

As with a data catalog, governance standards and tooling are federated across these domains (allowing for greater accessibility and interoperability), but unlike a data catalog, data discovery surfaces a real-time understanding of the data's current state as opposed to its ideal or "cataloged" state.

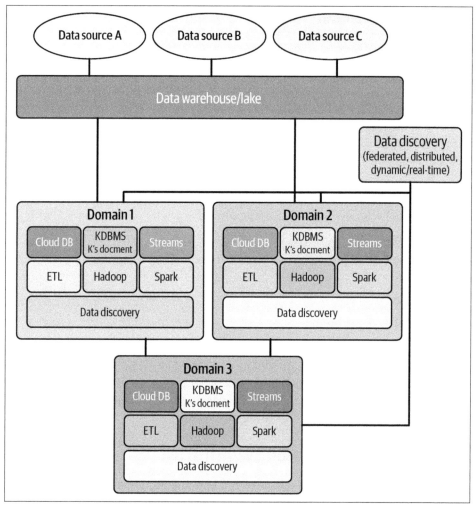

Figure 8-5. Data discovery provides real-time insights about data across different domains

It is especially useful when teams take a distributed approach to governance that holds different data owners accountable for their data as products, which allows data-savvy users throughout the business to self-serve from those products.

But as data becomes more accessible, how can downstream stakeholders determine what data sets have been served, transformed, and approved by a given domain's data team? How can one domain be sure a common set of data quality standards, ownership, and communication processes are being upheld across the organization?

For many teams, the answer lies in data certification.

Certifying Your Data

Data certification is the process by which data assets are approved for use across the organization after having met mutually agreed upon SLAs (*https://oreil.ly/lZtE5*) for data quality, observability, ownership/accountability, issue resolution, and communication.

Similar to the concepts of data quality, data validation, or data verification, data certification layers critical processes that align people, frameworks, and technology to central business policies. Data certification requirements vary based on the needs of the business, the capacity of the data engineering team, and the availability of data, but they typically incorporate features such as the following:

- Automated quality checks for freshness, volume, schema, and distribution
- Delivery SLAs with defined uptime
- Data owners who are accountable for investigating alerts
- Alerts routed to Slack (or email)
- Set communication process for outages

Seven Steps to Implementing a Data Certification Program

Data certification programs increase scalability by leveraging a consistent approach applied across multiple domains. They also increase efficiency by facilitating more trustworthy exchanges of information between domains with clear lines of communication.

Here's how it works.

Step 1: Build out your data observability capabilities

Implementing data observability—an organization's ability to fully understand the health of the data in their system—is an important first step in the data certification process. Not only do you need insight into your current performance to set a baseline, but you also need a systemic end-to-end approach for proactive incident discovery, alerting, and triaging as shown in Figure 8-6. Powered by observability, a data incident dashboard automatically surfaces anomalies, schema changes, deleted tables, and rule breaches.

If *anything* within the pipeline breaks—and it will break—you will be the first to know. This head start, along with a detailed understanding of the data ecosystem, will reduce time to detection and resolution by pinpointing where errors occur.

Figure 8-6. Data incident dashboard

Knowing what systems and data sets have a tendency to create the largest or most frequent problems downstream also helps inform the process of writing effective data SLAs (Step 4). Additionally, understanding the upstream dependencies of your most important tables or reports helps data teams understand what data to give the most attention. The bottom line is that a table or data set should be closely monitored for anomalies (ideally continuously learning and evolving via machine learning) to be considered certified.

Step 2: Determine your data owners

Each certified data asset should have a responsible party across its life cycle from the ingestion to analytics layer as shown in Figure 8-7. Modern metadata management tools allow data owners to be assigned to tables along with other tags, helping them keep tabs on the reliability of critical data sets.

Tags
Ownership, governance, documentation and other metadata

Key	Value
Certified	Gold
owner	Jordan Van Horn

Figure 8-7. Responsible parties should be assigned for each layer

Some data teams may choose to implement a RACI matrix; others may build it directly into the specific SLA along with the expected communication procedures and resolution times.

Step 3: Understand what "good" data looks like

By asking your business stakeholders the "who, what, when, where, and why," you can understand what data quality means to them and which data is actually the most important. This will enable you to develop key performance indicators such as:

- Freshness
    - Data will be refreshed by 8:00 a.m. daily (great for cases where the CEO or other key executives are checking their dashboards at 8:30 a.m.).
    - Data will never be older than X hours.
- Distribution
    - Column X will never be null.
    - Column Y will always be unique.
    - Field X will always be equal to or greater than field Y.
- Volume
    - Table X will never decrease in size.
- Schema
    - No fields will be deleted on this table.
- Lineage
    - 100% of the data populating table X will have upstream sources and downstream ingestors mapped and include relevant metadata.
- Data downtime (or availability)
    - The number of incidents multiplied by (time to detection + time to resolution). An example of a data downtime SLA could be table X will have less than Y hours of downtime a year.
    - SLAs that measure each of the components of data downtime can be more actionable. Examples include we will reduce our incidents X%, time to detection X%, and time to resolution X%.
- Query speed
    - Our friends at Locally Optimistic suggest (*https://oreil.ly/tSNhm*): "Average query run time is a good place to start, but you may need to create a more nuanced metric (e.g., X% of queries finish in <Y seconds)."
- Ingestion (great for keeping external partners accountable)
    - Data will be received by 5 a.m. each morning from partner Y.

This process also enables you to configure granular alerting rules tailored to what matters most to the business.

Step 4: Set clear SLAs, SLOs, and SLIs for your most important data sets

As highlighted in Chapter 6, setting SLAs for your data pipeline is a major step toward increasing your data reliability and is essential to a data certification program. SLAs must be specific, measurable by an SLO and SLI, and achievable.

Not only do SLAs describe an agreed-upon standard of service, they define the relationship between parties. In other words, they outline who is responsible for what during normal operations as well as when issues occur.

In our discussions with Brandon Beidel (*https://oreil.ly/1nKQN*), a Senior Data Scientist with Red Ventures, he suggested that an effective SLA is realistic. Simply saying "having reliable data at all times" is too vague to be useful; instead, Brandon suggested, teams should set SLAs that are focused: "Good SLAs are specific and detailed. They will describe why it's important to the business, what the expectations are, when those expectations need to be met, how they will be met, where the data lives, and who is impacted by it."

Beidel includes within his SLAs how the team should respond if the SLA isn't met. For example, the "data in table X will be refreshed every day by 8:00 a.m." will transform into, "Team Z will ensure the data in table X will be refreshed every day by 8:00 a.m. Within two hours of an anomaly alert, the team will verify, communicate to affected parties, and begin a root cause analysis of the issue. Within one business day a ticket will be created and the wider team will be updated on the progress made toward resolution."

To achieve this level of specificity and organization, teams should align early—and often—with stakeholders to understand what good data looks like. That includes within the data team as well as the business. A good SLA needs to be informed by the realities of how the business operates and how your users consume the data.

Beidel takes a slightly different approach and differentiates between what he considers the SLA of "Table x will be updated by 8 a.m." and the SLO of "We will aim to meet this SLA 99% of the time." However you decide to approach it, he recommends against boiling the ocean. Most of his customers are implementing their data certification programs as "go forward" first and cleaning up older assets in a second wave.

In fact, many of the best data teams will start certifying the most critical tables and data sets: the ones that add the most value to the business, have the most query activity, number of users, or dependencies. Some are also implementing tiers of certification—bronze, silver, gold—that convey different levels of service and support.

Step 5: Develop your communication and incident management processes

Where and how will alerts be sent to the team? How will next steps and progress be communicated internally and externally? While this may seem like table stakes, clear and transparent communication is essential to creating a culture of accountability.

Many teams opt to have alerts and incident triage discussions take place in Slack, PagerDuty, or Microsoft Teams. This enables rapid coordination while giving full transparency to the wider team as part of a healthy incident management workflow, as discussed in Chapter 6.

It's also important to consider how to communicate major outages to the rest of the organization. For example, if an alert turns out to be a huge production outage, how does the on-call engineer inform the rest of the company? Where do they make that announcement and how frequently do they provide updates?

Step 6: Determine a mechanism to tag the data as certified

At this point, you have created SLAs with measurable objectives, transparent ownership, clear communication processes, and strong issue resolution expectations. You have the tools and proactive measures in place to empower your teams to be successful. The final step is to certify and surface the approved data assets for your stakeholders.

We recommend decentralizing the certification process. After all, the certification process is designed to help make teams faster and more scalable. Having centralized regulations, enacted at the domain level, will achieve these goals and avoid creating too much red tape. For the certification process, data teams will tag, search, and leverage their tables appropriately using either data discovery solutions, a home-grown tool, or some other form of data catalog.

Step 7: Train your data team and downstream consumers

Of course, just because tables are tagged as certified doesn't guarantee analysts will stay in bounds. The team will need to be trained in the proper procedures, which will need to be enforced as necessary. Fine-tuning the level of alerts and communication is important as well.

Occasionally receiving alerts that don't require action is healthy. For example, you may have a table that grows significantly in size, but it was expected because the team added a new data source. Nothing is broken and in need of fixing, but it's still helpful for the team to know. After all, "expected" behavior to one person might still be newsworthy and critical to another member of the team—or even another domain.

However, alert fatigue is real. If the team is starting to ignore alerts, it can be a sign to optimize your approach by either adjusting your monitors or bifurcating communication channels to better surface the most important information.

When it comes to your data consumers, don't be shy! You have put in an incredibly robust system for data quality aligned to their needs. Help them move from a subjective to objective understanding of how your team is performing and start giving them the vocabulary to be part of the solution.

Data certification can be a beautiful process to see in action. The data engineer tags the table as certified along with the owner of the data set, and surfaces it within the data warehouse for an analyst to grab it and use in their dashboard. And voila! No more (or at least, a whole lot less) data downtime.

At its core, this process underscores that without the proper processes and culture in place, certifying reliability and building organizational trust in your data is extremely difficult. Technology will never be a replacement for good data hygiene, but it certainly helps.

Second perhaps only to implementing a data certification program with clear SLAs, modern data teams can best navigate the cultural and organizational hurdles of data quality by prioritizing a team structure that plays to the strengths and needs of their business.

Case Study: Toast's Journey to Finding the Right Structure for Their Data Team

About mortality, Shakespeare's Hamlet once said: "To be or not to be, that is the question." About her data team, a wise head of data at a startup once said: "To centralize or decentralize, that is the question." And it's an important one. Here's how some of the best data leaders apply an agile methodology to build data organizations that scale with the growth of their companies.

As startups increasingly invest in data to drive decision making and power their digital products, data leaders are tasked with scaling their teams—and fast. From knowing which roles to hire for (and when) to setting SLAs for data, today's data leaders are responsible for—quite literally—keeping their companies insight-informed at each stage of the journey.

Regardless of where you are in this marathon, one of the biggest challenges is determining the proper reporting structure for your data team. As data needs increase, so too do the bottlenecks imposed by centralized data teams—and the duplication and complexity introduced by decentralized ones. And just when you think you've figured out the *perfect* paradigm (i.e., a central data engineering team, distributed data analysts, and a few analytics engineers to bridge the gaps or a handful of data analysts reporting to the COO with data engineers working under the CTO), your entire strategy gets turned on its head when priorities shift.

So, what's a data leader to do?

To better understand how some of the best teams are tackling this problem, we sat down with Greg Waldman, Senior Director of Business Intelligence at Toast, a newly public provider of point-of-sale software for restaurants, to discuss the evolution of his company's data team and share his experiences navigating the never-ending tug of war between these centralized and decentralized structures.

Over the last five years, Greg led the Toast data team as it grew from one analyst (Greg himself) to a 20+ person organization, and has evolved from a centralized to a hybrid-decentralized model—and back again. Read on to learn how Greg's team lets business needs drive the data team structure, how he knew when it was necessary to make those changes, and the crucial role he wishes he had hired much sooner.

In the Beginning: When a Small Team Struggles to Meet Data Demands

When Greg joined Toast in 2016, the company already had 200 employees—but no dedicated analytics staff. Despite this shortage of specialized talent, the company had always prioritized using data to make decisions. Greg said:

> Our founding team was just really sharp. They ran the company on Excel documents, but eventually when they got to 200 people, they knew that approach wasn't going to scale. When I came on, the ask was basically, "We have too many meetings where one person thinks the number's five and the other person thinks the number's four, and then they just bicker about that the whole time. So, make that stop happening.

Immediately, Greg dug in and began building out tools, processes, and a basic data program. Over the first year, the Toast data team tripled—they now had three people. And the company continued to use data to drive its culture and decision-making. "Everybody says they have a data-driven culture, but I've worked at enough places to know the difference, and I see the juxtaposition compared to Toast," said Greg. "Our people throughout the company—especially our leadership—really look for data before they make big decisions."

But while the small data team tripled, Toast itself had doubled. By 2018, the company had 400 employees. The centralized data team couldn't keep up with the demands of the entire fast-growing, data-obsessed organization. "We had lines out the door," said Greg. "There was just an appetite for more data than we were able to provide. And I think that was a bit of an inflection point for us. Because if you don't figure out a way to serve that need, then the business might start operating in a different way—and be less data-driven if you can't get them the necessary data."

Supporting Hypergrowth as a Decentralized Data Operation

The shift to a decentralized structure began to take shape organically as departments began finding ways to meet their own data needs. "Eventually small pockets of analytics opened up in other parts of the company, like sales and customer success," Greg said. "Mostly because our small team just couldn't meet the needs of the growing business. And so they started their own teams, and that kind of worked!"

In 2018, this decentralized team of 10 data professionals worked within business units, meeting data needs and supporting Toast's head-spinning trajectory as the company nearly doubled again, growing to 850 employees. Greg and his team also rebuilt their data tech stack, migrating from an end-to-end data platform to a modern distributed stack including S3, Airflow, Snowflake, Stitch, and Looker.

Dedicated analysts working in their business units still maintained a close connection with Greg's core analytics team, giving Toast a hybrid between a fully centralized and fully decentralized data team structure. But as the organization continued to scale—reaching a headcount of 1,250 employees in 2019, with 15 data analysts, data scientists, and data engineers—problems began to arise from this hybrid model.

Data consistency was one concern. "There were various degrees of rigor across the organization when it comes to what constitutes good data. When you're small, you're scrappy, you're growing, and any data is better than no data. But eventually, we reached a scale where we knew that inaccurate data could be harmful."

And even with technically accurate data, Greg knew that strong communication between analysts, technical leaders, and downstream stakeholders was critical when it came to establishing a standard of data observability and trust across the entire company. "As the business got bigger and more complicated, you need analysts to start seeing the whole business," said Greg. "Even in a decentralized model you need to ensure analysts work in close collaboration with other analysts and technical leaders when it comes to setting the standards around performance and operability."

Regrouping, Recentralizing, and Refocusing on Data Trust

So Toast brought analysts that had been working under their respective Customer Success and Go-To-Market teams back under an analytics umbrella, as depicted in Figure 8-8. When evaluating how to structure his data team, Greg always weighs three options: centralized, decentralized, and hybrid, each of which they tried on for size over time. In the end, he found the hybrid model to be most effective for the size and scope of his analytics-heavy team.

"We ended up centralizing and a discussed but underrated benefit has been just how much folks on the team have learned from one another," said Greg. The team is now part of the Finance & Strategy department. But he knows the centralized structure may not be the long-term solution for Toast.

"The way I think about data teams, in a nutshell, is that you want everyone to add as much business value as possible," said Greg. "We've been very open to change and trying different things and understanding that what works with 200 people versus 500 people versus a thousand versus two thousand is not the same answer, and that's OK. It can be somewhat obvious when you've reached those inflection points and need to try something new."

	Centralized	Hybrid	Decentralized
Pros	• Consistent standards and expectations for analysts • Increased collaboration leading to more mentorship and faster growth • Simpler to move around resources when necessary • More likely to see the whole business in analysis • Reduced work duplication	• Possibility for the best of both worlds • Central hub can take the more challenging tasks while the spoke teams can do the basics	• Analysts get "feet on the ground" perspective • Output velocity is high and can fluctuate with the business • Teams can easily allocate different amounts of analytics resources • Direct OKR alignment
Cons	• Velocity is generally slower • Easier for things to get lost in translation due to lack of "feet on the ground" perspective • Jockeying for resources can be challenging • OKR alignment is more complex	• Can lead to confusion on where responsibilities lie between central hub and spokes • Governance: may get different answers from different places	• Inconsistent standards and expectations for analysts • Technical growth more difficult • Harder for analysts to see and understand whole business • Redundant work • Analysis can be driven by preconceived notions based on reporting structure

Centralized
Analytics stands as its own function. Analysts and/or teams may be dedicated to different departments or business units (BUs), or have dotted lines, but they report into a central hub.

Hybrid
Analytics has its own function, which is supplemented by dedicated analysts and/or teams embedded in some departments or BUs. There may be a dotted line back to the analytics hub. Most enterprises fall here, but what this means can vary widely.

Decentralized
Departments or BUs house their own analytics functions. These analysts and/or teams generally report to leaders of their department or BU.

Figure 8-8. Three potential data team structures. Source: Adapted from an image by Greg Waldman and Toast

At the end of the day, it's all about meeting the needs of the business—no matter what it means for your team's reporting structure—while ensuring that technical leads are enablers and not bottlenecks for analysts.

Considerations When Scaling Your Data Team

Ultimately, Greg's team settled on a centralized data team structure with a few distributed elements, affording them greater ownership and governance over their data products and the ability to build a scalable, modular data stack. Greg has some hard-won advice for data leaders facing similar challenges at hypergrowth companies—but every tactic goes back to his principle of focusing on what approach best meets the business needs of your company, which will likely change over time.

In short, he suggests, leaders should stay nimble and teams should be willing to adapt to the needs of the business. Here's how.

Hire data generalists, not specialists—with one exception

According to Greg, the first specialist you should hire is a data engineer:

> Early on, we basically just hired data athletes who could do a little bit of everything. We had those athletes playing analyst/data engineer. And I had a senior manager role open, and a data engineer applied, but she didn't have any interest in managing. When I talked to her, it became obvious how badly we needed the dedicated data engineering skill set on the team. And in retrospect, I should have been looking for someone like that a year earlier given our growth trajectory.

All too often, data teams are hamstrung by the lack of technical support needed to build and maintain ETL pipelines, as well as ensure that the data infrastructure underlying them can scale with the analytics needs of the company. Greg notes, "So while I still believe in hiring data athletes who can do a bit of everything, data engineers are the one exception. After you hire a few analysts, your first data engineer should follow close behind."

Prioritize building a diverse data team from day one

This goes without saying, but when it comes to setting up your team for long-term success, you need to invest (early) in candidates with diverse experiences and backgrounds. Homogeneity is a nonstarter for innovation and prevents data analysts and engineers from understanding the perspectives and needs of all data consumers. When you're moving quickly at scale, however, it can be hard to remember this—unless you put in place a set of clear hiring and growth KPIs that reflect this goal.

"Think about diversity early on," said Greg. "Because especially in these small data teams, if you're not careful, you'll just end up with a bunch of like-minded people from similar backgrounds. And you don't want a bunch of the same people—you need different perspectives."

It's one thing to say, "We need to build a diverse team," but something else entirely to do it. So how should data leaders get started? Here are a few tips:

- Partner with executives and your Human Resources team to write job descriptions that are inclusive of different experiences and backgrounds (i.e., avoiding excessively masculine language in favor of gender-neutral ones).
- Put together diverse hiring panels (even if they're not pulled from the data team) to embody the team you're striving to build.

- Cast a wide net to recruit for candidates who may not have traditional data titles or roles; it's a constantly evolving space!

- Implement a gender- and race-blind application process that screens based on qualifications and experiences.

- It can be much harder to build a diverse team later in the startup journey because people from different backgrounds want to join a team that has people from different backgrounds. If you don't think about that right out of the gate, it can be much more challenging.

Overcommunication is key to change management

This point is even more relevant in our remote-first world, in which many teams work from home and overcommunication over email, Slack, and carrier pigeon (just kidding!) is a necessary part of any job. According to Tomasz Tunguz, Managing Director at Redpoint Ventures, companies should repeat themselves (*https://oreil.ly/dR7YP*) (i.e., their core value propositions) with customers consistently, even if it seems unnecessary. The same goes for data leaders when it comes to communicating their work and any team changes with data stakeholders.

For instance, if your decentralized customer success analyst is migrating to report up into the head of analytics after three months working under the head of customer success, not only should you communicate that this change is happening, but also reiterate that this adjustment doesn't change the nature of your team's output. Stakeholders can still expect accurate, timely analysis that maps to core business objectives, even if the team is no longer distributed.

While structural changes inevitably impact the nature of the relationship between stakeholder (the functional team) and service provider (the data team), codifying, communicating, and repeating how this shift will not impact your team's KPIs will restore goodwill and help cross-functional groups overcome change.

"If you have analysts reporting into business leaders, make sure that they're empowered to push back based on the data they are seeing," said Greg. "Otherwise it can be a tricky dynamic where they are encouraged to show data that backs anecdotal hypotheses. When you bring those teams back under an analytics umbrella, your analysts are going to learn from one another, but influencing other departments can be challenging." Most recently, Toast has been running a largely centralized analytics model, which has performed well and met the needs of the business for the last year and a half.

Don't overvalue a "single source of truth"

The concept of a "single source of truth" or golden data is a powerful one—for good reason. Striving for metrics alignment and consistently clean data can help companies trust that their data is pointing them in the right direction. Still, as a data leader at a hypergrowth startup, you'll be pulled in to work on lots of experiments and projects at any given time—as long as you have directional observability into data trust (i.e., Is this table up to date? Do I know who owns this data set? Why did 50 rows turn into 500?), the need for a "single source of truth" isn't as pressing.

"I always tell people not to overvalue the whole 'single source of truth' concept," said Greg. "As a perfectionist, it took a long time for me to learn this. There are times when you need to be 100% correct, and then there are a lot of times where you don't. Often, directional accuracy is fine, and you'll just waste resources trying to be perfect. The 80/20 rule is key."

Data is always messy and rarely perfect. You'll get more done if you prioritize having an end-to-end view of data health and accuracy over more granular control.

Greg's final piece of advice for data leaders?

"Hire good people with strong communication skills and everything else becomes a lot easier. Good people will lead you to other great people, and you can hire the smartest people in the world, but if they can't communicate their analyses to less technical folks they simply won't be successful."

Increasing Data Literacy

We've discussed the "what" and "who" of democratizing data quality, but "how" do you actually build a culture of data quality? For many organizations, it all starts with data literacy, in other words, the ability to read, write, and communicate about data in a way that drives value and impact for the organization. After all, how can you understand the value of data quality if you don't even understand the value of data? Or, for that matter, know how to use it?

A good data literacy strategy will gain top-down buy-in and bottoms-up adoption by making data more accessible and easy to work with, leveraging self-service tooling and education for less technical team members. The way to make these data initiatives successful beyond the boundaries of the data function and impactful for the broader organization, then, is to meet data stakeholders where they are.

One CDO Barr spoke with at the MIT CDO Symposium a few years ago shared with the group that he created a new role called "Head of Data Literacy," serving the entire business. This person was responsible for ensuring that each business unit in this ~10K employee organization was "fluent in data."

For example, they are creating a scorecard for each business unit to measure the performance of the function in terms of data skills such as Excel, SQL, R, Python, etc. They are then helping each function define goals for their data literacy aspirations (i.e., what skills each person should know and to what level of depth and breadth);

training/educating the teams to help members improve their skills; and overall getting more "data-fluent" as an organization. It is quite powerful to have a single point of accountability in the organization on the hook for getting the entire company to be data-literate in a very concrete, measurable way.

To achieve "data-fluency," however, it's important for data managers to prioritize both data literacy and educating stakeholders about the value of data quality. After all, what good is knowing how to work with and interpret data if the data itself can't be trusted to deliver accurate insights?

In our talks with Wendy Turner-Williams, Chief Data Officer at Tableau, she stated:

> Simplifying and putting data in the hands of those who need it, when they need it is hugely important. In addition, literacy is equally important and goes into multiple things such as how you educate people inside your own company to use data and understanding how data is used across teams to give you insight into what you can do with data and drive value from it when it's trustworthy.

Several data leaders we've spoken to over the years say that their number one hurdle in terms of long-term sustainability of their data quality initiatives (and the success of their data teams) is lack of documentation. Too often, teams rely on tacit knowledge and outdated wiki pages to keep tabs on their data, and that's just not scalable or sustainable.

When we interviewed Amy Smith, Staff Business Analyst at Intuit, she said the best way to ensure that your data team is all on the same page is through knowledge sharing, early and often: "A lot of a data scientist's early success is through joining a team that is willing to take the time necessary to write down their knowledge," she said. "Putting the collective knowledge of a team into a form that someone new can read and get up to speed on is hugely important."

More specifically, lack of robust information about data and metadata is a major pain point for teams, but it's something that can be addressed. Some solutions that make these insights easier to access are:

Data catalogs
Smaller teams (2–5 people) may get by with an Excel spreadsheet, but as your data stack matures, consider investing in an in-house, third-party, or even open source solution (more to come in the next section, "Prioritizing Data Governance and Compliance").

Database management system (DBMS)
A DBMS is a software application or package designed to manage data in a database, including the data's format, field names, record structure, and file structure. While this won't replace a data catalog in terms of providing context, it will help you keep your data organized for easy access.

Data modeling tools
> Data modeling tools give teams the ability to discover and visualize data assets. These products can also help teams understand the relationship between various elements of your data stack.

Operational analytics dashboards
> Your data knowledge only matters if your data can be trusted. Operational analytics dashboards about your data platform solve many of the same issues as data catalogs, DBMSs, and data modeling tools, but they also provide insights into how the data is being used and which data matters most to the business based on consumption, number of data quality rules set, and other key indicators of data set importance.

In addition, teams who want to take knowledge transfer and accessibility a step further can make a point to build out their data operations with missing information and other context. To this end, data leaders should encourage their analysts to add missing dimensions to data when noticed, not only when required. Just because you're not using it now doesn't mean you or a colleague won't use it later.

Prioritizing Data Governance and Compliance

Perhaps there's no topic in all of the larger data quality discussion that draws as much confusion and ire as data governance, in other words, the management of data across and beyond an organization. Data governance is top of mind for many data leaders, particularly in light of GDPR, CCPA, IPOs, COVID-19, and any number of other acronyms that speak to the increasing importance of compliance and privacy when it comes to managing your company's data.

Traditionally, data governance refers to the process of maintaining the availability, usability, provenance, and security of data, and, as a data leader once told us, is the "keep your CFO out of jail card." Still, Gartner suggests that more than 80% of data governance initiatives will fail in 2022 (*https://oreil.ly/v5kJn*).

In our opinion, data governance gets a bad reputation, primarily because traditional approaches fail to scale with the needs of cloud-based data stacks. Over the past several years, data catalogs have emerged as a powerful tool for data governance. As companies digitize and their data operations democratize, it's important for all elements of the data stack, from warehouses to business intelligence platforms, and now, catalogs, to participate in compliance best practices.

Prioritizing a Data Catalog

When you think of data governance, data catalogs often come to mind. As you'll recall from Chapter 2, data catalogs have historically served as the basis of a data team's ability to store and curate metadata about data usage and location. Analogous to a physical library catalog, data catalogs (*https://oreil.ly/QgJf3*) serve as an inventory of metadata and give investors the information necessary to evaluate data accessibility, health, and location.

Since data catalogs provide a single source of truth about a company's data sources, it's very easy to leverage data catalogs to manage the data in your pipelines. Data catalogs can be used to store metadata that gives stakeholders a better understanding of a specific source's lineage, thereby instilling greater trust in the data itself. Additionally, data catalogs make it easy to keep track of where personally identifiable information (PII) can both be housed and sprawl downstream, as well as who in the organization has the permission to access it across the pipeline.

Traditionally, manual data catalogs and metadata management platforms have been the de facto approach to tackling data governance, but as systems evolve, we're finding this approach insufficient to keep up with the pace of data growth and the distribution of data across distinct domains. Fortunately, many vendors are getting smart to this new need and are embracing machine learning and knowledge graph–based technologies to make governance more accessible and scalable.

There are three major types of automated data catalogs on the market today, available as in-house solutions, third-party tools, or open source technologies.

In-house

Some B2C companies—we're talking the Airbnbs (*https://oreil.ly/emuHa*), Netflixs (*https://oreil.ly/mFcaA*), and Ubers (*https://oreil.ly/Q4bNQ*) of the world—build their own data catalogs to ensure data compliance with state, country, and even economic union (e.g., GDPR) level regulations. The biggest perk of in-house solutions is the ability to quickly spin up customizable dashboards, pulling out fields your team needs the most.

While in-house tools (like Uber's Databook, depicted in Figure 8-9) make for quick customization, over time, such hacks can lead to a lack of visibility and collaboration, particularly when it comes to understanding data lineage. In fact, one data leader I spoke with at a food delivery startup noted that what was clearly missing from her in-house data catalog was a "single pane of glass." If she had a single source of truth that could provide insight into how her team's tables were being leveraged by other parts of the business, ensuring compliance would be easy.

On top of these tactical considerations, spending engineering time and resources building a multimillion dollar data catalog just doesn't make sense for the vast majority of companies.

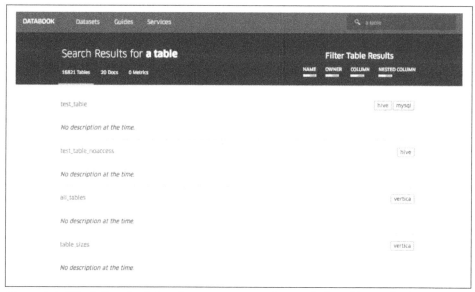

Figure 8-9. Uber's Databook lets data scientists easily search for tables and other critical assets across business domains

Third-party

Traditionally, data catalogs were managed manually and governed in silos, often requiring duplicated work between different analysts and data science teams. Now, there are a whole host of ML-powered data catalogs on the market that lend themselves to distributed governance, many with pay-for-play workflow and repository-oriented compliance management integrations. Some cloud providers, like Google, AWS, and Azure, also offer data governance tooling integration at an additional cost.

In our conversations with data leaders, one downside of legacy solutions came up time and again: usability. While nearly all of these tools have strong collaboration features, one Data Engineering VP I spoke with specifically called out his third-party catalog's unintuitive UI. If data tools aren't easy to use, how can we expect users to understand or even care whether they're compliant?

Open source

In 2018, Lyft became an industry leader by making their data discovery and metadata engine, Amundsen (*https://oreil.ly/1cBOl*), named after the famed Antarctic explorer, open source (Figure 8-10). Other open source tools, such as Apache Atlas (*https://oreil.ly/eWI1V*), Magda (*https://oreil.ly/iDseP*), and CKAN (*https://oreil.ly/Bmow9*), provide similar functionalities, and all three make it easy for development-savvy teams to fork an instance of the software and get started.

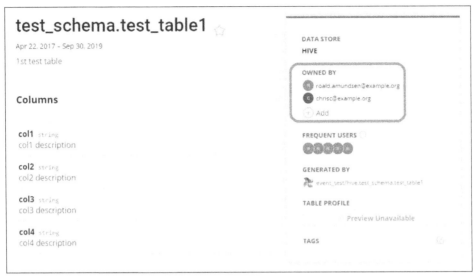

Figure 8-10. Amundsen, an open source data catalog, gives users insight into data set ownership

While tools like Amundsen allow teams to tag metadata (*https://oreil.ly/jgbMo*) to control user access, this is an intensive and often manual process that most teams just don't have the time to tackle. In fact, a product manager at a leading transportation company shared that his team specifically chose not to use an open source data catalog because they didn't have off-the-shelf support for all the data sources and data management tooling in their stack, making data governance extra challenging.

Beyond Catalogs: Enforcing Data Governance

As data organizations mature, however, data catalogs alone are unable to keep up with the requirements of modern data governance programs. To start, mitigating governance gaps is a monumental undertaking, and it's impossible to prioritize these without a full understanding of which data assets are actually being accessed by your company. Data lineage and observability help fill these gaps, as discussed in Chapter 2.

Data accessibility and security are also an important feature of data governance, particularly for organizations with distributed analytics teams or working with sensitive third-party information. As a result, data governance programs should also incorporate automated and distributed policy enforcement (whether built in-house or purchased via a third-party vendor) to manage PII identification and access controls.

Still, even with data catalogs, observability platforms, lineage, and data access controls, it's impossible to gain buy-in on governance (and all of data quality for that matter) without a data culture that prioritizes the right processes and workflows to make data reliable and secure at scale.

We talked to Zosia Kossowski, Group Product Manager, Business Intelligence at HubSpot, and she acknowledged that it is not an easy task to build a culture that prioritizes governance, particularly at scale:

> From a cultural aspect, it's tough when a community, especially as a company grows quickly and is used to having a certain level of autonomy in general, not just with data. As your company gets larger, you really have to implement more processes and regulations to make sure that you are bringing everyone along and having them understand the pain that a lack of governance and alignment can cause.

Zosia acknowledges that for most organizations data governance is also a cultural shift:

> If you are a data-driven company and it is a priority for your data to be clean and usable when a product is released that is part of the acceptance criteria, then it is a lot easier than if data is a byproduct or an afterthought that is troublesome when you have to come to an engineering team and you're like, "This is wrong." My recommendation is getting engineering leaders and anyone who's involved in producing data as part of your data governance conversations early on so they understand the pain that is caused as well.

Building a Data Quality Strategy

Over the past several sections, we've discussed the technical, process-driven, and organizational requirements necessary to scale a culture of data quality. Now, let's put it all together and lay the groundwork for building a data quality strategy from scratch. Here are the critical steps data engineering and analytics leaders must take when launching a data quality initiative at their company.

Make Leadership Accountable for Data Quality

Before you start trying to secure leadership and stakeholder buy-in, it's important to be transparent about the current state of your data quality strategy. Consider how you might answer the following questions:

- How do you measure the data quality of the assets your company collects and stores?
- What are the key KPIs or goals you're going to hold your data quality strategy accountable for meeting?
- Do you have cross-functional involvement from leadership and data users in other parts of the company?

- Who at the company will be held accountable for meeting your strategy's KPIs and goals?

- What checks and balances do you have to ensure KPIs are measured correctly and goals can be met?

In the same way that having visibility into your data pipelines makes it easy to ensure high data quality, transparency into both your strategy and its incremental progress will be critical when it comes to keeping everyone informed and accountable.

Set Data Quality KPIs

Before you tackle your data SLAs (as discussed in Chapter 6), it's critical to understand and align on each part of the data life cycle and how data brings value to your company. The outcome of each phase in this process will determine your corresponding data quality SLAs and measurements. For instance, raw data ingested by your data lake or warehouse needs to fulfill different requirements than transformed data rendered in a data warehouse.

Avoid focusing on data quality measurements. Instead, keep it simple. Measure for tangible metrics (*https://oreil.ly/gSexv*) like completeness, freshness, accuracy, consistency, and validity (*https://oreil.ly/Ov530*) as opposed to obscure "accuracy" scores or other homegrown measurements. These types of frameworks will only lead to confusion down the road as SLAs shift to meet company priorities.

Spearhead a Data Governance Program

If a data quality program launches but no one else at the company hears about it (including leadership), will it have an impact? Probably not. With the exception of a few noteworthy companies, data governance isn't often a formalized role, particularly in the context of data engineering.

To make sure that data users across the company are aware of why data quality matters, we suggest developing a program for data quality champions to carry the torch and shepherd others through data access, use, and storage best practices. Make participation and evangelism easy and accessible. Be sure to communicate how data quality affects their functional areas, from marketing to sales, and make it easy for them to share and enforce with their team. Focus on short-term or quick wins to get traction while promoting and executing on the long-term strategy.

Automate Your Lineage and Data Governance Tooling

With increasingly stringent compliance measures around data access and applications, a manual approach to data quality monitoring as a vehicle for data governance is not cutting it. Not only is manual data quality monitoring tedious and time-consuming, but these tools can't keep pace with the speed of innovation across the rest of the data stack (think: ML-enabled data modeling, speedy analytics dashboards, and the data mesh).

Instead, we suggest investing in automated tools that can quickly validate, monitor, and alert for data quality issues as they arise. Add the ability to set custom rules, and these technologies can truly unlock the potential of data for your organization.

Create a Communications Plan

Now that all of the pieces are in place, the final step is to put together a robust and comprehensive, program-level communications plan that will keep leadership in the loop, stakeholders aligned with your project's progress, and data stewards abreast of their marching orders. A good communication plan will be bidirectional and keep all involved in the loop on the status of relevant deliverables. A great communication plan will instill confidence in even skeptical parties that your team is in command of the situation, regardless of how far you are from your goals.

At the end of the day, the goal of your data quality strategy will be to ensure that teams across the entire company feel empowered to use data that is trustworthy. In fact, a robust and comprehensive data quality strategy makes all the difference when it comes to doing just about anything in data, from scaling an effective data team to building a great data platform.

Summary

Achieving data democratization is just as much of a technical process as it is a cultural one. Regardless of where you fall on the RACI matrix of data personas, chances are data quality plays an important role in your ability to succeed as a data practitioner.

Democratizing data quality requires these critical steps:

- Treating data with the diligence of a production software product
- Assembling a data team that can prioritize data quality at the source
- Making data literacy a first-class citizen
- Adopting process and technologies that can scale data governance

In our opinion, the most meaningful conversations we've had on this topic stem from experience: broken data pipelines, accidental compliance oversights, and stale dashboards. After all, without suffering the pain firsthand, it can be hard to muster the engineering energy and technical resources to prioritize it.

Fortunately, the tide is turning. Increasingly, companies are hiring data reliability engineers, data observability experts, and data literacy officers to spearhead these initiatives and make it easier for data engineers and analysts to apply data quality best practices to their day-to-day work.

CHAPTER 9

Data Quality in the Real World: Conversations and Case Studies

It's great to talk about data quality in theory, but what does this desired state actually look like in practice?

Over the past several chapters, we've walked through what it takes to achieve data reliability at scale, from how to design a DataOps workflow to common SQL tests to determine the volume and freshness of your data assets. We've sprinkled in a dose of real-world case studies, but as we all know, data quality isn't achieved in a textbook, and getting to "reliable data" depends on several other elements of your data analytics and engineering practice. As technologies advance and companies become more data-reliant, we need to consider how other industry-defining processes and technologies affect our ability to increase data reliability.

In this chapter, we'll discuss five topics that are top of mind for many of today's data leaders and share how data quality plays a critical part:

- The data mesh and where data quality fits in
- Data quality's role in the cloud-based data stack journey
- Knowledge graphs as the key to more accessible data
- Data discovery for distributed data architectures
- When to get started with data quality

Over the past several years, these five topics, technologies, and trends have become increasingly common, often giving organizations the advantage necessary to tackle data reliability in a more scalable and repeatable way. Let's dive in.

Building a Data Mesh for Greater Data Quality

In the age of self-service business intelligence (*https://oreil.ly/QnfLP*), nearly every company considers themselves a data-first company, but not every company is treating their data architecture with the level of democratization and scalability it deserves.

Your company, for one, views data as a driver of innovation. Your boss was one of the first in the industry to see the potential in Snowflake and Looker. Or maybe your CDO spearheaded a cross-functional initiative to educate teams on data management best practices and your CTO invested in a data engineering group. Most of all, however, your entire data team wishes there were an easier way to manage the growing needs of your organization, from fielding the never-ending stream of ad hoc queries to wrangling disparate data sources through a central ETL pipeline.

Underpinning this desire for democratization and scalability is the realization that your current data architecture (in many cases, a siloed data warehouse or a data lake with some limited real-time streaming capabilities) may not be meeting your needs. To address the limitations of these siloed infrastructures, many data teams are moving toward a more distributed model of "federated governance." Enter the data mesh.

Much in the same way that software engineering teams transitioned from monolithic applications to microservice architectures (*https://oreil.ly/fue6i*), the data mesh is, in many ways, the data platform version of microservices. As first defined by Zhamak Dehghani, a Thoughtworks consultant and the original architect of the term, a data mesh is a type of data platform architecture that embraces the ubiquity of data in the enterprise by leveraging a domain-oriented, self-serve design.

The data mesh concept utilizes Eric Evans' theory of domain-driven design, a flexible, scalable software development paradigm that matches the structure and language of your code with its corresponding business domain. Unlike traditional monolithic data infrastructures that handle the consumption, storage, transformation, and output of data in one central data lake, a data mesh supports distributed, domain-specific data consumers and views "data as a product," with each domain handling their own data pipelines. The tissue connecting these domains and their associated data assets is a universal interoperability layer that applies the same syntax and data standards.

Instead of reinventing Zhamak's very thoughtfully built wheel, we'll boil down the definition of a data mesh to a few key concepts and highlight how it differs from traditional data architectures.

If you haven't already, we highly recommend reading Zhamak's groundbreaking article "How to Move Beyond a Monolithic Data Lake to a Distributed Data Mesh" (*https://oreil.ly/Y6zGO*), checking out her recent book on the topic, or watching Max Schulte's tech talk on why Zalando transitioned to a data mesh (*https://oreil.ly/ zvpjo*). You will not regret it.

At a high level, a data mesh (Figure 9-1) is composed of three separate components: data sources, data infrastructure, and domain-oriented data pipelines managed by functional owners. Underlying the data mesh architecture is a layer of universal interoperability, reflecting domain-agnostic standards, as well as observability and governance. The data mesh gives teams the ability to operationalize data across functional domains, but with the ability to standardize governance (and what data quality looks like) across these domains.

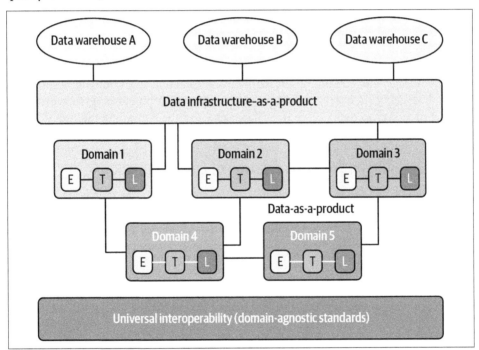

Figure 9-1. Data mesh visualization

Domain-Oriented Data Owners and Pipelines

Data meshes federate data ownership among domain data owners who are held accountable for providing their data as products, while also facilitating communication between distributed data across different locations.

While the data infrastructure is responsible for providing each domain with the solutions with which to process it, domains are tasked with managing ingestion, cleaning, and aggregation to the data to generate assets that can be used by business intelligence applications. Each domain is responsible for owning their ETL pipelines, but a set of capabilities is applied to all domains that stores, catalogs, and maintains access controls for the raw data. Once data has been served to and transformed by a given domain, the domain owners can then leverage the data for their analytics or operational needs.

Self-Serve Functionality

Data meshes leverage principles of domain-oriented design to deliver a self-serve data platform that allows users to abstract the technical complexity and focus on their individual data use cases.

As outlined by Zhamak, one of the main concerns of domain-oriented design is the duplication of efforts and skills needed to maintain data pipelines and infrastructure in each domain. To address this, the data mesh gleans and extracts domain-agnostic data infrastructure capabilities into a central platform that handles the data pipeline engines, storage, and streaming infrastructure. Meanwhile, each domain is responsible for leveraging these components to run custom ETL pipelines, giving them the support necessary to easily serve their data as well as the autonomy required to truly own the process.

Interoperability and Standardization of Communications

Underlying each domain is a universal set of data standards that helps facilitate collaboration between domains when necessary—and it often is. It's inevitable that some data (both raw sources and cleaned, transformed, and served data sets) will be valuable to more than one domain. To enable cross-domain collaboration, the data mesh must standardize on formatting, governance, discoverability, and metadata fields, among other data features. Moreover, much like an individual microservice, each data domain must define and agree on service-level agreements and quality measures that they will "guarantee" to its consumers.

Why Implement a Data Mesh?

Until recently, many companies leveraged a single data warehouse connected to myriad business intelligence platforms. Such solutions were maintained by a small group of specialists and frequently burdened by significant technical debt.

In 2020, the architecture du jour was a data lake with real-time data availability and stream processing, with the goal of ingesting, enriching, transforming, and serving data from a centralized data platform. For many organizations, this type of architecture falls short in a few ways:

- A central ETL pipeline gives teams less control over increasing volumes of data.
- As every company becomes a data company, different data use cases require different types of transformations, putting a heavy load on the central platform.

Such data lakes lead to disconnected data producers, impatient data consumers, and worst of all, a backlogged data team struggling to keep pace with the demands of the business. Instead, domain-oriented data architectures, like data meshes, give teams the best of both worlds: a centralized database (or a distributed data lake) with domains (or business areas) responsible for handling their own pipelines. As Zhamak argues (*https://oreil.ly/ZCWaS*), data architectures can be most easily scaled by being broken down into smaller, domain-oriented components.

Data meshes provide a solution to the shortcomings of data lakes by allowing greater autonomy and flexibility for data owners, facilitating greater data experimentation and innovation while lessening the burden on data teams to field the needs of every data consumer through a single pipeline.

Meanwhile, the data mesh's self-serve infrastructure as a platform provides data teams with a universal, domain-agnostic, and often automated approach to data standardization, data product lineage, data product monitoring, alerting, logging, and data product quality metrics (in other words, data collection and sharing). Taken together, these benefits provide a competitive edge compared to traditional data architectures, which are often hamstrung by the lack of data standardization between both ingestors and consumers.

To Mesh or Not to Mesh? That Is the Question

Nowadays, it seems like every data person falls into two camps: those who understand the data mesh and those who don't. Rest assured: if you're in either camp, you're not alone!

Rarely in recent memory has a topic taken the data world by storm, spawning a thriving community, hundreds of blog articles, and sighs of relief from data leaders across industries struggling with democratization and scalability. But with this new adoption comes new opportunities for misunderstanding around the true nature of a data mesh—and how to build one. Teams handling a large amount of data sources and a need to experiment with data (in other words, transform data at a rapid rate) would be wise to consider leveraging a data mesh.

Calculating Your Data Mesh Score

We put together a simple calculation to determine if it makes sense for your organization to invest in a data mesh. Please answer each question in the following with a number and add them all together for a total, in other words, your data mesh score.

- Quantity of data sources: How many data sources does your company have?
- Size of your data team: How many data analysts, data engineers, and product managers (if any) do you have on your data team?
- Number of data domains: How many functional teams (marketing, sales, operations, etc.) rely on your data sources to drive decision making, how many products does your company have, and how many data-driven features are being built? Add the total.
- Data engineering bottlenecks: How frequently is the data engineering team a bottleneck to the implementation of new data products on a scale of 1 to 10, with 1 being "never" and 10 being "always"?
- Data governance: How much of a priority is data governance for your organization on a scale of 1 to 10, with 1 being "I could care less" and 10 being "It keeps me up all night"?

In general, the higher your score, the more complex and demanding your company's data infrastructure requirements are, and in turn, the more likely your organization is to benefit from a data mesh. If you scored above a 10, then implementing some data mesh best practices probably makes sense for your company. If you scored above a 30, then your organization is in the data mesh sweet spot, and you would be wise to join the data revolution.

Here's how to break down your score:

- 1–15: Given the size and unidimensionality of your data ecosystem, you may not need a data mesh.
- 15–30: Your organization is maturing rapidly and may even be at a crossroads in terms of really being able to lean into data. We strongly suggest incorporating some data mesh best practices and concepts so that a later migration might be easier.
- 30 or above: Your data organization is an innovation driver for your company, and a data mesh will support any ongoing or future initiatives to democratize data and provide self-serve analytics across the enterprise.

As data becomes more ubiquitous and the demands of data consumers continue to diversify, we anticipate that data meshes will become increasingly common for cloud-based companies with more than 300 employees.

A Conversation with Zhamak Dehghani: The Role of Data Quality Across the Data Mesh

While writing this book, we sat down with Zhamak Dehghani (*https://oreil.ly/TMJva*) for a discussion about all things data mesh. During the conversation, Zhamak dispelled many of its biggest misconceptions, including whether or not the data mesh was a standalone technology, who should (or shouldn't) be building one, and if data mesh is just another word for data virtualization (hint: it's not).

Here are just a few of the key takeaways from our conversation.

Can You Build a Data Mesh from a Single Solution?

Zhamak defines the data mesh as "a socio-technical shift—a new approach in how we collect, manage, and share analytical data." The data mesh is *not* a technical solution or even subset of technologies—it's an organizational paradigm for how we manage and operationalize data, made up of several different technologies, whether open source or SaaS.

You couldn't build a microservice architecture with just a database. And you wouldn't build a data mesh with just a data warehouse or a BI tool. Instead, a data mesh can be powered in part by these technologies—and many, many others.

In a nutshell, a data architecture is a data mesh if it includes these four basic elements:

- Distributing ownership of data from one centralized team to the people who are most apt and suitable to control it—often, the business domains where the data comes from

- Giving those teams long-term accountability and equipping them with the product thinking they need to treat data as a product

- Empowering teams with a self-serve data infrastructure

- Addressing new problems that may arise with a new model of federated data governance

While it's easy to lose the forest for the trees, applying this methodology can ensure your mesh starts off on the right footing.

Is Data Mesh Another Word for Data Virtualization?

There's confusion in the data community about how decentralized data ownership actually works. As Lena describes, some technicians wonder if the concept of decentralized data ownership overlaps with the concept of data virtualization (*https://oreil.ly/Yf9JR*), in other words, an approach to data management that allows an application to retrieve and manipulate data across many silos.

According to Zhamak, it used to be the case that virtualization sits on top of your OLTP systems and your microservices or operational databases and exposes that data as is or with some minor transformation. And when it comes to applying this to the data mesh, it's probably not a wise idea. As Zhamak explained:

> Whether it's a data mesh or an API base, you're trying to expose a database that has been optimized for a transactional purpose for analytical purposes. And predictive analytics or historical trend modeling both require a very different view of the data. If you think about using virtualization on top of your microservices database and expose them and call that a mesh, that is probably a bad idea.

Does Each Data Product Team Manage Their Own Separate Data Stores?

According to Zhamak, the answer to this question is no. And we would have to agree—if each data product team manages their own store, the opportunity for duplication—and poor data quality—is exponentially higher. And don't get us started on cost. Zhamak explained:

> Data mesh would say that as a data product developer, I would want to have autonomy—to have all of the structural elements, the storage and compute, and query system, and all of the things that allow me to serve my data to data scientists. But that doesn't mean I have to now have my own geo-location-separated storage layer. In fact, if the mesh is an inter-organization setup with one cloud provider, you probably wouldn't do that. And you might have a single storage layer. However, they're independent schemas, they're independent access rights management, they're independent tenancy models that allow the data product to be deployed in an autonomous fashion.

The data store is often maintained by a central data engineering or infrastructure team responsible for ensuring that the data mesh is functional and operationalized for each domain. While analysts and data scientists in each domain are in charge of building and maintaining products (say, dashboards, models, and reports) on top of the data mesh, they're not the ones managing the infrastructure making the analytics, data science, and ML possible.

Is a Self-Serve Data Platform the Same Thing as a Decentralized Data Mesh?

Large organizations are already implementing self-serve platforms for infrastructure management, but according to Zhamak, the self-serve aspect of the data mesh is different in a few key ways:

> The majority of the service or data platforms built today are built for centralized data teams—they're built to help data specialists move through their backlog faster. They're built to serve a centralized team that's trying to optimize ingestion from all corners of the universe.

Data platforms, in their current state, are often optimized for a different purpose than the data mesh. Data platforms built to support the data mesh should be optimized to give autonomy to domain teams and give generalist technologists the ability to create data products. In short, data platforms should enable teams to manage their data from end to end and directly serve their data consumers: data analysts, data scientists, and other end users.

Is the Data Mesh Right for All Data Teams?

While more and more organizations are beginning to adopt or explore the data mesh, Zhamak believes the model is "still fairly nascent in its evolution." Organizations that face the problem of scaling data reliability are the organizations where adopting the data mesh makes the most sense. Early adopters tend to be engineering-focused and open to investing in "both building and buying technology, because not all of the elements are available to buy," Zhamak said.

According to Zhamak, if your stakeholders feel the pain around finding the right data and using it, and your innovation cycle is being slowed down, then you might be the right candidate for looking into the data mesh.

Does One Person on Your Team "Own" the Data Mesh?

Introducing the data mesh model requires more than just technology. It takes cultural buy-in across the organization. "I think data and all the data-driven initiatives and data platform investments are so highly visible and so highly political in organizations, especially large organizations, that there has to be top-down support and top-down evangelism," said Zhamak.

She attests that when organizations have a chief data officer or a chief data analytics officer reporting directly to the CEO, they're often more effective when it comes to data mesh adoption at scale. Still, the domains are the ones expected to take on ownership of their data, and as such will need to support this initiative, whether that means dedicated resources or interorganizational cheerleading. "If the domains aren't on board, all we're doing is overengineering the distribution of data among a centralized team," she said.

When you're trying to grow adoption for the data mesh at your organization, teams should get one to three domains that are aligned with the vision to serve as advocates pushing the design and implementation forward. Usually, the infrastructure teams—the practitioners and the engineers—aren't the difficult ones to convince since they're often the ones feeling the pain.

Does the Data Mesh Cause Friction Between Data Engineers and Data Analysts?

Again, the answer is: no. In fact, it's often the opposite!

Because the data mesh mandates the decentralization of data ownership, adopting this distributed, domain-oriented model often leads to healthy reconciliation in areas where there's historically been friction.

For instance, when organizations have an engineering team responsible for pipelines, and a data engineering group modeling data downstream, and then analysts further downstream that are consuming the data, incidents can often lead to finger pointing. But the data mesh's universal standard of data governance ensures that there is agreement around data quality, data discovery, data product schema, and other critical elements of data health and understanding.

According to Zhamak, such self-serve capabilities inherent to any good data mesh include:

- Encryption for data at rest and in motion
- Data product versioning
- Data product schema
- Data product discovery, catalog registration, and publishing
- Data governance and standardization
- Data production lineage
- Data product monitoring, alerting, and logging
- Data product quality metrics

When packaged together, these functionalities and standardizations provide a robust layer of observability—and trust. Zhamak explained:

> The evolution that we saw in the operational world started with our own ad hoc structured logging, which was a thing we already did as a good software engineering practice. I really hope that, with lineage and metrics and SLOs, we develop some open standards that we can use to convey these kinds of quality metrics, like your trust matrix, or tracing lineage in a standardized fashion and creating a healthy ecosystem of tooling on top of it.

In our opinion, organizational structures like data mesh actually allow for the right kind of autonomy and discussion around governance, forcing your team to answer such questions as: When and how should data be used? What are the standards that we care about that we want to enable everyone to have? Or even: Which responsibilities should each domain own?

Regardless of where you stand on the data mesh, there's no question the topic has inspired conversation around what it means to be a data professional, and what it takes to truly evangelize and operationalize data at scale for your organization. In fact, many companies we talk to have been applying data mesh concepts for longer than they realize; they just didn't have the words to describe it.

Case Study: Kolibri Games' Data Stack Journey

It's rare that you get a chance to sit down with a data leader to discuss the entire evolution of a company's data strategy. It's even rarer when said data leader was responsible for assembling their company's data stack from its earliest iteration. António Fitas, former head of Data Engineering at Berlin-based Kolibri Games (*https://oreil.ly/vK3OI*), is one such data leader. The company has had a wild ride, rocketing from a student housing–based startup in 2016 to a headline-making acquisition by Ubisoft in 2020.

While a lot has changed in five years, one thing has always remained the same: the company's commitment to building an insights-driven culture. With a new release almost every week, their mobile games are constantly changing and producing enormous amounts of data—handling 100 million events per day across 40 different event types, some with hundreds of triggers.

Along the way, the company's data organization grew from a team of one marketing analyst to 10+ engineers, analysts, and scientists responsible for ensuring that their data operations are reliable, scalable, and self-serve. To power this explosive growth, the team is building a data mesh architecture backed by a data-driven culture that would turn thousands of more mature companies green with envy.

Their story is a fascinating one and serves as a great resource for those getting started on their data mesh journey. In this section, we'll touch on how António's data organization evolved at every step, including what tech they used, which team members they hired, and the data challenges they faced.

First Data Needs

In 2016, the Kolibri Games founders started building a game out of their student apartments at the Karlsruhe Institute of Technology in Germany. They achieved early success with their first mobile game, Idle Miner Tycoon (*https://oreil.ly/R3W2W*), and the founders established some basic goals and objectives related to data.

The primary goal was to establish basic business reporting to determine whether the game was working properly, and whether the company was making any money, by:

- Reporting in-app purchase revenue
- Reporting ad revenue

- Reporting game-specific KPIs
- Reporting crashes and bugs

As a lean start-up, the founders relied entirely on third-party tools (Figure 9-2), including:

- Facebook Analytics
- Ad partners
- Firebase (to help fix app crashes and bugs)
- GameAnalytics (for in-game KPIs, such as retention)

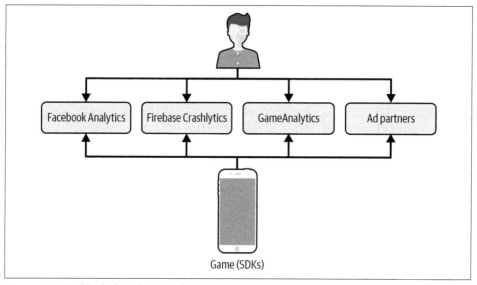

Figure 9-2. Kolibri's first data stack

Data quality wasn't the first priority for the Kolibri team, manifesting in several challenges down the road:

- Scattered analytics across different tools
- No transparency about how KPIs were calculated
- Reporting inconsistencies between different tools
- Tech problems due to SDK integrations
- Tech limitations, such as digging deeper into metrics and lack of flexibility

"This approach was far from perfect, but these were the first things we aimed to tackle," said António. "We were lucky that we got a lot of players in the game coming organically, but we wanted to get more. For that, we wanted to ramp up our marketing and user acquisition operations—with data."

Pursuing Performance Marketing

As Idle Miner Tycoon grew in popularity, so did the team (Figure 9-3) required to run the company—moving out of the student apartments into a proper office in Karlsruhe. And as the organization focused on acquiring new customers, the team set up data capabilities to measure and improve performance marketing.

Figure 9-3. The first "data team" at Kolibri, consisting of a single marketing manager

At this stage, the key objective for António's team was to ramp up performance marketing to get more users into the game while identifying which campaigns were profitable by:

- Calculating return on ad spend for campaigns
- Creating simple user lifetime value prediction
- Building up paid ad bidding script to optimize campaign performance

To gain insight into the company's return on ad spend and user lifetime value, the team added a third-party mobile measurement partner tool, AppsFlyer, a SaaS mobile marketing analytics and attribution platform, to their arsenal, as depicted in Figure 9-4. This tool helped the marketing manager know which user acquisition campaigns were performing well and how much they cost, as well as how much revenue the newly acquired players were generating. AppsFlyer also informed the scripts that were running locally to optimize bid management operations.

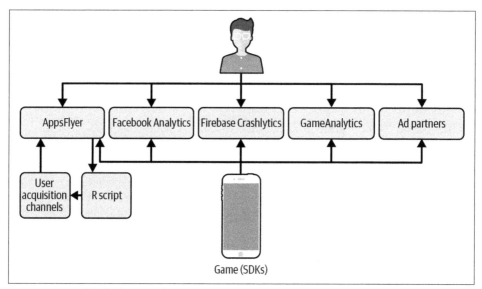

Figure 9-4. Kolibri's data stack in 2017

Key data challenges at this point in their journey included:

- Lack of transparency
- Proneness to error
- No version control
- Data even more scattered

"We were basically blindfolded around those operations," said António. "We didn't have any version control or engineering best practices around the code that we were running for setting our bids."

Still, Kolibri Games ended its second year with over €10M in annual revenue. To get to the next level, it was time to invest in some improvements.

2018: Professionalize and Centralize

In its third year, the young company moved to Berlin, hired more developers and designers—and António, who joined just in time for a splashy celebration of 50 million downloads. Together with another data engineer and the marketing team, a professional data organization began to take shape.

The primary goal was to centralize data and professionalize performance marketing by creating one tool to gather all information, provide transparency, and enable deeper dives into the data by:

- Investing in a proprietary solution to centralize data
- Collecting raw data
- Building up a central data warehouse
- Setting up dashboards

In 2018, Kolibri grew their team to include data engineers, a vital role that enabled greater scalability and flexibility for their data architecture. António and one additional data engineer (Figure 9-5) worked to build up the initial tech stack, while a marketing analyst focused on building dashboards to enable performance marketing.

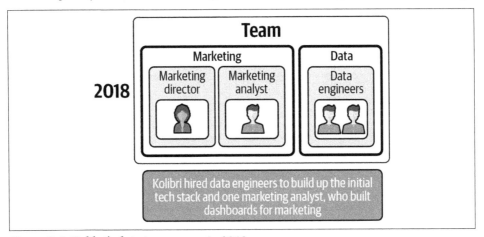

Figure 9-5. Kolibri's data team grows in 2018

As António and his team built the first iteration of their data platform (Figure 9-6), they used Azure for nearly all of their services. They built event telemetry that generated data points for specific events or actions in a game, set up batch jobs to integrate data from APIs into their data lake, and made their first tech switch: migrating from Power BI to Looker to gain another layer of data manipulation and out-of-the-box features like version control. At this point, the data platform included the following components:

- Data factory (Azure)
- Event hubs (Azure)
- Stream analytics (Azure)
- Data lake analytics (Azure)
- Power BI, then Looker
- SQL database

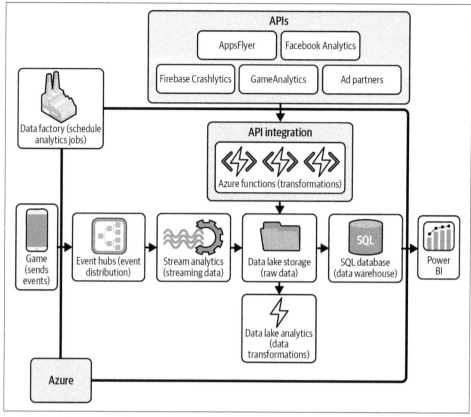

Figure 9-6. Data team begins to invest in cloud data technologies in 2018

Still, António and his team were dealing with a few key hurdles to truly becoming data driven, including the overall reliability of their stack:

> Our SQL database was becoming a limitation. The jobs that were integrating the data were writing the data at the same time that our dashboards were running, or that an analyst was doing an ad hoc query—and basically, the whole service started to become very unpredictable and very slow. And we started seeing that some of our jobs were failing a lot, and we had limited alerting or monitoring. We decided we wanted to get data-oriented and start addressing some of the problems that we had.

Getting Data-Oriented

With another successful game launch, a rebrand, and global recognition under its belt, Kolibri Games entered 2019 poised for even greater growth. The company hit the twin milestones of 100 million downloads and 100 employees in July. With more users and more products came more raw data, and António and his team knew they were just scratching the surface of how data could drive the company forward.

Goals at this point included creating insights for games by understanding player behaviors, conducting experiments backed by data, and maturing the data tech stack by:

- Building a monetization dashboard to show how much the company was earning with offers, shops, and ads
- Building progression and engagement dashboards to understand how players were interacting with the games (such as when they were dropping off and how they interacted with certain features)
- Running A/B tests
- Increasing performance of warehouse and maintainability of data pipelines

António knew they needed more people (Figure 9-7) to make their massive amounts of data useful. They added a head of game data and two BI developers to the data platform team. The data engineers worked closely with infrastructure—maintaining systems, integrating new tools, and maintaining streaming use cases—while building frameworks for BI developers to work with data integration, data modeling, and database visualization.

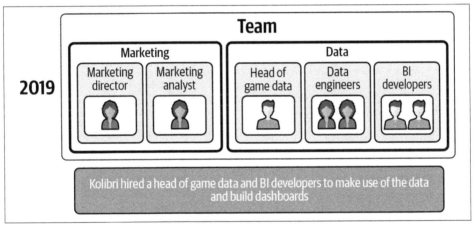

Figure 9-7. The state of Kolibri's data team in 2019

The growing data team needed more flexibility and easier collaboration, so António replaced some Azure services with Databricks (Figure 9-8). They tried using Spark to leverage their data lake as their data warehouse but found the people working on the platform preferred Python and SQL—and they didn't see the performance they expected in Looker while using Spark. So António and his team ended up replacing their SQL database with Snowflake, which became the main computation engine for all of their analytics.

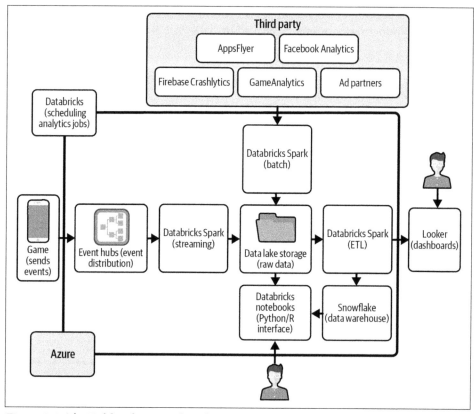

Figure 9-8. The Kolibri data team's architecture in 2019

Still, there were a few key challenges that prevented their stack from sufficiently scaling to meet the demands of their data science and BI teams:

- A/B tests were difficult to set up, missing transparency, and had no way to dashboard or present.
- No data-driven decisions were showing up in games.

"Most of the decisions were still made out of intuition and community feedback," said António. "We continued to generate even more data, but we knew that we could utilize it even more and build more use cases around it."

Getting Data-Driven

In early 2020, Kolibri Games was acquired by French gaming giant Ubisoft (*https://oreil.ly/KPH3s*). With more resources, António's team continued to grow, layered machine learning capabilities into their platform, and became inspired by conversations about data mesh architecture and domain-specific data ownership. To start building a data-driven culture, they introduced data-specific service-level agreements (*https://oreil.ly/m43vX*) and focused on increasing self-serve access to data.

A key initiative during this year was to make it easier for nondata teams to make decisions fully data-driven to unlock the full potential of the company's games, specifically by including product managers to help track that:

- 90% of all decisions on Idle Miner Tycoon needed to be backed by data.
- Time-to-insight needed to be less than one hour for 90% of questions.
- 90% of all changes needed to be validated with analytics.

To get there, the data platform team would:

- Improve the A/B testing process to help make informed decisions about features and changes to be implemented
- Improve personalization by creating game configurations for segments of players
- Use predictive analytics to predict lifetime value and churn to adjust the game accordingly
- Enable people to answer data-related questions without having to consult a data analyst

As the data organization (Figure 9-9) focused on domain-specific data ownership, it made sense to have new analyst hires embedded directly into the product team, working closely with product managers to understand needs and align priorities to reflect what the product actually needed. A third data engineer and two data scientists also joined the data platform team, working specifically on ML algorithms and A/B test data pipelines.

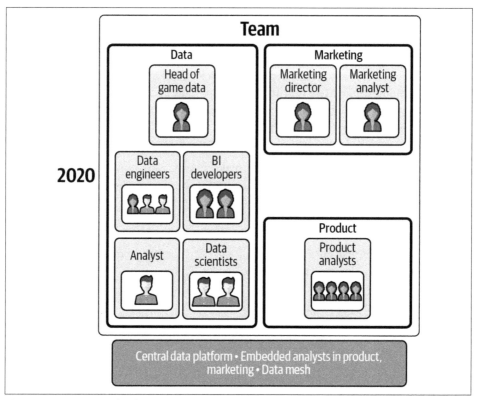

Figure 9-9. In 2020, the data team was now nine people strong (including two scientists and analyst)

With the company no longer in its infancy, António and his team needed faster cleaning and easier transformation, now directly in the warehouse. António's team added data warehouse architecture into Snowflake, better defining where they were applying business logic (Figure 9-10). They also moved from doing ETL to ELT, doing cleaning and transformation directly in Snowflake. They combined that with dbt, a data transformation tool, to collaborate between everyone working on the platform, increasing transparency and visibility.

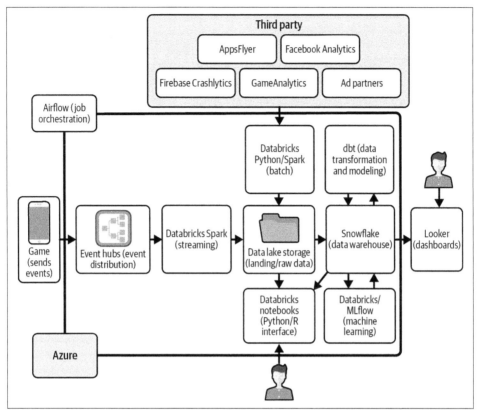

Figure 9-10. Data team architecture continues to expand in 2020

The data engineering team also focused on abstracting data pipelines so product analysts could essentially own the design and definition of new data events together with a game development team. By following the defined guidelines set out by data engineers, they could now get that data into the warehouse and model the data without requiring a data engineer. António and his team also introduced Airflow as the main orchestration for data integrations, all dbt models, and data validations.

At this stage in their data platform journey, a few key challenges rose to the top of the list:

- Data trust
- Software stability
- Scaling personalization

António explained:

> I think it was really good work when we tried to measure "Are we actually using data for our product development?" Getting those KPIs around our questions and measuring those kinds of things really helped people to think more about it and push more for it. I think the exercise by itself proved to be really fruitful in terms of getting more people to think about data....But what happened at this point was that we were getting much more data, and many more new use cases around data, and a lot of new models—but it was becoming difficult to monitor all of these and to make sure that things were correct.

Building a Data Mesh

As 2021 unfolded, António and his team focused on building data trust and reliability—which is crucial to their mission of achieving a data mesh architecture with domain-specific data ownership.

In 2021, the team's goal was to help the company scale with reliable data while building a data mesh architecture, increasing the speed of development and mitigation of incidents, decreasing the number of incidents, and increasing player personalization with further advanced analytics. António and his team planned to accomplish this by:

- Increasing testing capabilities
- Building common release and development process
- Implementing more monitoring and alerting
- Focusing on advanced analytics
- Collaborating to extend data platform capabilities around data monitoring and engineering best practices
- Building domain cross-functional teams

Inspired by the data mesh concept, the company planned to expand the domain teams (Figure 9-11) embedded with product and marketing by adding project managers who would help define the work for their team and BI developers to help integrate new and maintain existing data sources. The central data platform team would continue to focus on building solutions, frameworks, maintaining infrastructure, and advanced analytics.

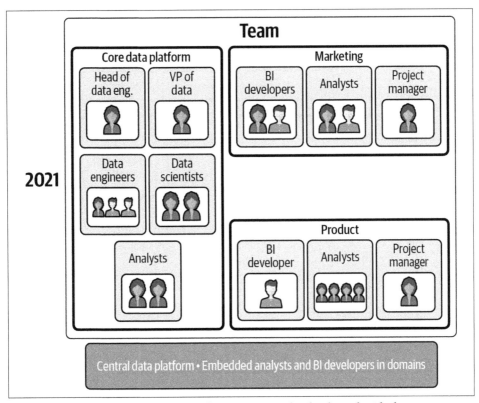

Figure 9-11. By 2021, António's team becomes more closely aligned with the ever-growing product and marketing teams

In 2021, the data team strived to centralize development and release processes (Figure 9-12) so that the data platform, marketing, and product teams all followed the same merge request and release into production processes. Kolibri's data tech stack invested in dbt and data observability to unlock greater benefits of the metadata layer for richer transformations and greater visibility into data quality.

And finally, to solve for data quality, they decided to invest in a monitoring solution that spanned the entirety of the data assets in their data warehouse, providing extra capabilities about understanding the end-to-end lineage of data to speed up troubleshooting and incident resolution.

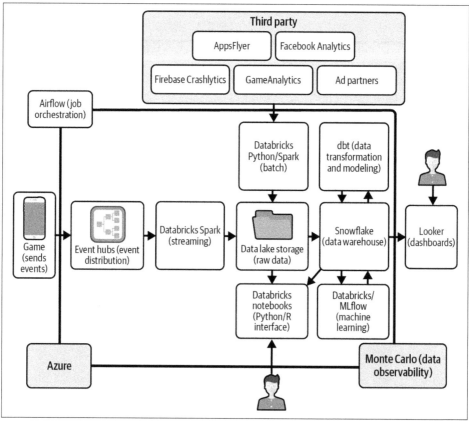

Figure 9-12. Kolibri's data tech stack continues to grow in 2021

Five Key Takeaways from a Five-Year Data Evolution

Building a data-driven company is a marathon—not a sprint.

For António, implementing a data mesh and achieving end-to-end data trust was a culmination of his team's journey. Here are his key takeaways when it comes to setting up your data team (no matter its shape or size) for success at each phase of its evolution:

- "Building your own data stack pays off, as it gives you all of these capabilities and enables you to be data-driven on your product development or working on your team."

- "We've been through a lot of iterations over our data platform, so you have to choose and be able to understand when it's the right time to change technology, for which right amount of data, for which process that you're running."

- "It's very important to have a higher degree of data observability if you want to establish trust in your data. It's important that you are able to understand when there is a problem, and that you're able to indicate that easily."

- "It's important to get the basics right before advancing to more advanced data applications. In our case, we should have hired analysts earlier to make more use of the data."

- "Establishing a data-driven culture is quite important and sometimes even more important than building the right tech stack."

As more organizations adopt the data mesh and distributed architectures, the opportunity for innovation, efficiency, and scalability has never been greater. Still, it's important to acknowledge that technology and process get you only so far when it comes to implementing a data mesh and building out a distributed data team. At the end of the day, becoming data-driven always starts—and ends—with culture. Now let's turn to how to use all that data to enhance the business.

Making Metadata Work for the Business

Over the last decade, data teams have become increasingly proficient at collecting large quantities of data. While this has the potential to drive digital innovation and more intelligent decision making, it has also inundated companies with data (*https:// oreil.ly/KLoyW*) they don't understand or can't use. All too often organizations hungering to become data-driven can't see the forest for the trees: data without a clear application or use case is nothing more than a file in a database or a column in a spreadsheet.

In recent years, we've seen the rise of data: now, companies are collecting more and more data about their data, in other words, metadata. By and large, this enthusiasm around metadata is a huge win for the industry. ETL solutions like dbt make it easy to track and use metadata, while cloud providers make interoperability of metadata more seamless between data solutions in your stack.

Still, as we become more metadata-dependent, it's important to remember not to repeat these same mistakes. Just as data without context is nothing more than a bunch of numbers, metadata by itself is useless—it's just more information about other information. Collect it all you want, but without a practical use case, metadata is largely meaningless.

Take for example, lineage, a type of metadata that traces relationships between upstream and downstream dependencies in your data pipelines. While impressive (neon colors! nodes! sharp lines!), lineage without context is just eye candy, great for a demo with your executives—but, let's be honest, not much else. The value of lineage doesn't come from the simple act of having it (Figure 9-13), but instead lies in its relevance to a particular use case or business application.

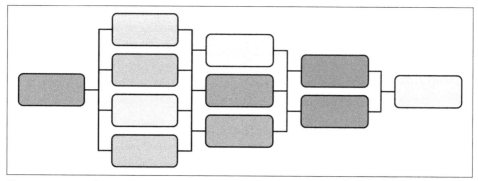

Figure 9-13. Without context and metadata, lineage is just eye candy

Where can lineage be actually useful? Aside from looking nice in a fancy demo or PowerPoint presentation, data lineage can be a powerful tool for understanding:

How to understand data changes that will impact consumers and determine the best course of action to resolve that use case
> Say for example you want to make a change to a particular field. Without lineage, you're likely making that change blindly—hoping there are no downstream repercussions (you: "Fingers crossed that no downstream consumers are going to be surprised by this change!").
>
> By using field- and table-level lineage, you can see which specific tables, reports, and—most importantly—users consuming those assets are going to be impacted by this change.

How to troubleshoot the root cause of an issue when data assets break
> In another scenario, you may be paged in the middle of the night about a broken dashboard your team is supposed to present to execs the next morning. You need a quick way to understand what broke upstream to render your Tableau graphs completely useless.
>
> But what exactly is the root cause of this problem? And which of the 100,000 tables you have in your data warehouse will you need to fix? With lineage, you can immediately identify the upstream assets contributing to this data downtime and pinpoint the root cause.

How to communicate the impact of broken data to consumers
> And finally, let's say data breaks (as it often does)—specifically, an ETL job was completed, but the data in this column is now 80% null—essentially, a silent failure. And now you need to highlight how this silent failure affects the users of this data.

How do you know who will be impacted and should be notified about this? Lineage provides a quick and easy way to communicate what happened and where so that you can keep stakeholders in the know while you resolve the issue.

Ultimately, lineage and metadata have the potential to be immensely valuable to data teams and companies at large—but only when it's applied directly to your business.

At the end of the day, your metadata (including but not limited to lineage) should answer more than the basic "who, what, where, when, why?" about your data (Figure 9-14). It should enable your customers (internal or external) to be equipped with up-to-date and accurate answers to questions that relate back to your customer's pain points and use cases, including:

- Does this data matter?
- What does this data represent?
- Is this data relevant and important to my stakeholders?
- Can I use this data in a secure and compliant way?
- Where does the answer to this question come from?
- Who is relying on this asset when I'm making a change to it?
- Can we trust this data?

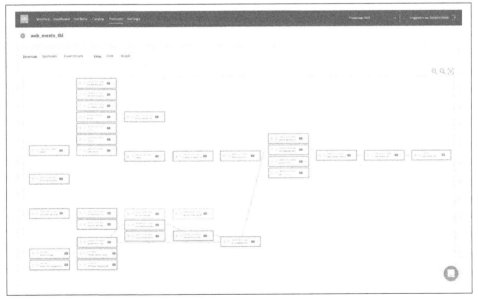

Figure 9-14. When captured holistically and in the context of business applications, metadata has the potential to serve as a force multiplier for your entire company

Many data teams are trying to answer these questions through a variety of solutions, including APIs that hook into modeling and pipeline transformation tools, data catalogs, documentation, and lineage. All four provide rich insights about your data, but they're missing one critical piece: its application to your business. Metadata without a use case is like an elephant riding a bicycle: interesting and impressive but not very useful (unless you're running a circus).

The true power of metadata lies in where, when, and how we use it—specifically, how we apply it to a specific, timely problem we are trying to solve. In addition to collecting metadata and building metadata solutions, data teams also need to ask themselves:

- What purpose is this metadata serving?
- How can I apply it to solve real and relevant customer pain points?

In our next section, we discuss a new approach to understanding and leveraging metadata with business value in mind.

Unlocking the Value of Metadata with Data Discovery

Over the past few years, cloud data warehouses and lakes have emerged as a must-have for the modern data stack. But while the technologies powering our access and analysis of data have matured, the mechanics behind understanding this data in a distributed environment have lagged behind.

Here's where data catalogs fall short and how data discovery tools (or federated catalogs) can help ensure your data environment doesn't turn into a data swamp. For more robust technical guidance about how to build and use a catalog, revisit Chapter 2.

Data Warehouse and Lake Considerations

One of the first decisions data teams must make when building a data platform (second only perhaps to "Why are we building this?") is whether to choose a data warehouse or lake to power storage and compute for their analytics.

While data warehouses provide structure that makes it easy for data teams to efficiently operationalize data (i.e., gleaning analytic insights and supporting machine learning capabilities), that structure can make them inflexible and expensive for certain applications. On the other hand, data lakes are infinitely flexible and customizable to support a wide range of use cases, but with that greater agility comes a host of other issues related to data organization and governance.

As a result, data teams going the lake or even lakehouse (*https://oreil.ly/KvCRz*) route often struggle to answer critical questions about their data such as:

- Where does my data live?

- Who has access to it?

- How can I use this data?

- Is this data up-to-date?

- How is this data being used by the business?

And as data operations mature and data pipelines become increasingly complex, traditional data catalogs often fall short of how you would expect a data discovery tool to answer these questions. Here's why some of the best data engineering teams are rethinking their approach to building data catalogs—and what types of data discovery tools data lakes need instead.

Data Catalogs Can Drown in a Data Lake—or Even a Data Mesh

Data catalogs serve as an inventory of metadata and provide information about data health, accessibility, and location. They help data teams answer questions about where to look for data, what data represents, and how it can be used. But if we don't know how that data is organized, all of our best laid plans (or pipelines, rather) are for naught.

As companies lean into lakes, they're often compromising the organization and order implicit in storing data in the warehouse. Data warehouses force data engineering teams to structure or at least semi-structure their data, which makes it easy to catalog, search for, and retrieve based on the needs of business users.

Historically, many companies have used data catalogs to enforce data quality and data governance standards, as they traditionally rely on data teams to manually enter and update catalog information as data assets evolve. In data lakes, data is distributed, making it difficult to document as data evolves over the course of its life cycle.

Unstructured data is problematic as it relates to data catalogs because it's not organized, and if it is, it's often not declared as organized. That may work for structured or semi-structured data curated in a data warehouse, but in the context of a distributed data lake, manually enforcing governance for data as it evolves does not scale without some measure of automation.

Similarly, data stored in traditional catalogs has difficulty scaling—and evolving—to meet the demands of distributed data architectures, like the data mesh. As discussed earlier in this chapter, the data mesh posits that analytical data is processed and transformed in distributed environments, with a universal layer of federated governance and discovery across all domains. Due to their manual nature, data catalogs generally have trouble updating and adapting to new information, making it hard to understand the current state of data at any given stage in its life cycle.

Moving from Traditional Data Catalogs to Modern Data Discovery

Understanding the relationships between disparate data assets—as they evolve over time—is a critical but often lacking dimension of traditional data catalogs. While modern data architectures, including data lakes, are often distributed, data catalogs are usually not, treating data like a one-dimensional entity. Unstructured data doesn't have the kind of predefined model most data catalogs rely on to do their job and must go through multiple transformations to be usable.

Still, companies need to know where their data lives and who can access it, and be able to measure its overall health—even when stored in a lake instead of a warehouse. Without that visibility into data lineage from a data discovery tool, teams will continue to spend valuable time on firefighting and troubleshooting when data issues arise further downstream.

Traditional data catalogs often can meet the demands of structured data in a warehouse, but what about data engineers navigating the complex waters of a data lake? While many data catalogs have a UI-focused workflow, data engineers need the flexibility to interact with their catalogs programmatically. They use catalogs for managing schema and metadata and need an API-driven approach so they can accomplish a wide range of data management tasks.

Moreover, data can enter a lake across multiple points of entry, and engineers need a catalog that can adapt to and account for each one. And unlike warehouses, where the data will be cleaned and processed before entry, data lakes take in raw data without any assumptions of end-to-end health.

Within a lake, storing data can be cheap and flexible, but that makes knowing what you have and how it's being used a real challenge. Data may be stored in a variety of ways, such as JSON or Parquet, and data engineers interact with data differently depending on the job to be done. They may use Spark for aggregation jobs or Presto for reporting or ad hoc queries—meaning there are many opportunities for broken or bad data to cause failures. Without a data discovery tool and data lineage, those failures within a data lake can be messy and hard to diagnose.

Within a lake, data can be interacted with in many ways, and a catalog has to be able to provide an understanding of what's being used and what's not. When traditional catalogs fall short, we can look to data discovery tools as a path forward.

Data discovery, in other words, a federated data catalog, is a new approach rooted in the distributed domain-oriented architecture proposed by Dehghani's data mesh model. Under this framework, domain-specific data owners are held accountable for their data as products and for facilitating communication between distributed data across domains. By doing the following, modern data discovery tools fill voids where traditional data catalogs fell short:

Automating to scale across your data lake

Using machine learning, data discovery tools automate the tracing of table- and field-level lineage, mapping upstream and downstream dependencies. As your data evolves, data discovery tools ensure your understanding of your data and how it's being used evolves, too.

Providing real-time visibility into data health

Unlike a traditional data catalog, data discovery tools provide real-time visibility into the data's current state, as opposed to its "cataloged" or ideal state. Since discovery encompasses how your data is being ingested, stored, aggregated, and used by consumers, you can glean insights such as which data sets are outdated and can be deprecated, whether a given data set is production-quality, or when a given table was last updated.

Leveraging data lineage to understand the business impact of your data

This flexibility and dynamism make data discovery tools an ideal fit for bringing data lineage to data lakes, allowing you to surface the right information at the right time, and drawing connections between the many possible inputs and out-flows. With data lineage, you can resolve issues more quickly when data pipelines do break, since frequently unnoticed issues like schema changes will be detected and related dependencies mapped.

Empowering self-service discovery across domains

Data discovery tools also enable self-service, allowing teams to easily leverage and understand their data without a dedicated support team. To ensure this data is trustworthy and reliable, teams should also invest in data observability, which uses machine learning and custom rules to provide real-time alerting and monitoring when something does go wrong in your data lake or pipelines downstream.

Ensuring governance and optimization across the data lake

Modern data discovery tools allow companies to understand not just what data is being used, consumed, stored, and deprecated over the course of its life cycle but also how, which is critical for data governance and lends insights that can be used for optimizations across the lake.

From a governance perspective, querying and processing data in the lake often occurs using a variety of tools and technologies (Spark on Databricks for this, Presto on EMR for that, etc.), and as a result, there often isn't a single, reliable source of truth for reads and writes (like a warehouse provides). A proper data discovery tool can serve as that source of truth. From an optimization standpoint, data discovery tools also can make it easy for stakeholders to identify the most important data assets (the ones constantly being queried!) as well as those that aren't used, both of which can provide insights for teams to optimize their pipelines.

As companies continue to ramp up their ingestion, storage, and utilization of data, technology that facilitates greater transparency and discoverability will be key. Increasingly, some of the best catalogs are layering in distributed, domain-specific discovery, giving teams the visibility required to fully trust and leverage data at all stages of its life cycle. Personally, we couldn't be more excited for what's to come with data discovery tools. With the right approach, maybe we can finally drop the "data swamp" puns altogether?

Still, it doesn't matter how "discoverable" your data is if you can't trust it. Often, when teams are building their data platform, data quality isn't the first item on the list (you have to be able to ingest, store, and process it, after all), but it helps to prioritize data quality early on in your company's data journey to avoid unnecessary—and inconvenient—bouts of data downtime.

In the next section, we'll discuss when it makes sense to start prioritizing data quality, and how modern data technologies and methodologies—such as data discovery tools and data mesh architectures—are more successful with data quality initiatives in place.

Deciding When to Get Started with Data Quality at Your Company

At this point in the book, you've become well-acquainted with the technologies, processes, and metrics teams must apply to achieve higher data quality at scale. We've also walked through real-world data reliability success stories of the data teams at leading companies like Fox, Toast, and Blinkist that have applied all three with promising results. Nevertheless, we've yet to address the "when." In fact, one of the most frequent questions we get from data leaders we talk to is: "When does it make sense to invest in data quality?"

Chances are, your first thought when building a data platform probably isn't "Can I trust this data?" You're likely more concerned with just driving adoption and getting the thing up and running. So when it comes to understanding when you should invest in data quality, the answer truly is "It depends." The reality is that building a data platform is a multistage journey and data teams have to juggle dozens of competing priorities. Data observability may not make sense for a company with a few dashboards connected to an on-premises database.

On the other hand, many organizations we've spoken with have increased their investment in developing their data platform without seeing a corresponding increase in data adoption and trust. If your company doesn't use or trust your data, your best laid plans for data platform domination are a pipe dream. To answer this question, we've outlined seven leading indicators that it's time to invest in data quality for your data platform.

You've Recently Migrated to the Cloud

Whether your organization is in the process of migrating to a data lake or between cloud platforms (e.g., Amazon Redshift to Snowflake), maintaining data quality should be high on your data team's list of things to do.

After all, you are likely migrating for one of three reasons:

- Your current data platform is outdated, and as a result, data reliability is low, and no one trusts the data.

- Your current platform cannot scale alongside your business or support complex data needs without a ton of manual intervention.

- Your current platform is expensive to operate, and the new platform, when maintained properly, is cheaper.

Regardless of why you migrated, it's essential to instill trust in your data platform while maintaining speed. You should be spending more time building your data pipelines and less time writing tests to prevent issues from occurring.

For AutoTrader UK, investing in data observability was a critical component of their initial cloud database migration (*https://oreil.ly/dEP6n*). "As we're migrating trusted on-premises systems to the cloud, the users of those older systems need to have trust that the new cloud-based technologies are as reliable as the older systems they've used in the past," said Edward Kent, Principal Developer, AutoTrader UK.

Your Data Stack Is Scaling with More Data Sources, More Tables, and More Complexity

The scale of your data product is not the only criterion for investing in data quality, but it is an important one. As with any machine, the more moving parts you have, the more likely things are to break unless the proper focus is given to reliability engineering.

While there is no hard and fast rule for how many data sources, pipelines, or tables your organization should have before investing in observability, a good guideline is more than 50 tables. That being said, if you have fewer tables, but the severity of data downtime for your organization is great, data observability is still a very sensible investment.

Another important consideration is the velocity of your data stack growth. For example, the advertising platform Choozle knew to invest in data observability as it anticipated table sprawl with their new platform upgrade.

"When our advertisers connect to Google, Bing, Facebook, or another outside platform, Fivetran goes into the data warehouse and drops it into the reporting stack fully automated. I don't know when an advertiser has created a connector," said Adam Woods, CTO of Choozle (*https://oreil.ly/nnhb8*). "This created table sprawl, proliferation, and fragmentation. We needed data monitoring and alerting to make sure all of these tables were synced and up-to-date, otherwise we would start hearing from customers."

Your Data Team Is Growing

The good news is your organization values data, which means you are hiring more data folks and adopting modern tooling to your data stack. However, this often leads to changes in data team structures (from centralized to decentralized), adoption of new processes, and knowledge with data sets living among a few early members of the data team.

If your data team is experiencing any of these problems, it's a good time to invest in a proactive approach to maintain data quality. Otherwise, technical debt will slowly pile up over time, and your data team will invest a large amount of their time into cleaning up data issues.

For example, one of our customers was challenged by what we call the "You're Using That Table?!" problem. As data platforms scale, it becomes harder for data analysts to discern which tables are being actively managed versus those that are obsolete.

Data certification programs and end-to-end data lineage can help solve these issues. It's important to note that while a growing data team is a sign to invest in data quality, even a one-person data team can benefit greatly from more automated approaches.

Your Team Is Spending at Least 30% of Their Time Firefighting Data Quality Issues

When we started our company, Monte Carlo, we interviewed more than 100 data leaders to understand their pain points around managing data systems. More than 60% indicated they were in the earlier stages of their data reliability journey, and their teams spend the first half of their day firefighting data quality issues.

Multiple industry studies have confirmed: data engineers are spending too much of their (valuable!) time fixing rather than innovating. During our research, we also discovered that data engineering teams spend 30 to 50% of their time tackling broken pipelines, errant models, and stale dashboards. Even organizations further along the curve that have developed their own homegrown data quality platform are finding their team spends too much time building and upgrading the platform—and that gaps remain.

Your Team Has More Data Consumers Than They Did One Year Ago

Your organization is growing at a rapid speed, which is awesome. Data is powering your hiring decisions, product features, and predictive analytics. But, in most cases, rapid growth leads to an increase in business stakeholders that rely on data, more diverse data needs, and ultimately more data. And, with great data comes great responsibility as the likelihood of bad data entering your data ecosystem increases.

That is the irony: the most data-driven organizations will have more data consumers to spot any error when it arises. For example, at AutoTrader UK, more than 50% of all employees are logging in and engaging with data in Looker every month, including complex, higher-profile data products such as financial reporting. Typically, an increase in data needs from stakeholders is a good indicator that you need to proactively stay ahead of data quality issues to ensure data reliability for end users.

Your Company Is Moving to a Self-Service Analytics Model

You are moving to a self-service analytics model to free up data engineering time and allow every business user to directly access and interact with data. Your data team is excited since they no longer have to fulfill ad hoc requests from business users. Likewise, your stakeholders are happy since a bottleneck is removed from having access to data.

While this is exciting for your data team, your stakeholders need to trust the data. If they don't trust it, they won't use it for decision making. And, ultimately if your end users don't trust the data, it defeats the purpose of moving to a self-service analytics model.

There are two types of data quality issues: those you can predict (known unknowns) and those you can't (unknown unknowns). As data becomes more and more integral to the day-to-day operations of data-driven organizations, the need for reliable data only increases.

Data Is a Key Part of the Customer Value Proposition

Every application will soon become a data application. As a data leader, it's exciting when your company finds a new use case for data, especially if it's customer-facing. Personally, we couldn't be more excited for this new norm.

Toast, a leading point of sale provider for restaurants, separates itself from its competitors based on the business insights it provides to its customers. Through Toast, restaurants get access to hundreds of data points, such as how their business has done over time, how their sales compared to yesterday, and who their top customers are.

"We say our customers are all Toast employees," said Noah Abramson (*https://oreil.ly/bgNQA*), a data engineering manager at Toast. "Our team services all internal data requests from product to go-to-market to customer support to hardware operations."

While this is a huge value add, it also makes their data stack customer-facing. That means it has to be treated with the same reliability and uptime standards as its core product. When data quality isn't prioritized the data team—and your customers—get burned.

Data Quality Starts with Trust

Much like gas companies need to trust their oil rigs daily to provide gas and oil to consumers, organizations need to trust their data to deliver clean and reliable data to stakeholders. By following a proactive approach to data quality, your team can be the first ones to know about data quality issues, well in advance of frantic Slack messages, terse emails, and other trailing indicators of data downtime.

Otherwise, valuable engineering time is wasted firefighting data downtime, your efforts at becoming a data-driven company will be hindered over time, and business users will lose trust in data. While each situation varies based on your business, it's best to bake data quality into your data platform as early as possible.

Summary

In this chapter, we put a fresh lens on some of the most critical technologies and topics when it comes to achieving high data quality, including the data mesh and data discovery tools. We also walked through how one lean startup, Kolibri Games, was able to build a data stack from scratch and retroactively address data reliability concerns using smarter and more automated solutions, as well as a domain-oriented approach to managing data.

We ended the chapter with a practical discussion of seven key indications that your team should invest in data quality—sooner rather than later. Of course, every data organization will differ when it comes to data needs, but we strongly encourage you not to overlook these considerations when designing your data strategy for scale.

In Chapter 10—our final chapter—we'll recap a few key learnings, share a powerful new approach to justifying the effort and resources necessary to give data quality its proper diligence, and share our predictions for the future of data reliability as they relate to broader industry trends.

Pioneering the Future of Reliable Data Systems

If *Data Quality Fundamentals* taught you anything about the larger state of analytics and data engineering, it's likely that data as an industry is going through a massive, irreversible sea change.

Only five years ago, it wasn't uncommon for data to live in siloes, accessed only by functional teams on an ad hoc basis for discrete tasks such as understanding how internal systems were being used, for example, or perhaps querying data about application usage over time. Now, analytical data is turning into the modern business's most critical and competitive form of currency. It's no longer a matter of if your company relies on data, but how much and for what use cases.

Still, it's simply not enough to collect more data; you also have to trust it. Solutions like cloud data warehouses and lakes, data catalogs, open source testing frameworks, and data observability solutions are building out additional features and functionalities to bring data reliability to the center of the conversation. Warehouses like Snowflake and Redshift make it easy to pull data quality metrics for freshness and volume, while open source tools like dbt and Great Expectations enable practitioners to quickly unit test their more critical data sets. Even catalogs like Alation and Collibra can provide some insight into data integrity and discovery at static points in time.

While these exciting new technologies have given data engineering teams more leverage when it comes to solving for and scaling data trust, new features and shiny tools can only get data teams so far; ultimately, data quality starts and ends with good culture, robust process, and stakeholder buy-in.

In our interview with Shane Murray, former SVP of Data and Analytics at the *New York Times*, he went so far as to say that data quality initiatives should often be prioritized before projects like catalogs and data discovery. Murray, who was with the *Times* for over eight years, was no stranger to the side effects of data downtime.

"At the end of the day, if you don't know whether the data you're leveraging to build products, power analytics, and help stakeholders make smarter decisions is up-to-date or accurate, you'll have a difficult time finding value in your stack," he told us. "Once data is being shared with downstream stakeholders, you really need to ensure that it can be trusted."

Data trust is critical to any successful data engineering or analytics initiative, yet it's often challenging to achieve, and even more difficult to maintain. As one of our colleagues, Michael Segner, says: "Data trust is hard to develop but easy to lose." And with any new process or initiative, driving adoption, resources, and budget for data quality can be even harder.

As a result, and despite the warnings from seasoned leaders like Murray at the *New York Times* and other experts cited throughout our book, making the argument to invest in data quality is often easier said than done: unless you can measure it. Unfortunately, most organizations don't start prioritizing data quality until after the damage is done: a schema change that causes a downstream report to generate wonky results, a freshness anomaly that pipes inaccurate data about user behavior to critical marketing channels, or even a failed dbt model that causes your CEO to scratch her head and question the validity of your analytics work.

In Chapter 5, we introduced an equation to calculate data downtime, which takes us one step closer to understanding its impact. The calculator for data downtime boils down to the number of data incidents times the average time to detection and the time it takes to resolve them:

$$DDT = N(TTD + TTR)$$

where DDT is data downtime, N is the number of incidents, TTD is time to detection, and TTR is time to resolution.

This calculation will tell you the amount of time it takes to identify and resolve a data quality incident—and while this is useful for understanding the cost of downtime, how do we actually assess the value of good data quality so that we can more easily make the case for it? Barring any data downtime disasters, how do you make the case for data quality?

As any engineering or product development team will tell you, adopting new processes and culture is a journey, not a sprint. And with data engineers and analysts juggling a million things every minute for even more stakeholders, it can be hard to carve out time for proactive measures.

Be Proactive, Not Reactive

Perhaps we need look no further than a May 2022 data downtime incident involving Unity Technologies, the gaming software company, to understand why architecting for data reliability—instead of tackling it reactively—is a valuable use of your team's time today, and not tomorrow.

On May 11, 2022, Unity stock crashed 36% (*https://oreil.ly/EyfVH*) after news came to light that stale data had been powering its ad monetization tool for well over a quarter. Compounding over several quarters, the data quality incident cost the company $110 million in lost revenue. If even some of the most innovative and tech-savvy companies can't prevent data downtime, the urgency is heightened for the rest of us. While having a data incident fresh in our minds can add fuel to the fire when it comes to prioritizing data trust, it pays to be proactive.

As Neil Diamond crooned in his 1978 hit, "Forever in Blue Jeans," "Money doesn't talk, it walks," and surely this applies to data quality, too. Only when money "walks" away as a result of bad data does it become crystal clear just how valuable good data is. So, the first step to making a case for data quality is to measure the financial impact of data reliability on your business.

To make it easier for you to make the business case for data quality—and take a proactive approach to preventing data downtime—we came up with an annual data downtime labor cost calculation. In other words, what is the rough cost of tackling data quality issues for your business? In short, this calculation boils down to: the number of data engineers × 1,804 × $62 × hours of data downtime.

First, we need to calculate the number of hours per year your company tackles data quality issues. As a proofpoint, the team at Monte Carlo discovered that 1 in 15 tables per year are affected by a data incident for any given environment across a pool of ~150 companies. Supplementing this data, in a 2022 survey with Wakefield Research (*https://oreil.ly/2AfGC*) that polled more than 300 data engineers, most respondents claimed 4 hours or more for time to detection and, once found, an average of 9 hours for resolution.

It can be days or even weeks before many data issues are detected. At that point, data teams launch a time-consuming root cause analysis process that involves several steps including checking the lineage (if it exists), the code, the data, the operational environment, and talking to peers. For the purposes of this calculation, let's estimate the average TTD and TTR to be a combined 8 hours for teams with low data quality maturity, 6 hours for teams with average data quality maturity, and 4 hours with high data quality maturity.

Our calculation caps its data downtime result at 8,760 hours, which is the total amount of hours in a year. If your organization has more than 16,425 tables that are important *and* a low data quality maturity, you are experiencing data downtime (the period where data is incomplete, erroneous, missing, or inaccurate) continuously all year round.

The math

(Tables / 15) × (TTD + TTR). The value cannot exceed 8,760.

The variables

8 hours for low data quality maturity, 6 hours for average data quality, 4 hours for high data quality maturity.

The justification

Customer conversations, an independent research survey, and in-depth experience in the root cause analysis process.

Our calculation for the financial impact of data downtime—in other words, the monetary cost of a data incident on your company—ranges between 20%, 35%, and 50% of a data engineer's time based on if an organization has low, medium, or high data quality maturity. That is then multiplied by the number of data engineers employed by the company multiplied by the average number of hours worked per year according to February 2022 Labor Department statistics (1,804) (*https://oreil.ly/i6n4Y*) multiplied by the average salary for a data engineer according to Glassdoor ($62 hourly) (*https://oreil.ly/b25H5*):

The math

Number of data engineers × 1,804 × $62 × % data quality time

The variables

50% for low data quality maturity, 35% for average data quality maturity, 20% for high data quality maturity

The justification

More than 150 formal data leader conversations, published case studies, the Wakefield Research survey, and multiple industry studies

Let's assume for the sake of explanation that you have 5,000 tables, average data quality hygiene (you clean and test your data sufficiently, but you don't floss every night), 5 data engineers, and an average TTD and TTR of 8 hours. By that logic, the amount of data downtime would be 2,664 hours per year, with a *cost of $279,620 worth of labor.*

Keep in mind that this calculation doesn't even factor in opportunity cost (in other words, the price you pay for making poor decisions with inaccurate data). As the industry matures, we anticipate algorithms far smarter than us to be able to generate predictions of the cost of these issues on the business.

Predictions for the Future of Data Quality and Reliability

Building sound data practices into your organization is about more than being proactive when it comes to data downtime. Understanding where the field is going and proactively managing your organization's goals and strategy is also critical.

As companies and employees increasingly democratize data access and make analytics a critical part of every function, it goes without saying that the requirements and approaches for solving data quality naturally evolve. In particular, we predict four key trends that will impact the future of data quality for teams everywhere.

Data Warehouses and Lakes Will Merge

Our first prediction relates to the building block of modern data systems: the storage layer. For decades, data warehouses and lakes have enabled companies to store (and sometimes process) large volumes of operational and analytical data. While a warehouse stores data in a structured state, via schemas and tables, lakes primarily store unstructured data.

However, as technologies mature and companies seek to "win" the data storage wars, companies like AWS, Snowflake, Google, and Databricks are developing solutions that marry the best of both worlds, blurring the boundaries between warehouse and lake architectures. Additionally, more and more businesses are adopting both warehouses and lakes—either as one solution or a patchwork of several.

Traditionally, data quality is easier to maintain in warehouses, where it's easier to natively track schema, volume, and freshness. Some warehouses will even handle some of the extraction, cleaning, and transformation for you. On the other hand, lakes are made up of several entrypoints, meaning layers where data is sorted and aligned for operational use. While data lakes offer greater use cases and flexibility, they also introduce additional pipeline complexity and more ways data can break.

Primarily to keep up with the competition, major warehouse and lake providers are developing new functionalities that bring either solution closer to parity with the other. While data warehouse software expands to cover data science and machine learning use cases, lake companies are building out tooling to help data teams make more sense out of raw data.

But what does this mean for data quality? In our opinion, this convergence of technologies is ultimately good news. Kind of.

On the one hand, a way to better operationalize data with fewer tools means there are—in theory—fewer opportunities for data to break in production. The lakehouse demands greater standardization of how data platforms work, and therefore opens the door for a more centralized approach to data quality and observability. Frameworks like ACID (atomicity, consistency, isolation, durability) (*https://oreil.ly/*

6TTFJ) and Delta Lake (*https://oreil.ly/lsmgM*) make managing data contracts and change management at scale easier.

We predict that this convergence will be good for consumers (both financially and in terms of resource management) but will also likely introduce additional complexity to your data pipelines. While this centralization of data compute and processing across SQL and non-SQL file formats tackles both BI and ML use cases, broader adoption means more data users, which often leads to more data duplication, errors, and downstream fire drills.

Emergence of New Roles on the Data Team

In 2012, *Harvard Business Review* named "data scientist" the sexiest job of the 21st century (*https://oreil.ly/wfts3*). Shortly thereafter, in 2015, DJ Patil, a PhD and former data science lead at LinkedIn, was hired as the United States' first-ever Chief Data Scientist. And in 2017, Apache Airflow creator Maxime Beauchemin predicted the "downfall of the data engineer" (*https://oreil.ly/ERFIT*) in a canonical blog post.

Long gone are the days of siloed database administrators or analysts. Data is emerging as its own company-wide organization with bespoke roles like data scientists, analysts, and engineers. In the coming years, we predict even more specializations will emerge to handle the ingestion, cleaning, transformation, translation, analysis, productization, and reliability of data.

This wave of specialization is not unique to data, of course. Specialization is common to nearly every industry and signals a market maturity indicative of the need for scale, improved speed, and heightened performance. Regardless of your role, however, data quality should remain a priority because your ability to use and trust the data directly influences what you can responsibly do with it.

The roles we predict will come to dominate the data organization over the next decade include:

Data product manager
    The data product manager is responsible for managing the life cycle of a given data product and is often responsible for managing cross-functional stakeholders, product roadmaps, and other strategic tasks.

Analytics engineer
    The analytics engineer, a term made popular by dbt Labs, sits between a data engineer and analysts and is responsible for transforming and modeling the data such that stakeholders are empowered to trust and use that data. Analytics engineers are simultaneously specialists and generalists, often owning several tools in the stack and juggling many technical and less technical tasks.

Data reliability engineer

The data reliability engineer is dedicated to building more resilient data stacks, primarily via data observability, testing, and other common approaches. Data reliability engineers often possess DevOps skills and experience that can be directly applied to their new roles.

Data designer

A data designer works closely with analysts to help them tell stories about that data through business intelligence visualizations or other frameworks. Data designers are more common in larger organizations and often come from product design backgrounds. Data designers should not be confused with database designers, an even more specialized role that actually models and structures data for storage and production.

So, how will the rise in specialized data roles—and bigger data teams—affect data quality?

As the data team diversifies and use cases increase, so will stakeholders. Bigger data teams and more stakeholders means more eyeballs are looking at the data. As one of our colleagues, Prateek Chawla, a founding engineer at Monte Carlo, says: "The more people look at something, the more likely they'll complain about them."

Even hiring a data reliability engineer won't "solve" your data quality problem. But helping these disparate team members and stakeholders understand how to work with data in a way that avoids breakages and makes collaboration painless is a step in the right direction.

Rise of Automation

Ask any data engineer: more automation is generally a positive thing. Automation reduces manual toil, scales repetitive processes, and makes large-scale systems more fault-tolerant. When it comes to improving data quality, there is a lot of opportunity for automation to fill the gaps where testing, cataloging, and other more manual processes fail.

Over the next several years, we foresee that automation will be increasingly applied to several different areas of data engineering that affect data quality and governance:

Hardcoding data pipelines

Automated ingestion solutions make it easy—and fast—to ingest data and send it to your warehouse or lake for storage and processing. In our opinion, there's no reason why an engineer should be spending their time moving raw SQL from a CSV file to your data warehouse.

Unit testing and orchestration checks

Unit testing is a classic problem of scale, and most organizations can't possibly cover all of their pipelines end-to-end—or even have a test ready for every possible way data can go bad. One company Ryan once worked for had key pipelines that went directly to a few strategic customers. They monitored data quality meticulously, instrumenting more than 90 rules on each pipeline. Something broke and suddenly 500,000 rows were missing—all without triggering one of their alerts. In the future, we anticipate teams leaning into more automated mechanisms of testing their data and orchestrating circuit breakers on broken pipelines.

Moving data from staging to production environments

Take, for example, this scenario. We have data in streams that we write to S3. To make that data available in our Snowflake environment, we need to manually log in to Snowflake and define the external table that points to the S3 data. Sometimes we would create the stream but forget to create the table in Snowflake. Or, there would be a manual error that would break jobs. Imagine a world in which the Snowflake table is created automatically when the stream is created. This proactive approach would prevent downstream schema breaks and more reliable pushes to production.

Root cause analysis

Often, when data breaks, the first step many teams take is to frantically ping the data engineer who has the most organizational knowledge and hope they've seen this type of issue before. The second step is to then manually spot check thousands of tables. Both are painful. We hope for a future where data teams can automatically run root cause analysis as part of the data reliability workflow with a data observability platform or other type of DataOps tooling. Ideally, such a solution would be able to aggregate metadata about the incident that teams can then use to piece together a picture of what happened, and from there, resolve the issue.

Data documentation, cataloging, and discovery

One of the next frontiers for the data stack is the semantic or descriptive layer. In Chapter 2, we discussed the benefits of and challenges with traditional data catalogs, but whether it's through using a catalog, data discovery, or other tool, there needs to be some sort of automated process for documenting data sets. We now have decades of evidence to show that if data documentation isn't automated, then it doesn't happen—at the very least not at the necessary scale. That's why we have the "You're using *that* table?!?!" problem and why we are treating data engineers like data catalogs by pinging them incessantly in Slack about which table to use. We need to automate context generation for our data in addition to upstream and downstream lineage.

While this list just scratches the surface of areas where automation can benefit our quest for better data quality, we think it's a decent start.

More Distributed Environments and the Rise of Data Domains

As discussed in Chapter 1, distributed data paradigms like the data mesh make it easier and more accessible for functional groups across the enterprise to leverage data for specific use cases. The potential of domain-oriented ownership applied to data management is high (faster data access, greater data democratization, more informed stakeholders, etc.), but so are the potential complications.

Data teams need look no further than the microservice architecture for a sneak peek of what's to come after data mesh mania calms down and teams begin their implementations in earnest. Such distributed approaches demand more discipline both at the technical and cultural level when it comes to enforcing data governance.

Generally speaking, siphoning off technical components can increase data quality issues. For instance, a schema change in one domain can cause a data fire drill in another area of the business, or duplication of a critical table that is regularly updated or augmented for one part of the business can cause pandemonium if used by another. Without proactively generating awareness and creating context about how to work with the data, it can be challenging to scale the data mesh approach.

While data mesh evangelizes a universal federation layer (in other words, agnostic governance) across domains, teams must abide by specific contracts and use dedicated APIs, which can lead to complexity and confusion. This is why companies determining whether to migrate to the data mesh should think long and hard about whether they'll be able to drive cross-organizational adoption and avoid the pitfalls of half-baked microservice rollouts.

So Where Do We Go from Here?

In the coming years, we predict that achieving data quality will become both easier and harder for organizations across industries, and we hope that this book has prepared the reader to navigate these challenges as they drive their business's strategy forward. Increasingly complex systems and higher volumes of data begets complication; innovations and advancements in data engineering technologies means greater automation and improved ability to "cover our bases," so to speak, when it comes to preventing data downtime. Regardless of how you slice it, however, striving for some measure of data reliability will become table stakes for even the most novice of data teams.

We anticipate that data leaders will start measuring data quality as a vector of data maturity (if they haven't already), and in the process, work toward building more reliable systems using many of the technologies and approaches outlined in this book.

In the coming months and years, we hope to see more data organizations prioritize data reliability as a foundational aspect of their data architectures, workflows, and team culture. And when they do, our readers will be well prepared.

Until then, here's wishing you no data downtime!

Index

A

Abramson, Noah, 268
accessibility, balancing with trust, 209-210
accountability, 208
accuracy, anomaly detection and, 112-115
Airbnb, 119
Alberini, Francisco, 143
alerting and testing, 55-63
  (see also data testing)
  dbt unit testing, 56-59
  Deequ unit testing, 60-63
  Great Expectations unit testing, 59-60
  machine learning and, 104
Amazon Redshift, 17
ambiguity, syntactic versus semantic, 52
Amundsen (data discovery and metadata
  engine), 226
analytical data
  batch versus stream processing, 45
  defined, 14
  operational data versus, 14-16
analytical data transformations
  ensuring data quality during ETL, 54
  ensuring data quality during transforma-
    tion, 55
  running, 54
analytics engineers, 205, 274
anomaly detection, 69-118
  accounting for false positives / false nega-
    tives, 105
  building an algorithm for, 72-87
  data incident management, 145-147
  defined, 69

designing data quality monitors for warehouses versus lakes, 117
detecting freshness incidents with data
  monitoring, 110
F-scores, 111
frameworks for, 108-110
improving alerting with machine learning,
  104
improving precision and recall, 106-110
incident detection and, 145-147
investigating a data anomaly, 94-99
known unknowns and unknown unknowns,
  70-71
model accuracy and, 112-115
monitoring for freshness, 73-78
scaling with Python and machine learning,
  99-115
for schema and lineage, 88-92
understanding distribution, 79-87
various useful approaches to, 116
visualizing lineage, 92
ANother Tool for Language Recognition
  (ANTLR), 180
Apache Airflow
  installing circuit breakers with, 66
  managing data quality with, 63-67
  scheduler SLAs, 63-66
  SQL check operators, 67
Apache Hadoop, 46
Apache Kafka, 46
  managing operational data transformations
    across, 53
  reasons to choose, 50
  stream processing and, 49

About the Authors

Barr Moses is the CEO and cofounder of Monte Carlo, a data reliability company. In her decade-long career in data, Barr has served as commander of a data intelligence unit in the Israeli Air Force, a consultant at Bain & Company, and VP of Operations at Gainsight, where she built and led their data and analytics team. The instructor of O'Reilly's first course on data observability, an emerging discipline in data engineering, Barr has worked with hundreds of data teams struggling with these problems. Inspired by her time in the analytics trenches, she is building a product dedicated to identifying, resolving, and preventing what she calls "data downtime," periods of time when data is missing, erroneous, or otherwise inaccurate. In other words: bad data. In this book, she shares her experiences and learnings on how today's data organizations can achieve high data quality at scale through technological, organizational, and cultural best practices.

Lior Gavish is CTO and cofounder of Monte Carlo. Prior to Monte Carlo, Lior cofounded cybersecurity startup Sookasa, which was acquired by Barracuda in 2016. At Barracuda, Lior was SVP of Engineering, launching award-winning ML products for fraud prevention. Lior holds an MBA from Stanford and an MSc in computer science from Tel-Aviv University.

Molly Vorwerck is the Head of Content at Monte Carlo. Prior to joining Monte Carlo, Molly served as editor-in-chief of the *Uber Engineering* blog and lead program manager for Uber's Technical Brand team, where she spent countless hours helping engineers, data scientists, and analysts write and edit content about their technical work and experiences. She also led internal communications for Uber's Chief Technology Officer and strategy for Uber AI Labs' research review program. In her spare time, she freelances for *USA Today*, reads up on all the latest trends in data, and volunteers for the California Historical Society.

Colophon

The animal on the cover of *Data Quality Fundamentals* is a grivet monkey (*Chlorocebus aethiops*).

A member of the *Cercopithecidae* family of Old World monkeys, the grivet is more closely related to apes than to New World monkeys such as lemurs and tarsiers. Unlike apes, however, the grivet possesses a tail; it is also smaller than most apes.

Highly adaptable to various rural and urban environments, grivets mainly inhabit the savanna woodlands of Sudan, Ethiopia, Eritrea, and Djibouti in eastern Africa. Though common throughout this range, grivets are most prevalent near rivers, which they rely on as sources of water during the dry season.

Grivet monkeys are primarily quadrupedal and terrestrial, traveling on four limbs as they forage and hunt along the ground during the day, and usually taking to the trees only at night to sleep. While foraging, they use their cheek pouches to store food until they can move on to a safe location and eat.

Like most primates, grivets are highly social, living in hierarchical groups that typically range from 6 to 20 individuals. They boast a broad repertoire of calls and strengthen social bonds through behaviors such as grooming and play. They can live for up to 30 years.

Interestingly, grivets have a long history of association with humans: they're one of five monkey species known to have been kept in ancient Egypt and have been depicted as pets on tombs. Today, despite some loss of suitable habitat due to large-scale farming and land development, grivets have been categorized by IUCN as being of least concern.

The cover illustration is by Karen Montgomery, based on an antique line engraving from *Mammalia*. The cover fonts are Gilroy Semibold and Guardian Sans. The text font is Adobe Minion Pro; the heading font is Adobe Myriad Condensed; and the code font is Dalton Maag's Ubuntu Mono.

Milton Keynes UK
Ingram Content Group UK Ltd.
UKHW012005050824
446578UK00004B/7